NATIONAL GEOGRAPHIC

TRAVELER

san francisco

NATIONAL
GEOGRAPHIC

T R A V E L E R

san francisco

by Jerry Camarillo Dunn, Jr.
photography by Gilles Mingasson

National Geographic
Washington, D.C.

CONTENTS

Pages 2–3: San Francisco cable car routes offer several stunning vistas; this one, climbing Nob Hill, gives riders an overview of Alcatraz and the Bay.
Opposite: Victorian houses adorn the Haight-Ashbury District.

TRAVELING WITH EYES OPEN

Alert travelers go with a purpose and leave with a benefit. If you travel responsibly, you can help support wildlife conservation, historic preservation, and cultural enrichment in the places you visit. You can enrich your own travel experience as well.

To be a geo-savvy traveler:

- Recognize that your presence has an impact on the places you visit.

- Spend your time and money in ways that sustain local character. (Besides, it's more interesting that way.)

- Value the destination's natural and cultural heritage.

- Respect the local customs and traditions.

- Express appreciation to local people about things you find interesting and unique to the place: its nature and scenery, music and food, historic villages and buildings.

- Vote with your wallet: Support the people who support the place, patronizing businesses that make an effort to celebrate and protect what's special there. Seek out local shops, restaurants, hotels, and inns. Use tour operators who love their home—who love taking care of it and showing it off. Avoid businesses that detract from the character of the place.

- Enrich yourself, taking home memories and stories to tell, knowing that you have contributed to the preservation and enhancement of the destination.

That is the type of travel now called geotourism, defined as "tourism that sustains or enhances the geographical character of a place—its environment, culture, aesthetics, heritage, and the well-being of its residents." To learn more, visit National Geographic's Center for Sustainable Destinations at *travel.nationalgeographic.com/travel/geotourism.*

san francisco

ABOUT THE AUTHOR & THE PHOTOGRAPHER

A third-generation Californian, **Jerry Camarillo Dunn, Jr.,** was born and raised in Los Angeles—a fact that elicits pity (at best) in San Francisco, but for which he makes no apology. San Francisco became a second home during college at nearby Stanford University. In later years, Jerry lived in the city and also in Marin County across the Golden Gate Bridge. He is the author of numerous books, including National Geographic's *Driving Guides to America: California and Nevada and Hawaii;* the Smithsonian *Guide to Historic America: The Rocky Mountain States; Idiom Savant: Slang as It Is Slung;* and National Geographic's *My Favorite Place on Earth: Celebrated People Share Their Travel Discoveries.* A former staff editor and writer for National Geographic *Traveler* magazine, he has won three Lowell Thomas Awards, the Oscars of the field, from the Society of American Travel Writers for his feature stories. Jerry lives with his wife, Merry, and two sons, Graham and Locke, in southern California. Their tucked-away valley is still filled with orange blossoms and not with smog.

Gilles Mingasson grew up in Grenoble, France, and moved to Paris to pursue photojournalism. After arriving in the United States on an assignment, he traveled through Latin America before making Los Angeles his home base. In 2005, his work on Latinos in the United States won him an American Photography award. His photography can be seen in the National Geographic *Traveler* guidebooks on Panama, the Dominican Republic, and France. Gilles Mingasson's website is *mingasson.com.*

Charting Your Trip

Set between the Pacific Ocean and a glittering bay, San Francisco is a gorgeous city that's fun to visit and easy to navigate. Its 852,000 residents live in neighborhoods with distinctive personalities: Chinese, Italian, bohemian, yuppie, Hispanic, techie, gay. All enjoy easy access to parks and shorelines, museums and theaters, shopping, and—very important to locals—great food and wine.

How to Get Around

Use public transportation in San Francisco. Driving is hell on wheels, especially downtown and in popular tourist areas such as Fisherman's Wharf. And parking costs a fortune. Instead, take the buses, streetcars, and cable cars that crisscross the city and reach every neighborhood; all are operated by Muni. Taxis are fairly easy to flag down in the city center, but may be scarce in other neighborhoods. Headquartered in San Francisco and operating citywide, Uber and Lyft are ride-hailing services that summon private car drivers through an app on your cell phone.

A high-speed rail network called BART links the San Francisco International Airport, located on the peninsula south of the city, to San Francisco and onward to cities across the bay. Ferries carry passengers around San Francisco and to locations north, south, and east of the city. For detailed transit information, see pages 239–240.

If You Have Only Three Days

Have you ever been to Disneyland, where various "lands" radiate from a central hub? In San Francisco, that hub is Union Square, your home base on **Day 1.** Get your bearings by sitting for a moment with office workers and shoppers taking a morning break in the square's terraced park. Cable cars clang their bells as they pass on Powell Street. On the square and surrounding streets, elegant boutiques send forth their siren calls. Wander east on tiny Maiden Lane to see the gallery at No. 140, San Francisco's only building designed by famous 20th-century architect Frank Lloyd Wright; you're welcome to peek inside. From Union Square, it's easy to reach fascinating neighborhoods nearby. Walk north up Grant Avenue to the colorful Chinatown Gate, the entrance to a world at once genuinely Chinese and unabashedly touristy. Along Grant, you can shop for jewelry, art pieces, embroidery, and all the tacky souvenirs you can carry. In this crowded

This corner in Haight-Ashbury was once the heart of hippie culture in San Francisco.

neighborhood, Portsmouth Square serves as an outdoor living room, where old men play card games and kids simply play. In narrow alley-ways, you'll find a fortune cookie factory and the Tin How Temple, scented with incense, that few tourists discover.

Keep walking north on Grant Avenue to Broadway, then turn right to Columbus Avenue, the heart of North Beach. Now you're in Little Italy, a neighborhood of Old World traditions, scented with wafts of garlic. Here, too, the Beat Generation of post–World War II writers gathered in coffee-houses to talk long into the night about poetry and Big Ideas. A neighborhood pulse point is City Lights Bookstore, a San Francisco institution that carries works by Jack Kerouac and authors of the Beat era.

Above North Beach on Telegraph Hill, head for Coit Tower, a 210-foot (64 m) landmark that offers a panoramic view. Inside, murals from the 1930s depict life in California during the Great Depression.

Or you can retrace your steps south to California Street and ride a cable car to the summit of Nob Hill, once the neighborhood of early San Francisco millionaires. End the day with a drink at the Top of the Mark, a sky-high cocktail lounge atop the Mark Hopkins hotel with a dazzling city view.

Day 2 is devoted to exploring San Francisco Bay and its attractions. Start by taking a scenic ride on the Powell-Hyde cable car to Fisherman's Wharf. The area is named for the working fishing boats that dock here. Older ships are docked at the San Francisco Maritime Historical Park, ranging from an 1880s square-rigger to a side-wheel ferry. At Pier 45, tour a World War II submarine or wander through the Museé Mécanique, a nostalgia-inducing display of antique arcade games and mechanically operated musical instruments.

Fisherman's Wharf is also a classic tourist trap. Along the brassiest stretch of Jefferson Street you'll find the Ripley's Believe It or Not! Museum with its

---

NOT TO BE MISSED:

Serious shopping around
  Union Square **58–59**

Riding a cable car **64–65**

Exploring the culture and busy
  streets of Chinatown **67–76**

The aroma of espresso in a
  North Beach café **83–85**

Touring the infamous prison
  island of Alcatraz **112–117**

Finding your favorite view of the
  Golden Gate Bridge **131–134**

Taking time out of modern life
  at the Japanese Tea Garden
  and museums within Golden
  Gate Park **164–171**

Visitor Information

The city's official **San Francisco Travel** website *(sanfrancisco.travel)* has in-depth information on things to do and see, hotels, restaurants, nightlife, shopping, the arts, and transportation; there are online tools for planning your trip and a virtual visitors guide.

Near Union Square, pick up brochures, maps, and a printed visitors guide at the **San Francisco Visitor Informa-tion Center** *(900 Market St., next to cable car turntable at Powell & Market Sts., tel 415/391-2000)*. Visitor information and entertainment listings are updated regularly on the **San Francisco Chronicle** newspaper's website *(sfgate.com)*.

See pages 238–240 in the Travelwise chapter for more travel information.

Ups & Downs

One word appears regularly on maps of San Francisco: "hill"—Nob, Telegraph, Russian, and 40 more. When the famous song "I Left My Heart in San Francisco" talks about little cable cars that "climb halfway to the stars," it's clear that traversing the city is an uphill struggle. So consider the topography when planning your activities. Mapped streets that look as flat as a sheet of paper turn out to be half vertical—useful to know if you're driving a car or parking (see p. 240). When you pack for the trip, don't forget walking shoes with good traction for steep, sometimes wet, streets.

strange-but-true displays, the Madame Tussauds wax museum, and endless souvenir shops.

Bay cruises depart from Fisherman's Wharf, as do trips to Alcatraz Island, the former federal penitentiary that held America's baddest bad guys, including 1920s Chicago mobster Al Capone and more recently James "Whitey" Bulger.

Have lunch at touristy Pier 39 or Ghirardelli Square, a former chocolate factory remodeled for dining and shopping. Then head west by bus or taxi through the sunny waterfront Marina District to the Presidio, a former Army base with a sprawl of historical buildings set amid a forest. In a restored barracks, the Walt Disney Family Museum tells the story of the animation pioneer. Also visit Fort Point, a pre–Civil War fortress located under an arch of the Golden Gate Bridge. Stop for snacks at the bayside Warming Hut at Crissy Field, a former airfield transformed into a shoreline park.

Still have some energy? Top off the day with an afternoon walk or bike ride across the Golden Gate Bridge and back. Allow a couple of hours for this spectacular trip and bring a jacket for the wind.

Day 3 takes you first to an outdoor haven from the busy city, Golden Gate Park, a 3-mile-long (5 km) swath of green stretching inland from the Pacific Ocean. The park's Japanese Tea Garden is a San Francisco favorite for its cherry trees, ponds, and relaxing tea pavilion. The San Francisco Botanical Garden showcases 8,000 types of plants from around the world. You can also go boating on Stow Lake, see a herd of shaggy American bison, and take a bike ride.

The park's outdoor features are matched by its indoor attractions. The California Academy of Sciences is the world's only combined natural history museum, planetarium, and aquarium. Facing it across a plaza stands the de Young Museum, a bold modern structure filled with an impressive collection of American art.

For a different experience of San Francisco culture, walk or drive east from the park into Haight-Ashbury, a neighborhood that was home to the hippie flower

When to Go

With its generally mild climate, the city of San Francisco is a year-round destination. Still, the weather is quirky. Summer can be unexpectedly foggy, yet on some days temperatures climb to 80°F (27°C). Fall is warm and clear, a very pleasant time to visit. The rainiest period is during the winter months. Cold winds can blow in almost any time. To outwit the changeable climate, carry a sweater or jacket when you go out all times of the year.

During summer's high tourist season, reserve hotels well in advance and expect long lines for cable cars and attractions. The city is less crowded in winter. See pages 238–239 for more information.

Take it to the bridge: Musicians rock the farmers market crowd at the Ferry Building on the bay.

children of the 1960s and the birthplace of psychedelic rock music. Along Haight Street, explore funky shops selling rock music posters and vintage clothing, fending off young panhandlers as you go, and travel back in time to a faded facsimile of the Summer of Love that turned the world's eyes toward San Francisco in 1967.

Alternatively, head west to Ocean Beach to watch the sunset. For a warm indoor view, go to the nearby Cliff House, whose bar and restaurants overlook the water.

If You Have More Time

It's worth spending extra days in the city to explore some of the many other neighborhoods. For museums grand and quirky, walk around SoMa (the area "South of Market" Street). The San Francisco Museum of Modern Art, with work by artists from Paul Cézanne to Andy Warhol is an artwork in itself—a stack of geometric forms backed with a tall, rippling white slab.

Along Mission Street, pick from a collection of fine small museums: the California Historical Society, the Museum of the African Diaspora, and the Contemporary Jewish Museum.

Locals enjoy picnicking on the grass outside SoMa's Yerba Buena Center for the Arts, an institution focused on contemporary visual and performing arts. Or they head northeast on Mission Street to the bayfront Ferry Building. The classic transit terminal has been reinvented as a sort of European market hall, with restaurants, food stalls, and a popular farmers market held on Tuesdays, Thursdays, and Saturdays.

Two other neighborhoods offer a chance to explore diverse cultures. Traditionally Hispanic, the Mission District grew up around Mission Dolores, founded by Franciscan padres in 1791. Street life along Valencia Street showcases a mix of Hispanic, hipster, lesbian, and techie cultures. In contrast, 24th Street remains the heart of San Francisco's Latino culture with its food, music, and brightly colored street murals.

Not far west, the Castro neighborhood is the hub of San Francisco's large, vibrant gay community. For a window into this world, take the Cruisin' the Castro tour, or just walk around and enjoy the street life, shopping, and dining. ■

History & Culture

Modern sculpture contrasts with the classical lines of the Legion of Honor. Opposite: The Tea House at the Japanese Tea Garden

San Francisco Today

It's little wonder that so many visitors do as the famous song says: They leave their hearts in San Francisco. Of course, the love affair may be purely physical: No American city offers such gorgeous sights, from the painted gingerbread trim on a Victorian house to a sparkling panorama of the bay with Alcatraz in the middle.

But San Francisco's appeal is far more than skin-deep. The constantly changing views, the interplay of water, hills, and sky, lend the city a rhythm, an effervescent beat, like jazz. You get the feeling that the city is improvising out of some deep well of experience and expressing a singular personality. It never ceases to come up with inspired new riffs on an old refrain.

The Palace of Fine Arts, built for the Panama-Pacific International Exposition of 1915, is the only structure from the exposition still situated on its original site.

Some San Francisco scenes are urban classics: When the fog rolls in off the Pacific Ocean, for instance, a cloak of mystery and romance drapes the city's shoulders, like fictional local detective Sam Spade's overcoat thrown around a blonde on a darkened street. Shadows fall, music rises, ice cubes clink in cocktail glasses, and anything goes. The city has a definite mystique. Of course, this mood is only one of many that make up San Francisco's multi-faceted personality. Other experiences that a visitor can take home to remember might include:

• riding a bike across the Golden Gate Bridge as a ship traces a white streak on the blue bay below;

• eating the creatively flavored ice cream at Bi-Rite Creamery, a popular spot in the Mission District;

• piloting your car downhill on steep, winding Lombard, the "world's crookedest street";

• drinking a classic cocktail in a lively bar, perhaps behind the unmarked door of Bourbon & Branch, a modern-day speakeasy;

Many visitors say that San Francisco is their favorite American city. Europeans often compare it to Europe, meaning they find it both picturesque and charming.

• walking from Coit Tower down the hidden Filbert Steps, past cottages and gardens;

• having a flashback to the 1960s Summer of Love in Haight-Ashbury, the legendary home turf of the hippies;

• buying a crab cocktail at Fisherman's Wharf from an Italian vendor who sports a big moustache;

• wondering what Rodin's "The Thinker" is thinking about, as he sits there among the artistic treasures at the California Palace of the Legion of Honor;

• dancing 'til you drop at a club like Ruby Skye;

• taking snapshots at Alamo Square, where old Victorian houses are set against the city's modern skyline;

• tucking yourself into bed at one of San Francisco's personality-filled boutique hotels after a big day of sightseeing;

• touching ancient, thick adobe walls at Mission Dolores, the city's oldest building.

Such experiences beguile those who come here with the city's iconic imagery long since hardwired into their minds. Many visitors say that San Francisco is their favorite American city. Europeans often compare it to Europe, meaning they find it both picturesque and charming. New Yorkers feel at home with the city's array of world-class hotels, restaurants, museums, and opera. Folks from small towns discover a city built on a human scale.

And no one loves San Francisco more than San Franciscans themselves. Sometimes the great city on the hill grows dewy eyed with self-appreciation. It could give itself a big hug. But you can't blame it, really. How many cities can boast such a spectacular setting and such a rich stew of cultural influences?

Part of the city's appeal lies in the way it manages to balance the old and traditional with the new and offbeat. The city is, paradoxically, both provincial and very worldly. San Francisco clings to its past, even while helping to create the future with booming tech companies and start-ups.

The Provincial

In many ways, San Francisco maintains itself in an insular world, guarded by its 43 hills and locked behind the Golden Gate. For more than half a century the city's symbols, now visual clichés, have remained the same: cable cars, the Golden Gate Bridge, Chinatown.

Provincial San Francisco carefully preserves its past. Lovingly restored Victorian houses and Edwardian buildings lend the city an old-fashioned look, even when their street affords a view of downtown skyscrapers. In fact, a street of Victorians seems like something out of a child's pop-up storybook.

San Francisco is also a city of provincial manners. Older citizens remember a time when ladies never ventured downtown without their hats and gloves. Even today, San Francisco is always called the City, and never "Frisco"—a gesture of civility.

To the knowing eye, San Francisco is a collection of traditional neighborhoods, districts that bind residents to the corner grocery stores and familiar faces they see every day. Home is home. It may be Pacific Heights, where the elite can walk their pedigreed pups in a hilltop park. Or Chinatown, where old women in bulky sweaters practice the slow meditative dance of tai chi chuan, or tai chi. Or North Beach, where aspiring poets who hope to emulate the 1950s Beats sit at café tables, scribbling in notebooks and sipping coffee for inspiration.

The Worldly

Among the many features that make San Francisco a beloved city, one of them can't be depicted in a color postcard. But it's there in the eyes of residents who return your friendly or curious gaze. This quality is open-mindedness, a receptiveness to new and different ideas, and a willingness to let you do your own thing.

For a century and a half, this West Coast port city has been opened up to the outside world through waves of immigrants, from Italian fishermen to Chinese herbalists. They have come from all directions: Europe, Asia, Latin America, Russia, the Philippines,

---

EXPERIENCE: Take Yourself Out to the Ball Game

The San Francisco Giants play their home games at AT&T Park, which offers visitors fantastic views of the bay. But there's more to a baseball game than watching the players and eating hot dogs. You can go on a behind-the-scenes tour of the $320-million ballpark: inside a dugout, luxury suite, batting cage, and press box *(tel 415/972-2400, sfgiants.com, $$$$).* On game day, join the **"knothole gang,"** random fans who gather by openings in the right-field wall to view the action for free. Another option: Rent a kayak *(citykayak.com)* and float in the bay near the right-field fence; if you're a fast paddler, you might even catch a home-run ball.

A cable car climbs the steep slope of California Street from the Embarcadero.

Traditional drummers perform during the annual Cherry Blossom Festival in Japantown.

and more. Their languages, religions, and cultures have helped to create a uniquely diverse and tolerant place to live.

San Francisco's broad-mindedness first took root during the California gold rush, when everyday life was a wild pageant. San Franciscans embraced all sorts of characters in this passing parade of colorful personalities. Ravishing entertainer Lola Montez (famous for her Spider Dance) strolled the streets with a riding whip to discourage male admirers who became too enthusiastic. Silk-cuffed gamblers and grizzled miners mixed with writers and millionaires. Around the infamous Barbary Coast, a character named Oofty Goofty wore fur and feathers left over from his days as a sideshow "wild man." He launched a new career by permitting anyone to kick him for a dime (whacking him with a baseball bat cost a quarter).

But San Francisco's most enduring character was its favorite (and only) monarch, Joshua Abraham Norton. After arriving in San Francisco in 1849 and losing his

fortune, he took to wearing an old blue army uniform and a dusty plumed hat. He proclaimed that he would henceforth be known as "Norton I, Emperor of the United States and Protector of Mexico."

San Franciscans played along happily with this bearded eccentric. When Emperor Norton entered a theater, the audience would rise to its feet. Newspapers published his letters, whose "crazy" suggestions included building the Bay Bridge, as well as decorating a colossal Christmas tree in Union Square for the children of San Francisco—a tradition that is still followed to this day. The emperor frequently asked city financiers for loans of millions of dollars, but happily settled for 50 cents.

Like Emperor Norton, over the decades countless other characters have shown that the city makes room for people of all social and political persuasions. Consider, for example, the Sisters of Perpetual Indulgence, a group of biking and skating "nuns" who are actually amusing guys in drag. The city has always fostered outrageous characters, individualists, and bohemians—from turn-of-the-20th-century painters and poets to the Beat Generation of the 1950s and the 1960s flower children who "did their own thing" during the Summer of Love. It's also a worldwide magnet for the LGBT (lesbian, gay, bisexual, transgender) community.

But even if you're a traditional, buttoned-down type, you'll find that San Francisco takes hold of you with all the giddy joy of riding a cable car down a dizzying hill, with the sunshine on your face and the bay breeze in your hair. Suddenly you come alive. What a rush! What freedom! What a beautiful city!

> **San Francisco's broad-mindedness first took root during the California gold rush, when everyday life was a wild pageant.**

Physical Setting

The city of San Francisco occupies the tip of a peninsula located between the Pacific Ocean and the San Francisco Bay. The bay is both an inlet that stretches for 50 miles (80 km) and an estuary fed by 16 rivers that drain the Sierra Nevada and Central Valley.

Geography: About 500,000 years ago, the ocean level offshore began to fall about 300 feet (90 m) as ice built up at the Poles during the ice ages. The San Francisco coastline was out near the Farallon Islands, 27 miles (43 km) west. What is now the bay was a dry, grassy valley in the Coast Range where mammoths grazed. A river flowed from the Sierra Nevada and through the valley into the Pacific, passing through the Golden Gate. Then about 12,000 years ago, the glacial ice melted and the ocean level rose. Water flooded inland to fill the ancient valley, which became San Francisco Bay.

The peninsula was left high and dry, with water on three sides, a setting that lends San Francisco an exhilarating beauty, especially when viewed from one of its 43 hills.

San Francisco's climate is maritime and Mediterranean, with both summer and winter temperatures moderated by the ocean air. But in a city famous for nonconformity, even the weather is eccentric. The warmest season is early autumn, rather than summer. At any time of year, fog and chill may envelop the Sunset District, while "banana belt" neighborhoods such as North Beach and Potrero Hill bask in sunshine. These weather pockets, or microclimates, are created as the result of cooled sea air entering the Golden Gate and being deflected off the city's irregular hills in divergent patterns.

Fog on the Bay

San Francisco's fog is a shape-shifting shaman that casts a spell of white magic over the city. At the headlands of the Golden Gate, moisture-carrying Pacific winds meet the upwelling chilly waters of the bay, causing the moisture to condense like droplets on an iced-tea glass. The result: fog. Common in summer, it pours through the Golden Gate at between 10 and 20 miles (16–32 km) an hour, sucked inland because high temperatures in the Central Valley cause air to rise there and pull the fog toward it. Conversely, on many winter mornings, a dense, low-lying tule fog forms inland and drifts toward the ocean, often blanketing the entire bay.

Earthquake Territory: San Francisco has a noisy neighbor with a bad reputation: the San Andreas Fault. Constantly threatening an earthquake, the much-feared fault runs from the northwest part of the state more than 700 miles (1,125 km) to the Gulf of California. It doesn't actually pass beneath San Francisco, but veers offshore between Point Reyes and Daly City. The fault is the unstable boundary between two tectonic plates—the Pacific and North American—which move in opposite directions against each other about 2 inches (5 cm) each year. Occasionally, the plates lock along the fault. Pressure builds, to be released in sudden cataclysmic fury.

In 1906, the earth shifted more than 15 feet (4.5 m) along the fault line, and the force shook buildings for 200 miles (320 km). The great earthquake was estimated at 8.3 (out of 10) on the Richter scale. Nowadays earthquakes occur every week, most of them less than magnitude 3.0 and therefore unnoticed (see sidebar p. 33 for the main exception). Seismologists predict that a "Big One" is coming. They just don't know when or where.

Viewpoints: Nearly everywhere you go in San Francisco, from the shoreline to the top of Coit Tower, you encounter a view that is affecting or downright jaw-dropping: the Golden Gate Bridge seemingly suspended in midair as its towers vanish into the fog; cherry trees in bloom at the Japanese Tea Garden; rows of pastel-hued houses against the backdrop of the blue bay. For great views of the city, take to the water, the hills, or a tall building.

A **bay cruise** (see p. 103) gives a fresh vantage point on both the city and Fisherman's Wharf, plus a look *under* the Golden Gate Bridge. **Alcatraz Island** (see pp. 112–117) has achingly fine views of San Francisco (which must have driven the prisoners nuts). At **Fort Point** (see sidebar p. 132), you see the Golden Gate Bridge

The North Tower of the Golden Gate Bridge rises above the dense fog that fills the bay.

from beneath, all metal and bolts, and the Golden Gate itself, with powerful currents surging through it. (Watch for windsurfers here.) From **Baker Beach** (see sidebar p. 134), there's a great view of the distant Marin Headlands, the Golden Gate Bridge, the Pacific waves—and probably some nude sunbathers on the sand.

Coit Tower (see pp. 90–92) has a 360-degree view of the Financial District and Chinatown (south); the Bay Bridge and East Bay (east); Fisherman's Wharf and Alcatraz (north); and Russian Hill and the Golden Gate Bridge (west). **Twin Peaks** (east of the Castro) gives you a clear shot of the city's northern and eastern sections. The Powell-Hyde cable car topping Nob Hill on the way to Fisherman's Wharf offers a classic view.

For another timeless San Francisco panorama, sip a cocktail at the Top of the Mark, a lounge on the 19th floor of the **Mark Hopkins hotel** (see p. 61), which shows off the twinkling city through huge windows. ∎

Food & Drink

San Francisco has some 4,450 restaurants—more per capita than any other American city—and eating out is a major recreation. Devoted foodies worship at such shrines as Gary Danko, Benu, and Saison. But the humblest Mexican taco stand or Italian trattoria may also turn out great meals, and at low cost. The city has enjoyed good food since the gold rush. If you were a lucky forty-niner with a pocketful of nuggets, you headed to San Francisco and splurged on oysters and French champagne.

A bartender at The Slanted Door restaurant in the Ferry Building prepares the day's fare.

Today's San Francisco cuisine has three distinctive elements that make it world-class: (1) tasty vegetables, fruit, meats, cheeses, nuts, herbs, and wines, all locally produced; (2) a melting pot of cooking styles that immigrants have brought to this port city from all over the world—particularly Italy, China/Asia, and Mexico/Latin America (although you'll also find Moroccan, Swiss, and even Istrian restaurants); and (3) groundbreaking new approaches to cooking, notably the "California cuisine" created in the early 1970s at Berkeley's Chez Panisse by Alice Waters, whose menus offered the freshest seasonal ingredients, cooked and presented with imagination and style.

Diners in San Francisco are—to put it mildly—obsessive about food. They'll ask a waiter exactly how organic, free-range, grass-fed, sustainably harvested, and fair-trade the entrée's ingredients are. Some menus have footnotes like academic journals.

Foodies also demand innovation and creativity. In San Francisco, luckily, culinary cross-fertilization produces some wonderful hybrid dishes. You'll find pumpkin ravioli with ginger, Caesar salad with Caribbean jerk chicken, and roasted salmon with red curry sauce.

The Napa and Sonoma Valleys, north of San Francisco, produce some of the world's great wines, along with very drinkable table varieties. Especially successful are Cabernet Sauvignon and Pinot Noir among the reds, Chardonnay and Sauvignon Blanc among the whites. Other drinks include beer (local Anchor Steam, various microbreweries), coffees (espresso, cappuccino, latte), and mineral water (Calistoga, from the Napa Valley).

During your visit, be sure to try some of these San Francisco specialties:

Cioppino: Italian fish-and-shellfish stew in a tomato stock.

Dim sum: Bite-size Chinese food that includes dumplings stuffed with seafood, meat, or vegetables. Served from carts. (There's no menu, so ask questions to avoid taking an unexpected bite of pig stomach or

---

EXPERIENCE: Find the Best Farmers Markets

What's a pluot?! Step right up and taste one—a cross between a plum and an apricot—at San Francisco's farmers markets, where produce from the countryside around San Francisco is displayed in colorful profusion. You can not only savor the visual spectacle and broaden your culinary education, but also take home some goodies. Some of the city's most popular markets: **Ferry Plaza,** at the Ferry Building (see p. 192); **Heart of the City,** at UN Plaza (see p. 181); and **Crocker Galleria,** in the Financial District *(50 Post St., Thurs.)*. Others: Upper Haight *(Wed.)*, Fort Mason Center *(Sun.)*.

INSIDER TIP:

I traveled 20,000 miles to find America's best burrito. The winner: the bundle of meat, pinto beans, sour cream, guacamole, and *pico de gallo* (but no rice) at La Taqueria (see Travelwise p. 256). Ask for it *dorado*, grilled golden crisp.

—ANNA BARRY-JESTER
Photographer, food writer

duck foot.) The bill is tallied by counting the plates on your table. A Chinatown bargain.

Dungeness crab: Light and delicate; goes with sourdough bread and white wine; in season mid-November through June.

Fortune cookies: Folded cookies with printed fortunes inside (see p. 76).

Ghirardelli chocolate: Created in San Francisco in 1852 and available at the company's historic factory, now a shopping-dining

complex called Ghirardelli Square (see pp. 110–111) at Fisherman's Wharf.

Hangtown Fry: Oyster-and-bacon omelette that dates back to gold rush days. You can try it for lunch at the downtown eatery once favored by mystery writer Dashiell Hammett, John's Grill *(63 Ellis St., tel 415/986-3274)*.

Irish coffee: A soul-warming blend of Irish whiskey, coffee, and whipped cream, introduced to the United States in 1952 at the Buena Vista Café (see p. 107).

Joe's Special: Eggs scrambled with ground beef, spinach, and onions; created at New Joe's restaurant. When a bandleader came in after a late show, the chef had only these ingredients left. Said the bandleader: "Mix 'em together!"

Sourdough bread: Crusty French bread with a sour tang (see sidebar p. 104). A large roll may be hollowed out as a "bread bowl" and filled with steaming clam chowder.

Walkaway crab cocktail: Dungeness crabs cracked and sold by Fisherman's Wharf vendors since 1916 (see p. 104); served with a sharp cocktail sauce.

History of San Francisco

Only 230 years ago, the San Francisco Bay area was a world unknown—at least, unknown to Europeans. It was the domain of Native Americans: Coast Miwok, Wintun, Yokut, and, most numerous, the 10,000 Ohlone who dwelled on the San Francisco peninsula, the East Bay, and south to Big Sur.

Indians & Early Explorers

The Native Americans enjoyed a bountiful diet of shellfish, deer, and acorn mush. They used tule, a marsh bulrush, to weave masterful watertight baskets. Ideas such as the wheel and agriculture never dawned, but neither did warfare. In this land of plenty, each tribe had its respective territory, with peace safeguarded by trade and marriage between groups.

Their splendid isolation couldn't last. Spain controlled an empire that included

A statue of Padre Junípero Serra, founder of the mission system, stands in Mission Dolores's garden.

Mexico, and in 1542, it sent Portuguese navigator Juan Rodríguez Cabrillo north to explore "Alta California." Cabrillo sailed past the entrance to San Francisco Bay, later named the Golden Gate, but didn't notice it.

Next came English freebooter Francis Drake, who in 1579 at the helm of the *Golden Hind* also missed the bay's entrance. Drake refitted his ship 25 miles (40 km) north in what was likely Drakes Bay, below Point Reyes. With grand words he claimed the area for Queen Elizabeth I, calling it "Nova Albion" (New Britain in poetical Latin). But the claim languished through English inactivity.

Two centuries passed before Spain realized that to keep dominion over Alta California, it must establish colonies. In 1769, an expedition under Capt. Gaspar de Portolá left Baja California bound for Monterey Bay. At length, suspecting that he had overshot his goal, Portolá sent Sgt. José Ortega with a party to scout the terrain. Ortega crested a ridge and saw a great body of water stretching north and south. Thus, the first outsiders spied San Francisco Bay. Remarkably enough, Portolá didn't recognize what this sighting meant, and doubled back toward Monterey.

> ## "I Am Alone"
>
> **From the historic Mission Dolores, look across Dolores Street at the former Notre Dame School, and try to imagine when it was part of the *rancheria,* or cattle compound, where Native Americans were corralled to live during mission times. Separated from their own people, forced to stay in one spot rather than roam, exposed to European diseases, they quickly succumbed. By 1850 (about 75 years after the mission was founded), only one local Indian remained. "I am all that is left of my people," he said. "I am alone."**

1775–1834: Spanish Settlement

Not until 1775 did the first European sail through the Golden Gate— Juan Manuel de Ayala in the supply ship *San Carlos*. He charted the bay and named features such as Angel Island.

Meanwhile, an expedition led by Capt. Juan Bautista de Anza was traveling overland to the bay. In 1776, he dedicated the site of the future Spanish *presidio,* or military post, at the tip of the peninsula near the entrance to the bay. Three miles (5 km) southeast, he situated the mission. And so the sword and the cross arrived together—emblems of Spanish power and aspiration.

Colonists celebrated Mass at the mission site on Laguna de los Dolores, or Lake of Sorrows, on June 29, 1776. In 1791, the mission that stands today was built of adobe bricks and redwood timbers. Formally named San Francisco de Asís, to honor the padres' patron St. Francis of Assisi, it is usually called Mission Dolores. Here Native Americans were yoked to Christianity and to field labor. In 1816, a French traveler noted that after a few months the converts "usually begin to grow fretful and thin, and they constantly gaze with sadness at the mountains." Some slipped away to their old life.

After Mexico's independence from Spain in 1821, the Mexican government secularized the missions and gave the Native Americans much of the mission land—which was quickly absorbed by Mexican property holders. Rootless, racked by European-imported smallpox and measles, stripped of their culture, the Native Americans were doomed. They drifted or worked on *rancherias*—cattle spreads on vast land grants that the government gave to settlers and retired soldiers. The favored families, known as *Californios*, dominated Alta California, holding fiestas while the Indians labored as virtual serfs. Neglected by Mexico, San Francisco's presidio fell into disrepair, although a few soldiers stayed on. Mission Dolores closed in 1834 and was later used as a tavern. Meanwhile, a settlement on a nearby cove was growing into a trading port that would soon bring the world to San Francisco.

1835–1848: Yankee Town

California cattle ranches produced hides and tallow, which Yankee ships carried from San Francisco to New England's leather tanners. The trade would soon end the settlement's isolation. Commerce centered on a sheltered cove at the northeastern edge of the peninsula with deep water for anchoring ships. The major businessman was English sailor William Richardson, who married the daughter of the Presidio's commander and started the first commercial boat service on the bay. In 1835, he put up the cove's first "house"—a tent made from a sail—and a trading post.

Whaling ships and other vessels called. More buildings rose along a dirt track grandly called Calle de la Fundación (Foundation Street, roughly equivalent to today's Grant Avenue). Richardson named the settlement Yerba Buena ("good herb"), after an aromatic, mintlike shrub that locals brewed to make a kind of tea. The Mexican authorities commissioned a Swiss grocer, Jean Jacques Vioget, to lay out streets for the expanding community. On the central plaza an adobe customhouse served the growing port.

At this time United States officials in Washington were starting to eye the fertile valleys and lucrative trade in California, taking note of the weak grip that Mexico had on its remote possession. Americans felt they had a Manifest Destiny to expand the nation from sea to shining sea. In 1846, war broke out with Mexico over Texas and California. On July 9, Capt. John B. Montgomery of the warship U.S.S. *Portsmouth* came ashore with 70 sailors and marines. Without meeting resistance, he raised the Stars and Stripes above Yerba Buena's plaza.

Mark Twain's San Francisco

In his late 20s, Samuel Clemens came to San Francisco and fell in love with "the livest, heartiest community on our continent." He wrote stories for any newspaper that would pay him, including the *Call*, where he turned out a profusion of articles. In later pieces for the journals *Golden Era* and *Californian*, he depicted the delights and foibles of 1860s San Francisco. His sense of humor made him a popular figure.

Inevitably, Clemens wrote about earthquakes, including a big one in 1865: "A lady sitting in her rocking and quaking parlor saw the wall part at the ceiling, open and shut twice, like a mouth, and then drop the end of a brick on the floor like a tooth." He also wrote a burlesque earthquake almanac in the style of a weather forecast. The prediction for October 23: "Mild, balmy earthquakes," and for November 2: "Spasmodic but exhilarating earthquakes, accompanied by occasional showers of rain, and churches and things."

Many features of his literary voice—tall tales, parody, a sense of justice—blossomed in San Francisco as Samuel Clemens transformed himself into America's storyteller, Mark Twain.

The Americans renamed the town San Francisco in 1847. Irish surveyor Jasper O'Farrell extended the street grid and added 120-foot-wide (36.5 m) Market Street, which sliced diagonally across the city blocks—creating difficulties in getting across town that plague residents to this day.

In 1847, John Augustus Sutter, who ran a trading post and fort in the area that became Sacramento, saw that the growing community of San Francisco would be needing lumber. So he hired carpenter James W. Marshall to build a sawmill on the American River at Coloma, in the foothills of the Sierra Nevada. When the Mexican War ended in 1848, the United States took possession of California. But a few days before the treaty signing, something happened that would transform sleepy California. On January 24, 1848, Marshall was inspecting the tailrace of the mill when he saw a gleam in the water. "I reached my hand down and picked it up," he said. "It made my heart thump, for I was certain it was gold."

> **The California gold rush had begun. Hopeful miners snatched up every pick and shovel in town and headed for the Sierra.**

1848–1859: Gold Rush Boomtown

Although San Francisco in 1847 was growing steadily, it was still a tiny settlement. Who could foretell that in two years it would explode from 500 people to 20,000, a boomtown whose name stoked gold fever in hearts around the globe?

Soon after his discovery, Marshall's workers were spending most of their time washing gravel for more nuggets. As word spread, San Francisco newspapers reported the find, but residents were at first skeptical. It took Sam Brannan to fan the flames of gold fever. The colorful Brannan had come to San Francisco heading a group of 200 Mormons but quickly became an entrepreneur. He founded the city's first newspaper, the *California Star*, and owned hardware stores in San Francisco and Sacramento. In May, Brannan strode through Portsmouth Square holding a small bottle filled with nuggets and hollering: "Gold! Gold! Gold from the American River!" San Francisco emptied like a theater on fire.

The California gold rush had begun. Hopeful miners snatched up every pick and shovel in town and headed for the Sierra. Sam Brannan became California's first million-aire. Before trumpeting the news of gold, he had cannily stocked his stores with all the equipment the miners would need, priced at a premium.

After President James Polk confirmed the rumors of an "abundance of gold" in California, the news electrified the East Coast and the world beyond. In 1849, an incredible 100,000 fortune seekers headed for California as if it were a golden magnet. In legend, they will live forever as the forty-niners. Some trekked overland across mountains and deserts. One emigrant tallied 469 wagons on a single 9-mile (14.5 km) stretch. At night, so many campfires flickered that they looked like the lights of a great city. Other argonauts came by sea, crammed onto ships around Cape Horn or crossing Panama at the risk of yellow fever. As fortune seekers arrived in San Francisco by ship, crews promptly deserted for the goldfields, leaving Yerba Buena Cove a forest of masts.

San Francisco provided food, mining equipment, and services, but not cheaply. Ham, eggs, and coffee cost $6, or a shovel $50. Land prices soared; one man sold a lot for $18,000 two years after trading a barrel of whiskey for it. Men walked the streets toting bags of gold dust. In 1848, when a day's wages east of the Mississippi averaged $1, a typical California miner made $10 to $15 a day. Crime flourished. Australian hooligans, called the Sydney Ducks, robbed people and set fires to distract attention so they could loot. Finally, entrepreneur Sam Brannan galvanized civic leaders to form a Committee of Vigilance to drive out the criminals. The "vigilantes" hanged several lawbreakers and murderers in 1851 and 1856, effectively cowing the undesirables.

About half the gold seekers were Americans, but the balance made San Francisco a cosmopolitan place, bursting with the languages and cultures of Mexico and Chile, Germany and France, Hawaii and Ireland, China and Italy. This diversity still marks San Francisco—a fine legacy from the days of 1849.

At first nuggets were easy to pluck from the rivers, and lucrative claims produced 5 pounds (2 kg) of gold a day. Men swirled dirt and gravel in frying pans, washing away the lighter material to leave the heavier gold. The "flash in the pan" of surface gold soon gave out, and more equipment was needed to extract the deeper-lying gold. Using cradles and wooden filter boxes, miners worked the deeper placers, which were largely exhausted by 1852. At this point corporate financing was required. Hydraulic nozzles called monitors blasted away hillsides to get at the gold—with disastrous environmental consequences.

Between 1848 and 1851, San Francisco was swept by six severe fires. The early city was a recipe for conflagration: wood-and-cloth houses, ocean winds, and whale-oil lamps and wood stoves used for light and heat. After the 1851 blaze—which burned a quarter-mile (0.4 km) swath and destroyed more than 1,500 houses—citizens rebuilt in more substantial brick and stone. Yerba Buena Cove was landfilled for a new financial district. Banks, churches, schools, theaters, and a horse-drawn streetcar line reflected a prosperous city grown up almost overnight from a frontier hamlet.

As gold production declined by the mid-1850s, the local economy turned to banking and manufacturing.

As gold production declined by the mid-1850s, the local economy turned to banking and manufacturing. But the city would never forget the gold rush, which turned San Francisco into an instant city, rich beyond its wildest dreams.

1859–1905: From Bonanza to Hard Times

In the waning days of California gold, a bonanza of a different color was discovered in 1859, northeast of Carson City, Nevada. History's richest silver find, the Comstock Lode produced more than $300 million from a stretch of ground a few hundred feet wide and 2 miles (3 km) long. The find brought fabulous wealth to San Francisco, whose citizens financed and controlled the mines, made or imported 90 percent of the miners' supplies, and reaped the profits. The four "Bonanza Kings" who controlled the big Consolidated Virginia mine raked in up to $500,000 per month: John W. Mackay, James C. Fair, James L. Flood, and William S. O'Brien. William C. Ralston of the Bank of California provided financing that kept the mines going despite flooding and debt, in return taking shares that made him rich. He and his partners stripped Lake Tahoe of trees for mine timbers and held a railroad monopoly to Virginia City, the main mining town.

The Comstock deluged San Francisco with capital. New banks, brokerage houses, and office buildings went up in the district around Montgomery and California Streets, which became the West Coast's financial center. When Andrew Hallidie introduced the cable car

In 1849, miners dubbed forty-niners sought riches at the dawn of the California gold rush.

in 1873, it stimulated development on Russian Hill and in Pacific Heights. Two years later, the 800-room Palace Hotel opened on Market Street.

Meanwhile, San Francisco was instrumental in building the 1869 transcontinental railroad. California business interests expected to benefit by this link to East Coast markets. The Union Pacific built westward to meet the Central Pacific heading east. Engineer Theodore Judah laid out the Central Pacific route from Sacramento across the Sierra Nevada to the meeting place at Promontory Point, Utah. Financing for the Central Pacific came from four canny Sacramento merchants: Leland Stanford, Mark Hopkins, Collis P. Huntington, and Charles T. Crocker. The "Big Four" earned huge profits and gathered vast amounts of real estate through government land grants along the railroad right-of-way. They built a transportation monopoly (known after 1884 as the Southern Pacific) that charged inflated rates and ran California politics, bribing politicians freely. Much hated, the Southern Pacific was known as the "Octopus" for its stranglehold on the West.

Although Californians expected the transcontinental railroad to bring trading advantages, instead it brought cheaper East Coast goods to San Francisco that undercut local high prices. Factories closed, unemployment rose, and the mid-1870s brought a depression. Chinese immigrants, whose labor was vital in building the Central Pacific, found themselves out of work when the project was finished. Thousands came to San Francisco and took low-wage jobs, angering unemployed white workers and provoking abuse, violence, and unfair laws such as the Chinese Exclusion Act of 1882, which blocked most Chinese immigration.

Despite turbulence, the 1880s blossomed into a so-called Gilded Age that turned the city into the "Paris of the West." The economy grew on fishing, whaling, and the shipping of wheat from California's Central Valley to Europe. Restaurants proliferated. Golden Gate Park played host to the 1894 California Midwinter Exposition.

On the flip side, the Barbary Coast district on the southern margin of Telegraph Hill peddled the seedier pleasures of the Victorian era—gambling and prostitution. The sordid could watch a woman have sex with a boar, or see a man called "Dirty Tom" who ate any disgusting substance offered. The area was rife with crime, and unwary men were "shanghaied," or kidnapped as seamen on departing ships. Under Mayor Eugene Schmitz and powerful boss Abe Ruef, political corruption rotted the fabric of civic life.

In 1898, a small industrial and shipping boom occurred when San Francisco became a base for military operations during the Spanish-American War. The new Ferry Building opened as an embarkation point to Marin and Oakland, while early skyscrapers rose in the business district. The arts also flourished. Bohemian poets lived on Russian Hill, Ambrose Bierce wrote his acerbic newspaper columns, and Mark Twain penned amused descriptions of the city.

1906–1915: Earthquake, Fire, & Recovery

Residents said it sounded like a cattle stampede, or a locomotive thundering at full speed. It was the sound of one of the worst natural disasters ever to hit a U.S. city. At 5:12 a.m. on April 18, 1906, citizens were jolted from sleep by tremors that lasted 65 seconds and unleashed the energy of 15 million tons of dynamite. The earthquake (later estimated at 8.3 on the Richter scale) took place along the notorious San Andreas Fault (see p. 20), a fracture in the Earth's crust that runs along the California coastline. It veers offshore around San Francisco, but if the fault had

The 1898 Ferry Building faces the Bay Bridge, which connects the city to Oakland.

run beneath the city, the catastrophe would have been much worse. People from Los Angeles to Coos Bay, Oregon, felt the earth move.

The temblor warped sidewalks, twisted streetcar rails out of alignment, and sent brick chimneys toppling through roofs. Several people were killed in their beds. Terrible damage occurred in reclaimed areas such as the former Yerba Buena Cove, where building foundations rested on unstable landfill. Downtown, whole fronts of buildings crashed to the streets. A woman's house was bumped 4 feet (1.2 m) down the street, making her feel like "corn in a popper."

Accustomed to occasional quakes, San Franciscans weren't panicked. Then they saw smoke rising across the city. Leaking gas pipes, broken electrical connections, and overturned wood stoves had started fires. Aid was hampered because the earthquake had not only knocked out the city's fire alarm system and killed the fire chief, but ruptured water mains so that the ample supply in reservoirs couldn't be delivered to fires. Telephone and telegraph lines went down, hindering emergency operations.

> **The temblor warped sidewalks, twisted streetcar rails out of alignment, and sent brick chimneys toppling through roofs.**

By noon, 52 fires raged in the city. Embers showered onto rooftops, spreading the blaze. That evening a witness reported "the whole front of San Francisco was ablaze, the flames shooting upward . . . with the glowing discharge of a blast furnace." The inferno reached 2,700°F, (1,482°C)

so hot that marble melted in buildings and silverware fused in kitchens. Smoke reached a height of 5 miles (8 km), and people 50 miles (80 km) away could see the fire's light and "desolating splendor." Brig. Gen. Frederick Funston dynamited buildings to clear a firebreak along the east side of Van Ness Avenue, but cinders blew across the street. Only a lucky shift in the wind turned the fire from continuing westward. Meanwhile, the mayor issued a proclamation that looters would be killed on sight.

After three days and two nights, the fire burned out. Four square miles (10 sq km) of the city were consumed, including the waterfront, business district, and industrial section—a total of 514 blocks and 28,000 buildings. The dead and missing numbered 674. Property damage was estimated at up to $500 million. Now the city had to house and feed 250,000 residents left homeless. They camped in tents in Golden Gate Park and the Presidio, and later occupied thousands of "refugee shacks" lined up in rows in the parks. Relief donations came in from around the country.

Optimistic San Franciscans rebuilt at an energetic pace. The first job was clearing streets of tons of debris, which legions of horse-drawn wagons hauled to the bay for dumping. The work was so arduous that 15,000 horses died. Three-quarters of the lost buildings were replaced within three years. Although civic leaders hoped to rebuild San Francisco in a more gracious layout planned by beaux arts architect Daniel Burnham, local businessmen quickly reoccupied their old locations, and little changed. At Civic Center Plaza, though, impressive new government buildings included the 1915 City Hall, with a dome taller than the Capitol's in Washington, D.C.

The 1906 earthquake and fire devastated the city. Property damage was estimated at $500 million.

1915–1941: An Era of Growth

Having resurrected San Francisco, residents were ready to show off their phoenix of a city to the world. Popular mayor "Sunny Jim" Rolph boosted the Panama-Pacific International Exposition of 1915, which celebrated the newly completed Panama Canal. Held in today's Marina District, this world's fair was a misty vision of gently lighted beaux arts buildings, with exhibits from many states and nations.

During this era, electric streetcars served the city. Housing was developed in the Richmond and Sunset Districts. San Francisco became a major financial center, providing capital for California's booming agriculture. To get water from the Sierra, the city built dams and reservoirs in the Tuolumne River watershed in Yosemite National Park. In 1934, a 156-mile (250 km) aqueduct began carrying water for San Francisco.

Despite the Great Depression, the city managed to complete some spectacular building projects—the Golden Gate Bridge, and the San Francisco–Oakland Bay Bridge, which was anchored to the world's largest man-made island. Here on Treasure Island in 1939, the city staged its third world's fair, the Golden Gate International Exposition, which focused on the cultures of the Pacific Rim and trade relations in Asia and the Pacific.

San Francisco became a union stronghold. Labor strife dated back to the Gilded Age, when sandlot orator Dennis Kearney criticized the rapacious railroad barons. In 1916, a bomb killed nine people during a parade supporting a military buildup before the U.S. entry into World War I. Many unionists opposed the buildup as an unfair load on the working class, and a court convicted labor activists Tom Mooney and Warren Billings for the bombing deaths. Later photos contradicted witnesses who placed Mooney at the crime scene, and his death sentence was commuted; both men were eventually released. In 1930, longshoremen held the biggest walkout in U.S. labor annals. The union gained better conditions, but only after strikebreakers sparked off rioting that killed two people.

World War II & After

During World War II, 1.6 million soldiers shipped out through the Golden Gate for action in the Pacific. The Bay Area filled with military installations. The Navy took over Treasure Island, constructing an airfield. Yards in Richmond and Sausalito built more than a thousand ships. At the Opera House, diplomats wrote the United Nations charter in spring 1945. That summer the cruiser *Indianapolis* sailed from the bay, carrying the atomic bombs that were later dropped on Japan.

Many wartime workers were women and members of minorities. The city's diverse population took shape as these workers and returning military personnel settled after the war. During the prosperous 1950s, bohemians disenchanted with conformity and mainstream society moved into North Beach, where the Beat Generation was led by writers such as Lawrence Ferlinghetti, Allen Ginsberg, and Jack Kerouac.

In 1965, another offbeat movement emerged with the hippies of Haight-Ashbury. Through them, San Francisco generated seismic shifts in American life (recreational drugs, "free love"), along with its own music (psychedelic or acid rock) and clothing style (thrift-store Victorian). The University of California at Berkeley, just across the bay, erupted with student activism and the Free Speech Movement, which among other things attacked racism and precipitated antiwar protests around the world.

By 1967, however, the flower children's ideals of sharing and "good vibes" had given way to media exploitation, hard drugs, and crime in Haight-Ashbury. A positive legacy for America was greater social tolerance as society opened more to women, gays, and minorities. San Francisco became a capital of gay liberation during the 1970s, and for the first time, a U.S. city elected out-of-the-closet politicians. In 2004, the mayor validated same-sex marriages, leading the way nationally on the issue (see sidebar p. 204).

The dot.com bubble burst in 2000, but San Francisco rose again, thanks to tech companies headquartered here and worth billions: Yelp, Uber, Pinterest, Dropbox, Airbnb. Thousands of Silicon Valley workers now live in San Francisco and commute daily. The astounding wealth they generate is changing the city—and creating the nation's highest apartment rents. Hopefully, the wealthy tech class will value and honor the culture, diversity, and free spirit that gave San Francisco its character. ∎

Loma Prieta Earthquake

On October 17, 1989, fans at Candlestick Park were waiting for the third game of the World Series when a tremor of magnitude 7.1 rocked the stadium—and the entire Bay Area. The force of the earthquake, the most powerful since 1906, jerked the Bay Bridge 5 inches (12.7 cm) north, shearing bolts and causing a 50-foot (15 m) upper section of the span to fall onto the lower section. On the Nimitz Freeway, a collapsing upper lane smashed automobiles and killed 43 people. In the Marina District, a number of houses and apartment buildings shifted off their foundations or collapsed. They stood on unstable landfill (made of rubble from the 1906 quake) that liquefied during the tremor. Fire spread, and as in 1906, residents formed bucket brigades to help firefighters. In all, 68 people died and damages exceeded $6 billion. The quake had one positive effect, however. The Embarcadero Freeway that blighted the waterfront was so damaged that it was torn down, opening up a panoramic view of the bay.

The Arts

It's no accident that the city where Jack London was born also inspired Jack Kerouac and the Grateful Dead. San Francisco seems to draw out the artistic adventurers, the questioners, the seekers of an alternative view. The best of the city's creative output turns things on their heads, makes you see the world afresh—either openly, as in Allen Ginsberg's poem "Howl" (see sidebar p. 81), or more subtly, as in the photographs of Ansel Adams.

Literary San Francisco

San Franciscans have always liked to read. The city had a newspaper by January 1847, when colorful Mormon leader turned entrepreneur Sam Brannan launched the weekly *California Star*. The paper later merged with the rival *Californian* as the

A sculpture by Claes Oldenburg and Coosje van Bruggen decorates the Embarcadero waterfront.

Alta California, the West's first daily. Pioneer newspapers were produced on hand-presses. When newsprint was scarce, they were printed on any handy substitute, from Chinese tea paper to brown manila.

Writers developed their craft in the city's literary journals. The first was the *Golden Era* (1852), which ran early poems and sketches by its typesetter, Bret Harte. Harte's short story, "The Luck of Roaring Camp," made him famous. He romanticized the life of the mining towns, portraying the gambler and the "prostitute with a heart of gold"—before they were stock characters. Harte's romanticism was counterbalanced by the satire of Mark Twain (see sidebar p. 26), who moved to San Francisco in 1864, stayed more than two years, and made his early reputation with a tall tale ("The Celebrated Jumping Frog of Calaveras County") and an account of his travels in the West called *Roughing It*.

San Francisco's literary and bohemian circles included the future poet laureate of California, Ina Coolbrith (see sidebar p. 97); she nurtured many writers, including the young Jack London (1876–1916). The unlikely son of an astrologer and a spiritualist medium, London worked in a cannery, became an "oyster pirate," and sought adventure on a schooner in the South Pacific. He wrote more than 50 books (including *The Sea-Wolf, The Call of the Wild,* and *Martin Eden*) and more than a hundred short stories, in which he tackled stark action and themes of social philosophy.

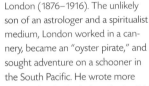

Pioneer newspapers were produced on handpresses. When newsprint was scarce, they were printed on any handy substitute, from Chinese tea paper to brown manila.

Poet Cincinnatus Heine Miller changed his name to Joaquin (inspired by bandit Joaquin Murrieta) and wrote about larger-than-life Western characters: frontiersmen, Indians, outlaws. He strode around in tall boots, a red flannel shirt, and a sombrero. Known as the Poet of the Sierra, he was more famous for his eccentricity than for his poetry.

By the 1880s, the city's dominant literary voice was that of Ambrose Bierce, whose "Prattle" column attacked people and issues with a bludgeon of black wit. He also produced the acerbic *The Devil's Dictionary*. During this period, Robert Louis Stevenson and Rudyard Kipling passed through and wrote about San Francisco. On the light side, in the mid-1890s, Gelett Burgess edited the gleefully anarchic *The Lark,* which published stories and poems with a silly streak. His "Purple Cow" became a classic of nonsense verse, and he wrote a response to the unsought fame it brought: "Ah yes, I Wrote the 'Purple Cow' / I'm sorry, now, I Wrote it!/But I can Tell you Anyhow/I'll Kill you if you Quote it."

At the turn of the century, Frank Norris set his realist novel *McTeague* in San Francisco, while *The Octopus* showed the Southern Pacific railroad's stranglehold on California. During the

1920s, Dashiell Hammett lived in San Francisco, the shadowy setting for *The Maltese Falcon*. He finished this hard-boiled detective classic in an apartment on Leavenworth Street.

The Beats and Beyond: The best known literary movement to come out of San Francisco spun out of North Beach and the 1950s Beat Generation. The Beat vibe was best exemplified by Jack Kerouac. He wrote *On The Road* (1957) in the spontaneous style of jazz in a three-week burst of almost continuous typing on a long roll of teletype paper. Kerouac's success spread Beat ideas of wandering the open road, partying, and yearning for freedom to the larger American culture, previously dominated by conformity and complacency.

A poetry renaissance began in 1955, when Allen Ginsberg erupted with "Howl" (see sidebar p. 81) at the Six Gallery on Fillmore Street. (An obscenity trial followed its subsequent publication by Lawrence Ferlinghetti.) Among other local poets were Kenneth Rexroth, the Zen-influenced Gary Snyder, and Ferlinghetti, whose City Lights Bookstore in North Beach was, and still is, a hub of literary life.

During the mid-1970s, Armistead Maupin wrote stories of young San Franciscans, both straight and gay, collected in the book *Tales of the City*. Other local writers include Herbert Gold *(Fathers),* Alice Walker *(The Color Purple),* and Amy Tan, whose *The Joy Luck Club* unfolds partly in Chinatown. In 2002 Dave Eggers *(A Heartbreaking Work of Staggering Genius)* co-founded 826 Valencia, a storefront nonprofit in the Mission District that helps young people develop writing skills and enthusiasm for the literary arts.

> **The best known literary movement to come out of San Francisco spun out of North Beach and the 1950s Beat Generation.**

In the Movies

As photogenic as a movie star, San Francisco has been the setting or subject of more than 500 films. Among early ones are *Frisco Kid* (1935, James Cagney), *San Francisco* (1936, Clark Gable), *After the Thin Man* (1936, William Powell), and *The Maltese Falcon* (1941, Humphrey Bogart). Later films include *Vertigo* (1958), *The Birdman of Alcatraz* (1962), *Bullitt* (1968), *Dirty Harry* (1971), *What's Up Doc* (1972), *The Conversation* (1974), *Towering Inferno* (1974), *Escape From Alcatraz* (1979), *Pacific Heights* (1990), *Sister Act* (1992), *Mrs. Doubtfire* (1993), *Golden Gate* (1993), *Zodiac* (2007), *Milk* (2008), *Rise of the Planet of the Apes* (2011), *Blue Jasmine* (2013), and *San Andreas* (2015).

Theater & Ballet

San Francisco's love for the performing arts dates back to the gold rush. In June 1849, the city's first theatrical event featured a New York actor doing impressions in the Portsmouth Square schoolhouse. By 1850, Shakespeare productions competed with less elevated saloon shows and circuses. Illiterate cab driver Tom Maguire opened the first of several Jenny Lind Theaters and then Maguire's Opera House. Spanish dancer Lola Montez came to town with her Spider Dance, which involved shaking whalebone "spiders" from her skimpy costume and stomping on them. The city was also a stop for touring East Coast performers such as actor Edwin Booth.

(continued on p. 38)

EXPERIENCE: Imbibe High Culture & Cocktails

Some of San Francisco's hottest nightspots these days are museums and arts organizations. After work hours, they serve up cultural offerings with drinks and food. Some programs are free with admission; check the organizations' websites for details and schedules. Here are some starters for you to consider during your visit to the city.

Seen on Facebook: "Great times and great tunes. I can't wait for Marc Fong to DJ again." But the fan wasn't raving about a dance club—the entry was about the **California Academy of Sciences** (see pp. 167–169) Its "NightLife" series on select Thursday evenings invites adults to explore the academy, enjoy music, science programs, and sip cocktails with like-minded urbanites.

The Artists Drawing Club, held one Thursday a month at the **Asian Art Museum** (see pp. 183–186) has a guest artist draw inspiration from the collection, the building, or the neighborhood to create an interactive event for the public. Example: Artists promenading through the galleries, wearing or holding pieces based on objects in the museum. Events often include a DJ and bar.

Friday night programs at the **de Young Museum** (see pp. 164–167) offer lectures, films, performance art, and workshops, all with strategically situated cocktail bars.

"A field trip for adults"— that's "After Dark," taking place every first Thursday at the **Exploratorium** (see p. 193). The innovative science museum shakes up a beaker of alcohol, conversation, and intriguing programs on topics from music to electricity to sex. Along with performances, films, and music, there's the opportunity to play with hands-on science exhibits. Other Thursdays offer small programs—e.g., a 3-D film on the secret life of cats.

Events at the **American Conservatory Theater** (see Travelwise p. 262) range from "Out With A.C.T." parties for LGBT patrons to "Theater on the Couch," a post-show Q&A session where psychoanalysts probe the play's psychological dimensions.

Every third Thursday of the month, SoMa's **Yerba Buena neighborhood** offers the chance to wander among museums and galleries to enjoy art and music, while bars and restaurants serve extended happy hour drinks and food. An endless variety of events have included a salsa dance concert and a light-sculpture installation.

"SoundBox" brings an underground club vibe to a backstage space at the **San Francisco Symphony** (see Travelwise p. 262). Advanced electronics

Revelers await a Friday-night SoundBox performance at the San Francisco Symphony.

(25 microphones and 85 speakers) create a perfect acoustical environment for anything from Gregorian chants to contemporary experimental music. Held on irregular Fridays, with cocktails and gourmet snacks.

Downtown art galleries stay open late for casual open houses every **First Thursday** of the month. For a map and list of galleries that participate, visit *firstthursdayart.com*.

Shows in today's theater district, west of Union Square, range from avant-garde to mainstream musical. The Geary Theatre runs repertory works by ACT/American Conservatory Theatre. Other venues include the San Francisco Playhouse (off-Broadway), the Magic Theatre (new plays), and the Lorraine Hansberry Theatre (African-American shows). Campy *Beach Blanket Babylon* (see p. 96) plays at Club Fugazi in North Beach. The San Francisco Mime Troupe has presented satirical pieces for more than 50 years. The San Francisco Shakespeare Festival gives free performances outdoors in the Presidio.

Founded in 1933, the San Francisco Ballet ranks among the nation's top companies. It was the first company to stage *The Nutcracker* in the United States, and at Christmas it mounts a spectacular production of this ballet.

Psychedelic Concert Posters

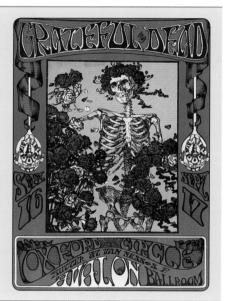

A revolution in graphic design, San Francisco concert posters of the 1960s blended swirling kaleidoscopic imagery, the intense optical vibration of pop art, elaborate lettering, and rubbery distortions. To mimic LSD hallucinations, Victor Moscoso adopted the flowing curves of art nouveau and the clashing colors of painter Josef Albers, his art instructor at Yale. Stanley Mouse and Alton Kelly appropriated commercial images (like the Zig-Zag man on cigarette rolling papers) and also designed the Grateful Dead's skull-and-roses motif. The posters resonated with hippies who turned on, tuned in, and dropped out to a sound track of psychedelic music.

Music

The sound track for the 1960s was partly played by San Francisco bands, which blossomed with the flower children and marijuana-LSD culture of Haight-Ashbury. The San Francisco Sound (aka psychedelic or acid rock) was created by major groups (the Jefferson Airplane, the Grateful Dead, Big Brother and the Holding Company with Janis Joplin) and many long-forgotten others.

A common thread was experimentation with LSD and other psychedelics. As a result, the bands' songs became longer and more improvised, with extended jams. New electronics altered rock music with echo, fuzztone, and wah-wah effects. Concerts were often accompanied by hallucinatory light shows.

In the late 1960s, the hippie scene was exploited in songs such as Scott McKenzie's "San Francisco (Be Sure to Wear Some Flowers in Your Hair)" and Eric Burdon and the

Animals' "San Franciscan Nights." The seminal Grateful Dead, though, stayed active for decades, keeping the spirit of the '60s alive.

In more traditional music forms, the dazzling San Francisco Opera at the War Memorial Opera House features top performers and imaginative sets. (There are video screens above the stage.) The San Francisco Symphony performs at the Louise M. Davies Symphony Hall. (Violinists Yehudi Menuhin and Isaac Stern debuted with the orchestra.) The Herbst Theatre presents chamber and baroque music. The annual San Francisco Jazz Festival is intelligently programmed, with top stars in intriguing venues.

Painting, Photography, & Sculpture

The visual arts in San Francisco form a composite image of the city's life and times. The oldest "work of art" is Mission Dolores (1791), whose Mexican altars and bronze bells reflect the era of the mission-founding padres, while its painted ceiling decorations evoke the basketry patterns of the Ohlone people.

The California gold rush brought an influx of influences and cultural styles from the world outside, notably from Europe. Painter Charles Christian Nahl used classical technique to depict life in the mining camps. His canvases, such as "Sunday Morning in the Mine" (1872), show telling details and wry humor, and, like the stories of Bret Harte, offer a living picture of early California.

At mid-century, a school of landscape took root, its best known painter being Albert Bierstadt (1830–1902), who first traveled west with a surveying expedition. His monumental canvases depict the vast gorges and towering mountains of the West. Thomas Hill painted Yosemite and other outdoor subjects, while William Keith produced tranquil, dappled landscapes of oak groves, hills, and brooks.

San Francisco's newly rich art patrons were a rather conservative, stiff-collared lot who preferred works that would decorate their mansions and lend prestige. (California's railroad and mining millionaires, such as Mark Hopkins and James Flood, scoured Europe for works of art, furniture, and tapestries.)

A group of painters helped form the Bohemian Club in 1872, about the same time that the San Francisco Art Association opened a gallery and school. Later, the association occupied the Mark Hopkins mansion on Nob Hill, then moved to Russian Hill. Its members included painters Bierstadt and Keith, and pioneering photographer Eadweard Muybridge, whose motion studies of a galloping horse (1872), taken by a series of still cameras, made photographic history.

Around the turn of the 20th century, Douglas Tilden created many heroic sculptures, including the "Mechanics' Monument" on Market Street, depicting muscled men wrestling with a lever and wheel. His pupil Robert Aitken created the figure of "Victory" that graces the Dewey Monument in Union Square. Meanwhile, Arthur Putnam produced snarling bronze jaguars and mountain lions, and various other creatures, all carefully observed. (His previous experience with animals included driving cattle and working in the backcountry.)

New artistic styles and influences flowed into San Francisco after the Panama-Pacific International Exposition of 1915, where works by Claude Monet and Edgar Degas were shown. When passing through San Francisco, Henri Matisse made colorful pictures of tropical fish at the Steinhart Aquarium. Mexican muralist Diego Rivera came to paint frescoes, including one at the San Francisco Art Institute. His style and technique influenced the government-subsidized artists who decorated the interior of Coit Tower during the 1930s Depression.

Watercolorist Dong Kingman used a bright palette to depict San Francisco scenes. In 1932, Ansel Adams, Edward Weston, and other photographers founded the influential Group f/64, whose ultrasharp images were a reaction against the romantic soft focus then in fashion. Sculptor Beniamino Bufano dotted the city's parks and playgrounds with huge stylized figures, including one of Sun Yat-sen (1938) in St. Mary's Square. But San Franciscans rejected his proposal to erect a 156-foot-tall (47.5 m) statue of St. Francis atop Twin Peaks. (The stainless-steel saint would have had his arms upraised, prompting a critic to quip: "It looks like a holdup.")

After World War II, abstract art came to the city under the tutelage of Mark Rothko and Clyfford Still at the San Francisco Art Institute, where they influenced students Sam Francis and Robert Motherwell. In reaction, Bay Area figurative painters such as Richard Diebenkorn produced representational work. (Diebenkorn's "Seated Woman" is part of the de Young collection; see pp. 164–167.)

The 1960s were reflected in work by artists such as Wayne Thiebaud, who portrayed features of popular culture. Since the 1970s, street muralists in the Mission District have painted buildings, alleyways, schools, and garage doors with colorful depictions of Latino life, work, dreams, and heritage. Some works are officially sanctioned and funded by arts programs, while others have the joy-of-graffiti quality of in-your-face street art.

San Francisco's art scene currently focuses around galleries near Union Square and the SoMa axis: the San Francisco Museum of Modern Art, specialized museums, and the Center for the Arts at Yerba Buena Gardens.

Architecture

The earliest structures around San Francisco Bay have long vanished—the huts of the Ohlone and Coast Miwok people, which were fashioned of a marsh bulrush called tule. European architecture was introduced after 1776 by Franciscan padres of the mission period. For their California missions they employed 17th- and 18th-century Spanish designs and construction methods, adapting them to a remote frontier with limited building materials: mud and wood. The Mission style was distinguished by thick walls of adobe (mud stabilized with straw), massive timbers, tile floors, and red-tile roofs. The only original example in San Francisco is Mission Dolores, the city's oldest building (1791). Three-foot-thick (1 m) walls have kept it standing despite earthquakes. Of the original Spanish *presidio*, or military post, nothing remains but adobe wall fragments now part of the Officers' Club.

> The Mission style was distinguished by thick walls of adobe (mud stabilized with straw), massive timbers, tile floors, and red-tile roofs.

With the California gold rush of 1848, wooden buildings predominated. After a series of fires raged through the canvas and wooden structures downtown, solid brick buildings were erected, often with iron shutters. Some commercial buildings survive in Jackson Square, next to the Financial District. Notable are the Golden Era Building (1852) and the Hotaling Warehouse (1866).

For the rest of the 19th century, Victorian architecture (see pp. 42–43) dominated.

Mission Dolores, dedicated in 1791, sits next to the parish basilica.

Architects of the ensuing arts and crafts style emphasized a natural appearance by using redwood, stone, and dark-stained shingles, often adapting decorative devices from Japan.

After the turn of the 20th century, San Francisco was caught up in the City Beautiful movement to redesign America's urban environments more aesthetically. The dominant style was beaux arts, derived from principles taught at the École des Beaux-Arts in Paris. A revival of classical and Renaissance design, the style was used chiefly for public buildings. Highlights include the Bank of California and the Fairmont Hotel, whose resurrection after the 1906 earthquake was overseen by Julia Morgan. The 1915 City Hall has a classical dome, Doric pillars, and Greek temple motifs. The pinnacle of beaux arts achievement in the city is the Palace of Fine Arts, sole survivor of the 1915 Panama-Pacific International Exposition. The California Palace of the Legion of Honor (1924) was designed by George Applegarth, who studied at the École des Beaux-Arts in Paris.

Modern architectural innovations appeared as early as the 1890s, when steel frames helped San Francisco buildings rise high. In 1917, Willis Polk produced a design four

(continued on p. 44)

San Francisco's Painted Ladies

San Francisco's exuberance during the second half of the 19th century found perfect expression in Victorian architecture, with its excessive ornamentation. Victorian houses ran riot with fanciful towers, bay windows, gingerbread decoration, turned posts and spindles, shingles, and gables. Oddly, most houses were mass-produced with similar floor plans on narrow plots of land. Their individuality came from the choice of embellishments and mixture of colors with which they were dressed up.

A Victorian house on Filbert Street sports a colorful Gothic Revival facade.

Ornamentation and structural framing were of wood—redwood, pine, fir—which was in plentiful supply in nearby coastal forests and therefore inexpensive. Houses were designed to fit San Francisco's narrow lots, generally 25 feet (7.6 m) wide by 100 feet (30.5 m) deep, a size that allowed developers to squeeze more houses onto a parcel of land . . . and more profits out. Bay windows eased the sense of narrowness by affording more sunlight, fresh air, and floor space.

About 15,000 Victorian houses still stand in San Francisco, many of them in Pacific Heights, the Western Addition, Haight-Ashbury, the Mission District, and the Castro District. These areas, situated west and south of downtown, escaped both the 1906 fire and subsequent redevelopment. In recent years, numerous Victorians have been lovingly restored, in many cases after various ill-conceived "modernizations" have first been corrected. Homeowners often paint the facades and trim with a vibrant palette of colors, quite unlike the pale hues typically used in the Victorian era itself. (The period takes its name from the virtuous and duty-bound Queen Victoria, who ruled Great Britain between 1837 and 1901.) Four major styles of architecture appeared successively in San Francisco during the Victorian period.

Gothic Revival: Popular in the 1850s and 1860s, this style (also known as Carpenter Gothic) draws on features of Medieval Gothic architecture and is distinguished by its use of spacious porches and balconies, pointed arches, and especially by carved or pierced bargeboards (trim attached to the projecting edges of gable roofs). Many dwellings of this style were modest cottages, usually painted white. (The house at 1978 Filbert Street is a good example.)

Italianate: A feature of the 1870s, the Italianate style evoked the villas and palazzos of Italy. Straight rooflines were topped with high cornices (horizontal molded projections). Neoclassical decorations framed the doors and windows, and porches often had pediments (triangular elements of classical Greek style). The facade was flat and formal, with symmetrically placed windows. The overall effect was a palatial look, even for a small house. As the style developed, later designs also incorporated bay windows. (The Pacific Union Club at 1000 California Street, originally a private mansion, is built in an Italianate style.)

Stick: In vogue in the 1880s, this style is also called Stick Eastlake (in honor of Charles Locke Eastlake, a British writer and designer who influenced furniture and architectural tastes of the late Victorian era). It can be identified by its strong vertical lines, which are created by long "sticks" of ornamental wood trim. Other characteristic features include square bay windows, square corners, false gables, and ornately decorative brackets. Embellishments were created by skilled wood-carvers. (Houses at 111–115 Liberty Street are excellent examples of Stick architecture.)

Queen Anne: Widely favored during the 1890s, this inventive, exuberant style showed off contrasts in texture (decorative shingles, stone, clapboard, brick, sunburst patterns, and other ornamentations) and form (turrets, pointed roofs, corner towers with witch's cap roofs, pediments, Venetian windows). Designs were asymmetrical, with stronger horizontal lines than in earlier styles. (Good examples of Queen Anne architecture include the Haas-Lilienthal house, 2007 Franklin Street, and the much photographed strip of houses on Alamo Square, 710–720 Steiner Street.)

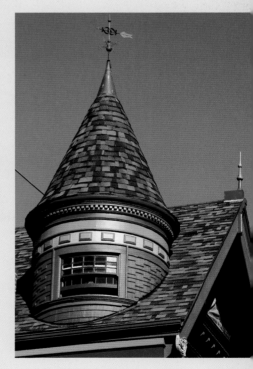

A turret caps this example of Queen Anne architecture near Alamo Square.

The new wing of the renovated San Francisco Museum of Modern Art

decades ahead of its time for the eight-story Hallidie Building, the grandfather of modern steel-and-glass skyscrapers; its glass curtain wall was a radical innovation. Among early skyscrapers, the 30-story Pacific Telephone and Telegraph Company headquarters (1925) appeared to soar heavenward, an effect achieved with stepped-back levels. Other notable buildings included 450 Sutter Street, an art deco building in Maya style, and the neo-Gothic Russ Building (1927), whose E-shaped footprint allowed light and air to penetrate to the offices.

Major construction in San Francisco took a 30-year hiatus, mostly caused by the Great Depression and World War II. In the 1960s, urban renewal in the Western Addition saw thousands of pre-1906 houses, flats, and shops razed to make way for multiple-family units. (The loss of so many early buildings helped give rise to the city's historic preservation movement.) The downtown skyline began to bristle with office towers, notably the Crown Zellerbach building (1959), which rests upon piers, and the cross-braced Alcoa building (1964). Later came the Bank of America headquarters (1969), with 52 floors and almost two million square feet (185,800 sq m) of offices, and the Hyatt Regency hotel (1973), with one of the world's largest atrium lobbies. The Transamerica Pyramid (1972) rises 853 feet (260 m), the city's tallest building—until the 1,070-foot (326 m) Salesforce Tower is completed in 2018—and a most recognizable emblem.

The Main Public Library (1995) is a postmodern take on beaux arts design. Notable contemporary architecture includes AT&T Park (2000), the copper-clad de Young museum (2005), and the Museum of Modern Art (1995, 2016). ∎

The Financial District—framed by Market and Kearny Streets, Pacific Avenue, and the Embarcadero

Financial District

John C. Portman's "The Tulip" sculpture at the Embarcadero Center

Financial District

You can almost hear the money piling up in the bank vaults of this powerhouse center of the city's financial life. Steel-and-glass skyscrapers of megacorporations tower above turn-of-the-20th-century banking halls that resemble Roman temples of commerce. Skyscrapers from the 1920s still soar gracefully. Both old and new buildings represent imposing feats of engineering and, in some cases, high points of American architecture.

The district's roots go back to the 1830s, when it was the site of Yerba Buena Cove, a small trading settlement. American forces under Capt. John Montgomery took it over from Mexico in 1846. The next year Jasper O'Farrell extended the street layout of the fledgling city. He laid out Market Street, a wide boulevard that slices across the downtown grid at a 36-degree angle. Market Street later became a line of social demarcation, with financial institutions and the upper class to the north, and industry and the working class to the south.

During the gold rush, droves of forty-niners (see pp. 27–28) transformed what was a backwater settlement of 500 people into a teeming throng of 20,000. The city's eastern shoreline lay at Montgomery Street, from which wharves were built into the bay to serve the merchants' warehouses. Soon the mudflats between the wharves were filled in with sand, trash, and abandoned ships whose crews had lit out for the goldfields. More than a hundred such ships were buried beneath the city as the shoreline pushed steadily eastward to today's Embarcadero.

As San Francisco got rich on gold and silver in the 1850s and 1860s, new financial institutions arose on the old waterfront, earning the area around Montgomery Street the title of the "Wall Street of the West." When the Bank of California opened in 1866 on California Street, this became the area's most prestigious commercial address.

Around 1890, the downtown area began to grow up—literally. The first steel-frame skyscrapers began to rise, among them the Mills Building, a Romanesque Revival design by Daniel Burnham that still stands on Montgomery Street. Most of the Financial District was reduced to rubble and ashes in the 1906 earthquake and fire, but it was quickly rebuilt. Today, apart from the area around Jackson Square, little remains of the city created by the gold rush. By the 1920s, innovative taller buildings were scraping the sky. Like other tall art deco buildings, the Shell Building incorporated stepped-back towers and vertical design elements that made it appear to rocket upward.

But the advent of the 1930s Great Depression put a lid on this new thrust. Not until the end of the 1950s did construction start again.

NOT TO BE MISSED:

It began with the Crown Zellerbach Building in 1959, and culminated in the late 1960s and 1970s with the Bank of America headquarters and Transamerica Pyramid. Still more towers rose upward in the 1980s. About 38 million square feet (3.5 million sq m) of office space is contained within these few blocks.

Wander around the Financial District at lunchtime with office workers enjoying the fresh air. Step aside as power brokers stride past. Peek into the often exceptional lobbies of the buildings. Stroll the streets and gaze upward to see the art of building at its loftiest. But watch out for speeding bicycle messengers! ∎

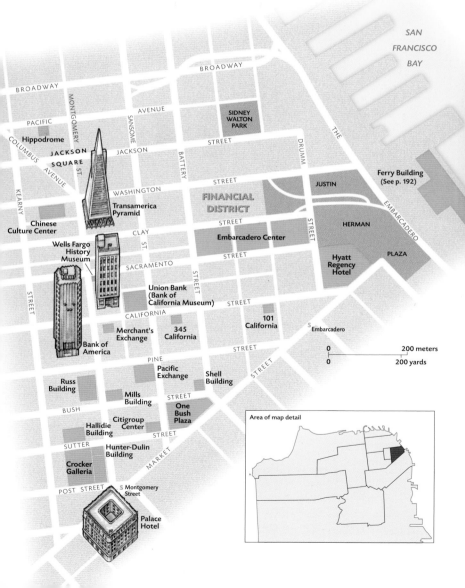

Around the Financial District

The Financial District is an open-air textbook of architectural periods, with stunning new skyscrapers and resplendent old banking halls that draw on classical styles. These are working buildings, so they may not provide access for travelers.

A city view features the Financial District and the iconic Transamerica Pyramid at center.

Transamerica Pyramid

 Map p. 47

✉ 600 Montgomery St.

🚋 CC: California St.; Bus: 1, 15, 42; BART: Montgomery

Transamerica Pyramid

This is the most easily recognized building in the city. Built in 1972 with 48 stories and a spire, it rises 853 feet (260 m)—taller than any other building in San Francisco (until the Salesforce Tower opens in 2018, with 61 stories). Why a pyramid? Architect William Pereira realized that its slender shape would allow more light to reach the street than a standard box design. Transamerica, an insurance and financial company, realized that as a corporate logo, the pyramid would put them on the map.

Here are amazing Pyramid facts, from the ground up: The base is a 30,000-ton (30,000 tonnes) concrete slab laced with more than 300 miles (480 km) of steel reinforcing rods. The walls slope at five degrees; their 3,000 quartz aggregate panels weigh 3.5 tons (3.1 tonnes) each and are spaced to allow movement in an earthquake. Exactly 3,678 windows pierce the building. The largest floor is the fifth at 145 feet per side (44 m); the smallest is the 48th, only 45 feet (13 m) per side. The 212-foot (65 m) spire is hollow and illuminated from inside. On the east side, this skyscraper has a California redwood grove.

The pyramid occupies the site of the 1853 Montgomery Block, once the biggest building west of the Mississippi. With offices for lawyers, businessmen, and newspapers, it was visited by everyone from Mark Twain to Sun Yat-sen.

California Street

The former **Bank of America Building** (1969) soars 52 stories upward (779 ft/237 m) and contains almost two million square feet (185,800 sq m) of office space, where 5,000 people work. The facades zigzag to make bay windows and are clad in polished carnelian granite, creating a looming, deep red presence in the cityscape. The building appeared in the 1970s movies *Dirty Harry* and *The Towering Inferno*. In the California Street plaza, a massive granite lump of a sculpture, "Transcendence" (1969) by Masayuki Nagare, is nicknamed "The Banker's Heart."

Bank of America founder Amadeo P. Giannini started his bank in 1904 for Italian immigrants whom other banks wouldn't serve. His Bank of Italy (as it was first called) accepted deposits as small as a dollar. During the 1906 fire, Giannini himself hauled deposits to safety, hidden in fruit crates. Giannini created

the branch banking system; by 1945, the Bank of America was the nation's largest (it no longer is).

In 1864, William Ralston and Darius Mills founded the **Bank of California** (*now Union Bank, 400 California St.*). Ralston had made a fortune investing in Nevada's Comstock mines, and used it to finance projects such as the city's first iron mill. This banking temple (1907, Bliss and Faville) has Corinthian columns, a marble interior, and windows soaring toward a 60-foot-high (18 m) coffered ceiling. The basement **Bank of California Museum** displays

INSIDER TIP:

Every April 18 at 5:12 a.m., the date and time of the 1906 earthquake, a ceremony is held at Lotta's Fountain on Market Street.

—SUSAN WINBLAD NELSON
Third generation San Franciscan

gold rush and Comstock artifacts: nuggets, banknotes, and privately minted coins.

The entrance of **345 California Center** (1987, Skidmore, Owings & Merrill) retains the fronts of two historic buildings (1919, 1920) that housed the Dollar Lines steamship company. The top 11 floors make up the elegant Loews Regency, with twin towers linked by dizzying glass "sky bridges." **101 California** (1982, Johnson & Burgee) is a

Bank of America Building

- Map p. 47
- 555 California St.
- CC: California St.; Bus: 1, 15; BART: Montgomery

Bank of California Museum

- Map p. 47
- Union Bank, 400 California St.
- Closed Sat.–Sun.
- CC: California St.; Bus: 1, 42

**Wells Fargo
History Museum**

⬛ Map p. 47
✉ 420 Mont-
    gomery St.
☎ 415/396-2619
🕐 Closed Sat.–Sun.
💳 CC: California
    St.; Bus: 1, 12,
    15, 42

**wellsfargohistory
.com**

round glass silo. A slanted glass gallery cutting across the lower floors gives the tower above a weightless appearance.

Montgomery Street

The 31-story **Russ Building** (235 Montgomery St., private) was designed in 1927 in Gothic Revival style by George Kelham, whose E-shaped plan

---

A Visit to the Bar With the Priceless Painting

The cocktail lounge Maxfield's in the venerable Palace Hotel hides an unexpected artistic treasure: "The Pied Piper." In 1909, celebrated illustrator Maxfield Parrish painted this 7-by-16-foot (2.1 x 4.8 m) canvas of the Pied Piper leading children along a rocky path with a mountain castle above. The fairy-tale scene is aglow with Parrish's trademark golden light. A tip: It's okay to pop in just to admire the painting, which hangs above the bar.

---

allows light and ventilation to penetrate to the offices. The lobby has inlaid floors, stone vaults, and ornate bronze elevator doors. The city's first all-steel-frame structure, the 1891 **Mills Building** (220 Montgomery St., private) was designed by Daniel Burnham in the Chicago-school style, with an exterior of marble, buff brick, and terra-cotta, and a Romanesque entry arch. A 21-story tower by Lewis Hobart was added in 1931.

Also in this area, the **Wells Fargo History Museum** tells of the company that Henry Wells and William Fargo established in 1852 to provide banking, express,

and mail services to the West. You'll see an 1860s Concord stagecoach, a re-created Wells Fargo office, raw gold and coins, and Wells Fargo strongboxes.

Other Buildings

Designed by George Kelham in 1929, the soaring art deco **Shell Building** (100 Bush St.) is clad in terra-cotta. Its entrance is topped with a scallop shell, one of many such motifs honoring the client, Shell Oil. The design was influenced by Eliel Saarinen's second-place entry in the Chicago Tribune Tower competition, a design never executed but of great impact.

The city's first international style building is **One Bush Street Plaza,** with its green glass tower set atop stilts and its low round pavilion. Designed in 1959 (Skidmore, Owings & Merrill for Crown Zellerbach), it also has a sunken plaza and an elevator tower of uniform mosaic.

Citigroup Center (1 Sansome St.), a 1984 design by William Pereira, preserves part of a 1910 beaux arts bank. Its forecourt displays a 1983 copy of the 1870 A. Stirling Calder statue from the 1915 Panama-Pacific International Exposition, "Star Girl," a woman in diaphanous gown and radiant star headdress. A block west, the 1926 **Hunter-Dulin Building** (111 Sutter St.) is where Sam Spade has his office in Dashiell Hammett's mystery stories.

Next door is the glass-roofed **Crocker Galleria** (1982, Skidmore, Owings & Merrill), an arcade of boutiques and cafés. ∎

Jackson Square

In Jackson Square, you can imagine you're in the gold rush era of San Francisco. Miners once weighed glittering nuggets on Gold and Balance Streets. Wells Fargo coaches rattled into livery stables on Hotaling Place. The district—bounded by Washington Street, Columbus Avenue, Pacific Avenue, and Sansome Street—preserves masonry buildings and cast-iron facades dating back to the 1850s. The streets are narrow and most buildings are under 40 feet (12 m) high.

In the 19th century, this part of town, particularly Pacific Avenue, was infamous as the **Barbary Coast** (named after pirate waters off North Africa). In this rough-and-tumble ten-derloin, men were men and women were prostitutes—hundreds of them working in tiny "cribs." The most depraved acts became entertainment: On stage, women had sex with horses. For a few pennies a man named Oofty Goofty let people beat him with a baseball bat; another man ate any disgusting glop presented to him.

The streets jumped with saloons called the Morgue, Devil's Kitchen, and the like. "Give it a wide berth as you value your life," said an 1878 tourist guide, describing "the precise locality, so that our readers may *keep away*." Dance hall entertainers included the Little Lost Chicken, who cried at the end of her songs and later picked the pockets of the crowd. A sister act called the Dancing Heifer and the Galloping Cow made the audience—and the boards of the stage—groan. Of all the dance halls, the old **Hippodrome** (*555 Pacific Ave.*) still shows off its bas-relief facade of busty girls.

Buildings here largely survived the 1906 earthquake and fire. In 1908, San Francisco's first gay bar, The Dash, opened at Pacific Avenue and Kearny Street. But after 1913, the government

Jackson Square
🅰 Map p. 47
🚌 Bus: 12, 15, 42, 83

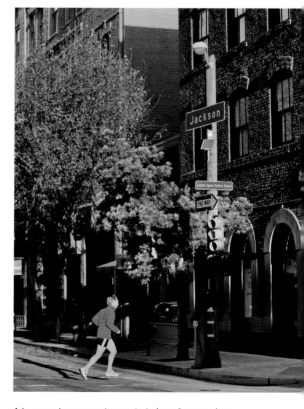

A jogger enjoys a morning run in Jackson Square, where historic brick buildings recall California's gold rush days.

expunged sin from the Barbary Coast. When the Great Depression lowered rents, artists moved in. Twenty years later, the district was taken over by interior decorators, then antiques shops, galleries, and ad agencies. Today, invading tech companies and start-ups have driven up rents, forcing out long-time dealers and bringing many upscale restaurants.

One axis is Montgomery Street. Among past tenants of the 1851 building at **722 Montgomery** were an auctioneer, a Turkish bathhouse, and a theater where frontier chanteuse Lotta Crabtree performed. In the late 1950s, a flamboyant lawyer, the late Melvin Belli, moved in. Whenever he won a big tort case, the building flew a Jolly Roger flag. The three-story brick building at **728 Montgomery** (1854) occupies

EXPERIENCE: Go on the Hunt for Antiques

You're seeking out some of the remaining Jackson Square antiques shops when something in a window catches your eye. A 1930s travel poster? You must be outside **Sarah Stocking** (368 Jackson St.), which also carries posters from bygone world's fairs and the performing arts. An ancient Greek urn displayed near a 1950s abstract expressionist painting? You're browsing at eclectic **Foster-Gwin** (38 Hotaling Pl.). As you explore the shops in this neighborhood's restored 1850s buildings, you'll also find 17th-century European furniture, California landscape paintings, antique scientific instruments, and botanical prints. If you're not in a buying mood, think of the shops as fascinating small museums.

the site where California's first Masonic Lodge meeting took place in 1849. Reputedly, Bret Harte wrote his short story "The Luck of Roaring Camp" here in the 1850s. Artists later occupied the top floors, where they entertained Oscar Wilde in 1882. More literary history was made at **730–732 Montgomery,** the 1852 Golden Era Building, home to the literary weekly that published early work by Harte and Twain.

The **400 block** of **Jackson Street** is lined with historic buildings. The former French consulate at **472 Jackson** (1852) has simple brick walls and its original iron shutters upstairs for fire protection. The 1860s masonry buildings on each side of Hotaling Place—**445, 455,** and **463 Jackson**—were the domain of liquor distiller Anson Hotaling, purveyor of booze to the Barbary Coast. When his Italianate warehouse survived the 1906 fire, a local wit wrote the famous jingle: "If, as they say, God spanked the town/ For being over-frisky/Why did He burn all the churches down/ And spare Hotaling's whiskey?" Possible answer: Firemen worked *really* hard to save this particular building. In 1893, Domingo Ghirardelli opened his pioneering chocolate factory (see pp. 110–111) in an 1853 building at **415 Jackson.**

Off Jackson, **Balance Street** was reputedly named for a ship buried here as landfill, a common practice during gold rush fever. ∎

Palace Hotel

It would be accurate to describe the Palace Hotel as a phoenix, because the building you see today rose out of the ashes of an earlier one and carries on some of its extraordinary style.

The opulent Palace Hotel's Garden Court Restaurant

Occupying a whole block, the city's grande dame original Palace Hotel was financed by William Ralston of the Bank of California in 1875. Guests entered a central courtyard edged with tiers of balconies and capped by a vast skylight. With seven stories and ample white paint, the hotel was compared to a combination of riverboat and wedding cake. There were newfangled elevators. Guests ranged from President Ulysses S. Grant to actress Sarah Bernhardt, who arrived in 1887 with her pet baby tiger.

In 1906, tenor Enrico Caruso checked in with 40 pairs of boots and an equal number of portraits of himself, but fled in a bath towel when the great earthquake struck. The Palace withstood the temblor, but burned in the ensuing fire.

Overextended, banker Ralston apparently drowned himself.

The hotel rose again in 1909, with a new design by New York's Trowbridge and Livingston (famous for the St. Regis Hotel). The former carriage entrance was transformed into the beaux arts style **Garden Court restaurant,** crowned by a spectacular dome of 70,000 pieces of leaded art glass. Austrian crystal chandeliers twinkle above the potted palms and Ionic columns of fine Italian marble.

After a 2015 remodel, guest rooms kept their original crown moldings and other features, but added stylish new colors and touches such as nightstands resembling vintage travel trunks. The 1,000-square-foot (92 sq m) Royal Suite boasts expansive city views and a beautiful carved marble fireplace. ■

Palace Hotel

🅰 Map p. 47

✉ 2 New Montgomery St. at Market St.

☎ 415/512-1111

🚍 Bus: 7, 9, 21, 31, 66, 71; Streetcar: J, K, L, M, N

sfpalace.com

NOTE: See Travelwise pp. 241–242 for more hotel information.

More Places to Visit in the Financial District

City Club

This private club, which can be visited only through City Guides (see Travelwise p. 240), in the former Stock Exchange Tower contains Diego Rivera's mural, "Allegory of California" (1931), his first commission outside Mexico. The model for warrior queen Califia was tennis great Helen Wills Moody. The club has notable art deco ornamentation. ✉ 155 Sansome St. 🚇 CC: California St.; Bus: 3, 4, 15, 42

Embarcadero Center

This cluster of four 30- and 45-story office towers linked by pedestrian bridges was designed by John Portman and Associates from 1967 to 1982 and partly financed by David Rockefeller. This is San Francisco's largest redevelopment project; it includes more than 150 shops and restaurants.

INSIDER TIP:

Visit the Old Ship Saloon (Pacific Ave. & Battery St.) to learn the story of early San Francisco's sunken ships.

—TOM ROCKWELL
Director of Exhibits, Exploratorium

Don't miss the magnificent 17-story atrium of the **Hyatt Regency hotel** (see Travelwise p. 241; *California St. at Drumm St.*), one of the world's largest hotel lobbies. The vast irregular space incorporates a "creek" and trees, an immense spherical sculpture by Charles Perry ("Eclipse," 1973), cafés, and twinkling, capsule-shaped glass elevators. On the bay side, **Justin Herman Plaza** is popular with skaters and features the Vaillancourt Fountain of monumental square tubes with flowing water. 🗺 Map p. 47 🚇 CC: California; Bus: 1, 32, 42

Hallidie Building

With the design of this 1917 building, architect Willis Polk made history. This was the world's first example of the glass curtain wall, a truly amazing innovation at a time when walls were always assumed to be solid and substantial. The facade is a grid of panes suspended in front of the seven-story concrete structure, so it bears no weight. Decades ahead of its time, the design found wide use in urban architecture. Decorative iron fire escapes frame the expanse of glass. Restored in 2013, the building is named for Andrew Hallidie, developer of the cable car. 🗺 Map p. 47 ✉ 130–150 Sutter St. 🚌 Bus: 4 🕐 Closed to the public

Merchant's Exchange Building

Designed by Willis Polk, this 1903 building was once the hub of San Francisco commerce. In the Grain Exchange Hall, traders, investors, and shipowners made deals for merchandise arriving on ships—which were spotted by lookouts on the roof of the 15-story building. Visitors are allowed access to the present-day bank, where fine paintings by William Coulter trace the maritime history of San Francisco. 🗺 Map p. 47 ✉ 465 California St. 🚌 Bus: 3, 4, 15

Pacific Exchange

Formerly occupied by the largest stock exchange in the United States outside New York (and now a fitness club), this is the 1915 U.S. Subtreasury building, a columned granite hall remodeled and expanded in 1930 by Miller & Pflueger. At the entrance to the building are Ralph Stackpole's monumental sculptures in 1930s social-realist style: "Man and His Inventions" and "Mother Earth." 🗺 Map p. 47 ✉ 301 Pine St. 🚇 CC: California St.; Bus: 3, 4, 15, 42

Union Square, San Francisco's heart and shopping hub, and nearby Nob Hill, with its stunning views of the bay and Financial District

Union Square & Nob Hill

A cable car travels Powell Street at Union Square.

Union Square & Nob Hill

If San Francisco were a theater, its main stage would be Union Square. Nob Hill would be a box seat for viewing the urban drama from lofty heights, both geographically and socially. The two districts are linked by the Powell and California cable car lines.

Union Square

Union Square is the heart of traditional San Francisco. It is a lively hub of elegant stores, bell-clanging cable cars, and, of course, curious travelers.

Union Square Park in 2002 got a $25 million makeover—a granite plaza with a terraced stage big enough to hold a symphony, a café, and grassy terraces for relaxing. It's a rest spot shared by office workers, homeless people, and shoppers. Stores range from Macy's and Neiman Marcus to Tiffany and Chanel. East of the park are boutiques; west are hotels and theaters.

The neighborhood wasn't always commercial. When Union Square Park was given to the city in 1850 by Mayor John Geary, churches, Victorian houses, and private men's clubs clustered round it. When residents moved away from fashionable Sutter Street in the late 19th century, their houses were converted to stores. The City of Paris department store appeared in 1896, and the St. Francis Hotel opened in 1904.

Nob Hill

After the cable car conquered San Francisco's hills in 1873, Nob Hill began to look like prime real estate. In 1876, Leland Stanford of the "Big Four" (see sidebar p. 61) erected an Italianate mansion, soon overshadowed by an edifice of Gothic towers and gables built next door by Stanford's partner, Mark Hopkins. Collis P. Huntington and Charles Crocker of the "Big Four" also had ornate Nob Hill mansions. The mansions of James Fair and James Flood, two of the "Bonanza Kings" (see p. 28), were filled with fine European antiques.

Most mansions on so-called Snob Hill were built of wood and destroyed in the 1906 fire. Only the brownstone Flood Mansion (now the Pacific Union Club) on California Street survived. Over time, rebuilding brought Edwardian houses, apartments, luxury hotels, and the vast Grace Cathedral. ■

NOB
HILL
LEAVENWORTH
SACRAMENTO
CALIFORNIA
PINE
HYDE
STREET
EDDY

Area of map detail

JACKSON   STREET

Cable Car
Museum

WASHINGTON   STREET

STREET

CLAY   Fairmont
                        Hotel
Grace Cathedral   HUNTINGTON   Pacific
                      PARK   Union
                                  Club
STREET   Stanford
                                  Court Hotel

STREET

                    Huntington   Mark
                    Hotel   Hopkins
                                  Hotel
STREET   POWELL

                                                        STREET   GRANT   KEARNY
BUSH   TAYLOR   MASON   Medical and
                                  Dental Building
                                                STOCKTON STREET
SUTTER   Sir Francis
                                  Drake Hotel   Ruth Asawa   STREET
                Bohemian Olympic   Fountain
                Club   Club   Tiffany's
                                                              140 Maiden Lane
POST   Isadora   AVENUE   STREET
           Duncan's   Westin   UNION
           Birthplace St. Francis SQUARE   STREET
                Clift   Hotel   Macy's   Neiman Marcus
                Hotel   Macy's
GEARY   Curran   Geary   STREET
            Theatre Theater   STREET
                                                        MARKET
O'FARRELL

                                  Cable Car
TENDERLOIN   BOEDDEKER   Turntable
             PARK
                                  Powell
        STREET   Street

0   300 meters
0   300 yards

Union Square Walk

Stroll among grand hotels, theaters, and throngs of shoppers in San Francisco's most famous retail district. Credit card ready? Cha-a-a-arge!

Begin in the lobby of the **Westin St. Francis Hotel** ❶ *(335 Powell St., tel 415/397-7000).* Its marble and gilt reflect the opulent vision of railroad millionaire Charles T. Crocker, who promoted the idea of a world-class hotel for the city. Opened in 1904, the St. Francis has welcomed monarchs and U.S. presidents. The lobby's 1856 Viennese Magneta clock, with its carved rosewood cabinet, is a meeting spot for social San Franciscans. Off the lobby, make sure you see the restored pink marble staircase.

Across Powell Street is **Union Square Park** ❷, a central place to rendezvous with friends or to rest your weary feet and people-watch.

NOT TO BE MISSED:

Westin St. Francis Hotel • Union Square Park • 140 Maiden Lane

Once a sandbank, the 2.6-acre (1 ha) park was set aside as open space in Jasper O'Farrell's 1847 plan of the city. Named when pro-Union rallies were held here before the Civil War, the park has provided a soapbox for public expression since 1930s labor demonstrations. In 1958, beatniks in sandals and beards paraded here to a bongo-drum beat on the "Squaresville Tour," designed to express wry annoyance at having become tourist attractions in North Beach. In 1987, a group of gay activists called the Sisters of Perpetual Indulgence protested Pope John Paul II's visit.

The park's **Dewey Monument** honors Adm. George Dewey for his 1898 victory in Manila Bay during the Spanish-American War. Atop its 97-foot (29.5 m) Corinthian column stands Robert Aitken's 1903 bronze figure of "Victory." Beneath the park is a pioneer underground parking garage built in 1942. Along Geary Street sprawls an immense **Macy's** department store. At Stockton stands the postmodern **Neiman Marcus** ❸ (1982, Johnson and Burgee), clad in multicolored Italian granite. Step into the rotunda to see a 2,600-piece stained-glass dome of pale gold and white, preserved from the 1909 City of Paris store, on whose site it stands. The ship it depicts is the emblem of Paris, France, whose Latin municipal motto *(Fluctuat nec Mergitur)* translates, "It floats but does not sink." In 1982, the fine beaux arts City of Paris did sink, however, to the sorrow of San Franciscans.

As you walk up Stockton Street, here's a typical scene: A homeless man sits by an open

Good eateries abound near Union Square.

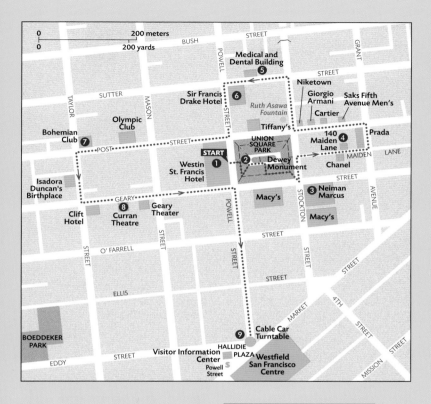

Map labels:
0 200 meters
0 200 yards
BUSH STREET
STREET
GRANT
POWELL STREET
Medical and Dental Building **5**
Niketown
SUTTER
Sir Francis Drake Hotel **6**
Giorgio Armani
Saks Fifth Avenue Men's
STREET
Cartier
TAYLOR
MASON
Ruth Asawa Fountain
Olympic Club
Bohemian Club **7**
STREET
POST
Tiffany's
UNION SQUARE PARK
140 Maiden Lane **4**
Prada
MAIDEN LANE
START
2
Dewey Monument
Chanel
Westin St. Francis Hotel **1**
STREET
Isadora Duncan's Birthplace
Neiman Marcus **3**
AVENUE
STOCKTON
Macy's
GEARY STREET
Clift Hotel
Curran Theatre **8**
Geary Theater
Macy's
STREET
STREET
O'FARRELL STREET
STREET
POWELL
STREET
ELLIS
STREET
MARKET
4TH STREET
BOEDDEKER PARK
EDDY STREET
Cable Car Turntable
9
Visitor Information Center
HALLIDIE PLAZA
Westfield San Francisco Centre
Powell Street S
STREET
MISSION STREET

See also area map pp. 56–57
Westin St. Francis Hotel
2 hours
Less than 1 mile (1.6 km)
Powell St. at Market

suitcase full of black kittens. Behind him in a store window, a mannequin slouches in a chic black dress. Enter **Maiden Lane,** an ironic name, considering that at the turn of the 20th century harlots lined the narrow street. Beckoning from windows and naked from the waist up, they charged passing men a dime to fondle one breast, or two for 15 cents; further intimacies cost a quarter. With sex came violence; the street averaged one murder a week. All this sin was reformed by the 1906 earthquake and fire. Today, the lane is lined with upscale shops and café tables. The highlight is **140 Maiden Lane 4** The city's only building designed by Frank Lloyd Wright (1949), it has been called one of the gems of 20th-century American architecture. The facade of honey-hued brick has a splayed entry arch of glass and brick that funnels passing shoppers inside. The sweeping

circular ramp to the mezzanine is an early version of Wright's design for the New York Guggenheim Museum. Circular wall cutouts and other round motifs echo the building's original use—as a china shop. The architect signed his creation on a red tile at the left of the entrance.

At Grant Avenue, turn left to Post Street. Turn left here and explore a block of stores both traditional and chic that include Cartier, Saks Fifth Avenue Men's, Giorgio Armani, and Niketown. Near Post and Stockton you'll find the **Ruth Asawa Fountain,** set outside the Grand Hyatt hotel. The 1973 fountain is faced in

EXPERIENCE:
Celebrate at Glide Memorial Church

Sunday church services that attract 2,000 people? Join a remarkably diverse congregation at Glide Memorial Church near Union Square in the Tenderloin, clapping and swaying while a band and a hundred choir singers belt out a mix of gospel, soul, jazz, blues, and pop music *(330 Ellis St., tel 415/674-6000, glide.org/celebrations, arrive 30 minutes early for Sun. services 9 a.m. & 11 a.m.).* The joy and soulful feeling are contagious. Glide, affiliated with the United Methodist Church, is known for its liberal philosophy and social service programs, such as preparing 787,000 free meals a year for the city's poor.

whimsical San Francisco scenes including the Cliff House, Transamerica Pyramid, and Victorian houses.

Continue up Stockton to Sutter and turn left to the **Medical and Dental Building** ❺ *(450 Sutter St.; 1928, Miller & Pflueger)*, an art deco skyscraper whose facade and gilded entrance canopy are rampant with Maya designs. The elevator lobby is a fantasy temple with a stepped roof and hanging lamps adorned with Maya faces. At Powell Street, turn left downhill past the 1928 **Sir Francis Drake Hotel** ❻ *(450 Powell St.)*, whose doorman famously wears a red Beefeater uniform.

At Post Street, turn right and walk two blocks to see two of San Francisco's elite private clubs. Housed in a Renaissance-style palazzo, the **Olympic Club** *(524 Post St.)* is the nation's oldest amateur athletic organization (1860). Heavyweight champion "Gentleman Jim" Corbett was once the boxing instructor; the Australian crawl was first demonstrated to Americans in the glass-roofed swimming pool. Next door, at the corner of Taylor and

Post Streets, stands the **Bohemian Club** ❼. Founded in 1872 by artists, writers, and journalists, the group's early members included luminaries such as Jack London and Ambrose Bierce. Today, business leaders fill the ranks.

Turn left down Taylor to see the **birthplace of Isadora Duncan** *(501 Taylor St.)*; the free-spirited dancer of the early 20th century was the first to interpret music through improvised movement. At the corner of Geary Street, the **Clift Hotel** *(tel 415/775-4700)* is a San Francisco classic redone by hotelier Ian Schrager and designer Philippe Starck. The lobby has wildly eclectic chairs and a coffee table by surrealist Salvador Dalí. The 1933 Redwood Room is paneled entirely from one 2,000-year-old redwood tree.

You are now in the theater district. Walk along Geary Street toward Union Square to reach the **Curran Theatre** ❽ *(445 Geary St.)*, with its mansard roof and Romanesque arches

INSIDER TIP:

The Fairmont Hotel near Union Square has a tiki bar with a bargain $10 all-you-can-eat buffet at happy hour.

—SUSAN WINBLAD NELSON
Third generation San Franciscan

(1922, Alfred Henry Jacobs). Next door is the ornate facade of the **Geary Theater** *(415 Geary St., tel 415/749-2228)*, where masks of comedy and tragedy decorate the entrance doors. Designed by Bliss & Faville in 1909, it has showcased stars from Fanny Brice to Helen Hayes. The theater is home to the celebrated ACT/American Conservatory Theater.

Continue to Powell Street at Union Square. If you turn right to Market Street you will see the **Powell Street cable car turntable** ❾, a device with which a single-ended cable car can be rotated by hand.

Hotels of Nob Hill

The grandeur of Nob Hill's mansions, once home to the city's rich and famous, turned to smoke in the 1906 fire. In their place rose swank hotels that echo the area's affluent heritage.

The Mark Hopkins hotel, built on the site of Mark Hopkins's turreted mansion, sits atop Nob Hill.

The **Stanford Court Hotel** occupies the mansion site of Leland Stanford, who financed the California cable car line. A stained-glass dome crowns the hotel's lobby.

Of Mark Hopkins's $3 million Victorian mansion, only granite retaining walls survive. These edge the **Intercontinental Mark Hopkins hotel.** In the hotel's Top of the Mark bar, World War II servicemen bound for the Pacific whispered goodbyes to their sweethearts.

The **Fairmont Hotel** occupies land once owned by Comstock silver king "Bonanza Jim" Fair. The Renaissance Revival building was gutted by the 1906 fire before opening day. Architect Julia Morgan oversaw its resurrection.

The brick-and-ivy **Scarlet Huntington Hotel** occupies a 1924 apartment house designed by Weeks & Day. Known for discretion and service, it blends old-style luxury with bright, contemporary design. ■

Nob Hill

 Map pp. 56–57

CC: All lines; Bus: 1

NOTE: See pp. 243–247 for information on hotels.

The "Big Four"

Four Sacramento merchants—Leland Stanford, Mark Hopkins, Charles Crocker, and Collis P. Huntington—made one of the shrewdest business deals in U.S. history, financing the Central Pacific Railroad (later the Southern Pacific) to build the 1869 transcontinental rail line. The "Big Four," called "robber barons" for their unscrupulous tactics, soon controlled California transportation and politics. All owned Nob Hill mansions.

Grace Cathedral

The nation's third largest Episcopal cathedral measures 329 feet long (100 m), with a spire rising 247 feet (75 m). It is modeled on Paris's Notre Dame, and, like a European cathedral, took many years to complete (1928–1964). Unlike European cathedrals, it was built not of stone but of reinforced concrete—a strange material for a sacred space, used for earthquake safety.

Grace Cathedral

 Map p. 57

✉ 1100 California St. at Taylor St.

☎ 415/749-6300

🚊 CC: All lines; Bus: 1

gracecathedral.org

The French Gothic architecture by Lewis Hobart sets off some fine features. In the **east portal** are copies of Lorenzo Ghiberti's bronze "Doors of Paradise" created for the Baptistry in Florence in 1445, with panels of Old Testament scenes. Above the 2.75-ton (2.5 tonne) doors glows a rose window made in Chartres. In the **Singing Tower,** a carillon has 44 bronze bells from England that weigh 12 pounds (5.4 kg) to 6 tons (5.4 tonnes). A joyful noise rises in the cathedral as they ring or when the baroque organ (1930, Aeolian-Skinner Co.) thunders through its 1,422 pipes. To the left of the main altar, the **Chapel of Grace** has a limestone French altar from 1430. The Gospel windows in the nave are by Charles Connick (1930) and contain 20,000 pieces of colored glass. Other windows depict Jesus Christ and a baffling range of other figures, including Henry Ford and Albert Einstein.

A **labyrinth** on the floor duplicates the limestone original at Chartres Cathedral. The single looping path symbolizes a pilgrimage. An identical labyrinth of terrazzo is on the cathedral grounds, north of the Taylor Street doors *(open to the public 24 hours a day).*

Between the Diocesan House and the Chapter House stood the cottage of undertaker Nicholas Yung, who refused to sell his lot to railroad baron Charles Crocker. Thwarted in owning the entire block, Crocker erected a 30-foot-high (9.1 m) "spite fence" around three sides of Yung's property. Crocker's heirs obtained the parcel on Yung's death in 1880. After the 1906 fire, the family donated the block for Grace Cathedral. ■

Women from nearby Chinatown practice their daily ritual of tai chi in front of Grace Cathedral.

Cable Car Museum

It seems impossible: The steel ropes that whiz in and out of this building power every cable car in San Francisco (see pp. 64–65). The 1909 brick structure contains the system's powerhouse, repair shop, car barn, and a museum on the world's first (and last) working cable cars.

A cable car has no power of its own, but is towed by an endless loop of cable moving beneath the street. Downstairs in the **Sheave Room,** you'll see the cables come in underground and thread around large grooved wheels called sheaves. The cables figure-eight their way upstairs, then around other huge sheaves whose electric motors drive the system. Plaques and a video explain how everything works.

On display is **Cable Car #8,** the sole survivor of San Francisco's first cable car line, the 1873 Clay Street Hill Railroad. It looks like a comic-strip Toonerville Trolley, with simple wooden benches and a grip that's nothing more than a screw and nut attached to a handwheel. Other museum attractions include a couple of early cars, historical

The Cable Car Museum contains the Sheave Room, where electric motors and giant wheels still power the city's cable cars.

photos, transit apparatus (ticket punches, coin changers), model cable cars, and a gift shop run by the nonprofit Friends of the Cable Car Museum.

At night, the city's cable cars are garaged in the barn on the building's upper level. ∎

Cable Car Museum
- 🅜 Map p. 57
- ✉ 1201 Mason St. at Washington St.
- ☎ 415/474-1887
- 🚋 CC: Powell-Hyde, Powell-Mason

cablecarmuseum.org

Hallidie's Folly

In 1869, London-born Andrew Smith Hallidie watched in horror as an overloaded streetcar slipped backward down a San Francisco hill, cruelly dragging the horses trying to pull it.

Hallidie was a maker of wire rope, with a factory near today's Fisherman's Wharf, and he had designed cable systems for the gold country—including an overhead loop with a system for attaching ore buckets by gripping and

ungripping. He imagined that a loop of wire rope could be made to move under the street, and that a rolling car could be attached or released at will.

People laughed at "Hallidie's Folly." But on August 1, 1873, the world's first cable car made its maiden run. The conductor chickened out when he saw the steep grade down five blocks of Clay Street, so Hallidie himself took over the controls.

Cable Cars

A San Francisco trademark, the cable car is an endearing marvel of 19th-century mechanical ingenuity. Climb aboard a colorful Victorian car with its Bombay roof and clanging bells, and you slow down to the pace of an earlier day, taking time to enjoy the trip and views of city and bay. Cable cars have appeared in movies, television commercials, and even wedding pictures.

A cable car crests the top of Nob Hill, with Alcatraz Island lost in the distance.

Introduced by Andrew Hallidie in 1873 (see sidebar p. 63), the cable car replaced the horse-drawn streetcar. Horses couldn't struggle up a number of the city's hills and left tons of manure in the streets. Cable cars solved these problems. In the system's heyday, eight cable car lines crisscrossed the city with 112 miles (180 km) of track.

By the early 1890s, more efficient electric streetcars made cable cars seem past their prime. But they remained in the hearts of San Franciscans. When officials decided to replace cable cars with buses in 1947, citizens launched a successful protest. ("San Francisco without its cable cars would be like a kid without his yo-yo!" said a radio comedian.)

Three lines survived along 10.5 miles (17 km) of Hyde, California, Mason, and Powell Streets. In 1964, the system became the nation's only moving landmark on the National Register of Historic Places. In 1982, the system shut down for rehabilitation, reopening in 1984 with a gala celebration.

Among the system's 40 cars (of which 26 operate at one time), there are two types. Single-ended cars run on the two Powell lines, and must be manually reversed on a turntable at the end. Double-ended cars operate on the California line and don't require turning around; they can be driven in either direction.

What Makes Cable Cars Go?

A cable car has no motor—it is towed by a cable moving beneath the pavement. A complex network of pulleys supports and guides the cable around sharp turns and through crossings.

To make a cable car move, the gripman pulls a lever, or grip, that passes through a slot in the pavement and clamps jaws onto the whizzing cable, like a pair of pliers. The car's speed depends on how loosely or tightly the grip is closed. (The cable moves at a steady 9.55 miles/15.3 km an hour) To stop, the gripman lets the cable drop, and the brakeman applies the brakes. The two coordinate through bell signals.

Cable car operators are chosen for their strength and outgoing personalities. The job must be a thrill, especially when a cable car rolls down the seemingly vertical stretch of Hyde Street between Bay and Francisco Streets, the system's steepest grade at 21.3 percent.

Cables & Grips

Each 1.5-inch-diameter (3.8 cm) steel cable is made up of six strands of 19 wires, which are woven around a core of sisal manila rope for more flexibility. Worn-out cables are replaced at night when the system is shut down. The old cable is cut and attached at one end to the new cable, then pulled through the entire channel and back to the

Where the Cars Go

Three cable car lines serve the city:
California Line: Market Street to Van Ness Avenue. Sights include the Financial District, Chinatown, and Nob Hill.
Powell-Hyde Line: Market Street to Victorian Park near Fisherman's Wharf. Sights include Union Square, Nob Hill, Cable Car Museum, and Russian Hill, as well as stunning city and bay views.
Powell-Mason Line: Market Street to Bay Street near Fisherman's Wharf. Sights include Nob Hill, Cable Car Museum, North Beach, and city and bay views.

See "Getting Around" on p. 239 for more information on the cable car system and how to use it.

powerhouse. The California line's cable is 21,500 feet (6,553 m) long. Skilled splicers fasten the ends of the new cable into a loop, interweaving strands for 90 feet (27.4 m) —a job that takes five hours.

Under constant stress, a cable lasts 100 to 300 days. The grip's soft metal dies, which clamp the cable, must be replaced every four days.

More Places to Visit in Union Square & on Nob Hill

Huntington Park

Opposite the Pacific Union Club, this slightly elevated 1.3-acre (0.5 ha) park was designed by John McLaren (superintendent of Golden Gate Park) on the site of the 1872 mansion of David Colton, attorney for the Big Four railway millionaires. The neoclassical mansion later belonged to Big Four member Collis P. Huntington, whose widow gave the land (bereft of the house, which burned in the 1906 fire) to the city. The **Fountain of the Tortoises** was a copy of a fountain in Rome. Map p. 57 ⊠ Bounded by California, Taylor, Cushman, & Sacramento Sts. CC: All lines; Bus: 1

The 42-room brownstone Flood Mansion, built in 1886, today is an exclusive men's club.

Pacific Union Club/Flood Mansion

In 1886, silver king James Flood built a 42-room mansion for $1.5 million. Around it he erected a bronze fence that cost $30,000 and required a full-time employee just to keep it polished. The mansion's walls of Connecticut brownstone survived the 1906 fire, while other Nob Hill palaces—built of wood—went up like kindling. After the Pacific Union Club bought the landmark building in 1907, architect member Willis Polk added

INSIDER TIP:

Attend yoga classes with 60 or 80 locals every Tuesday night at Grace Cathedral near Union Square.

—KAY RABIN
City guide, San Francisco Public Library

two wings in 1908. In the basement he installed a pool with Minoan columns and a ceiling of stained glass, which historian Randolph Delehanty ranked "among the most astounding private rooms in the city."

The best time to view the exterior is in early evening, when the windows of the shaded, hulking mansion shine warmly, as if turn-of-the-20th-century gas lamps were aglow inside. You won't get inside, though. The all-male Pacific Union Club (an amalgam of the 1852 Pacific Club and the 1854 Union Club) is strictly private, its rich-and-powerful membership consisting of leaders of industry and politics. Over the years, the roster has ranged from telegraph pioneer Samuel F. B. Morse to technology innovators William Hewlett and David Packard, U.S. Secretary of Defense Caspar Weinberger, and the founder of Bechtel Corporation. Map p. 57 ⊠ 1000 California St. Closed to the public CC: All lines; Bus: 1

Chinatown—often called a "city within a city," its narrow streets crowded with people

Chinatown

Chinese lanterns and lampposts adorn Grant Avenue in Chinatown.

Chinatown

Step through the jade green Chinatown Gate on Grant Avenue and you enter another world, a place at once exotic and ambiguous. Ahead stretches what appears to be a Cantonese marketplace, all pagoda roofs with upturned eaves (to ward off evil spirits), colorfully painted balconies, and signs in Chinese calligraphy.

Yet there is an underlying layer of turn-of-the-20th-century America in Chinatown's Edwardian buildings, not to mention a spot of carnival midway, with popping firecrackers and shops selling gimcracks ranging from plastic kung-fu weapons to wicker "finger traps." Potbellied Ho Tai, the god of happiness, smiles in ivory and porcelain from a hundred store windows.

More than one cultural Chinatown exists within the traditional borders of Bush, Broadway, Powell, and Kearny Streets. The first is the colorful tourist attraction that stretches along Grant Avenue. Visitors from around the world come to sample exotic foods such as fishball soup. Tourists also shop for trinkets, as well as jade carvings, gold jewelry, and silk gowns.

But this is also a true neighborhood, rather than a kind of improvised theme park. More

than 15,000 people live in just 24 blocks, making this second Chinatown not only the most densely populated section of San Francisco, but also one of the most congested neighborhoods in the nation. Because of housing conditions—too many people per room, too little plumbing—this Chinatown has been characterized as a ghetto. The average income here is low; the number of people who don't speak English is high. The majority of residents were born outside the United States. Women in small garment factories work long hours at whirring sewing machines for low wages. Residents must make use of whatever space they can find. Elderly men gather in Portsmouth Square, which functions as a community living room for chatting and playing Chinese chess. Children scamper in narrow alleys. On Stockton Street, locals shop for groceries, eat dim sum, and attend high school.

The third Chinatown forms a heartland for Chinese Americans who live elsewhere in the city. They come to buy snow peas, bamboo shoots, roast duck, oyster sauce, and other ingredients for holiday feasts. They read Chinese newspapers or see a Chinese movie. They enjoy big family dinners in upstairs banquet halls. On Waverly Place, they climb stairs to temples where incense rises above altars and oranges are left as offerings.

All three Chinatowns join together in joyful celebration of festivals such as Chinese New Year. Drums beat a cadence, dancing dragons weave along the street, and costumes of embroidered silk come out of closets to lend an air of the Far East to San Francisco. To see Chinatown, you must venture on foot. Slowly, all three Chinatowns will reveal themselves to you. ■

NOT TO BE MISSED:

Walking through the colorful Chinatown Gate, entryway to an intriguing foreign world   72

Shopping for souvenirs and art pieces on Grant Avenue   72

Tin How Temple, worth climbing three flights of stairs to visit   73

Hanging out in Portsmouth Square, the Chinese community's outdoor living room   75

Sipping hot samples at the Ten Ren Tea Company   75–76

The only fortune cookie factory you're ever likely to see   76

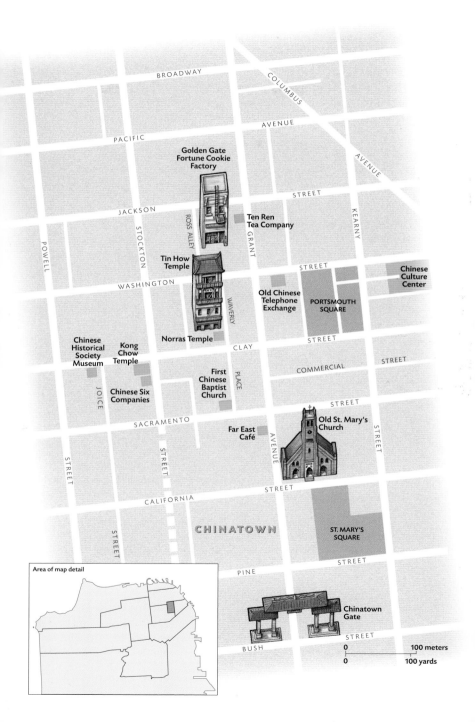

BROADWAY

COLUMBUS

AVENUE

AVENUE

PACIFIC

Golden Gate Fortune Cookie Factory

STREET

JACKSON

ROSS ALLEY

STOCKTON

GRANT

KEARNY

Ten Ren Tea Company

POWELL

Tin How Temple

Chinese Culture Center

WASHINGTON

WAVERLY

Old Chinese Telephone Exchange

STREET

PORTSMOUTH SQUARE

Chinese Historical Society Museum

Kong Chow Temple

Norras Temple

CLAY

STREET

JOICE

Chinese Six Companies

First Chinese Baptist Church

PLACE

COMMERCIAL

STREET

SACRAMENTO

Far East Café

AVENUE

STREET

Old St. Mary's Church

STREET

STREET

CALIFORNIA

CHINATOWN

ST. MARY'S SQUARE

Area of map detail

PINE

STREET

Chinatown Gate

STREET

BUSH

0   100 meters

0   100 yards

Chinese San Francisco

Chinese treasure seekers arrived in California in the late 1840s and headed for the gold diggings. (California was known as Gum San, or "golden mountain.") Most passed through San Francisco, and by 1849 the city's first Chinese restaurant opened, followed by laundries. Within 35 years San Francisco had 7,500 Chinese laundries.

Roasted ducks hang in the window of a restaurant on Stockton Street, much frequented by locals.

By the late 1850s, the Chinese had gathered around Portsmouth Square, which American merchants had abandoned for new commercial districts. Most Chinese were unmarried male laborers, fleeing floods and famine in southern China's Guangdong Province, whose capital was Canton (now called Guangzhou). The Cantonese newcomers wore knee-length trousers and quilted jackets, with wide hats of split bamboo. As sojourners, most planned to save money and return home with improved chances for business and marriage.

Most men were indentured servants, having borrowed their ship passage from brokers in Asia, and were now compelled to work off their obligation. They joined associations that secured jobs, repaid their passage, provided a social life, and, if the men died, even organized the shipping of their bodies back to China for interment. In return, members paid dues. District associations recruited arrivals from various geographical regions of Guangdong, while family associations assembled men with the same family names (Lee, Eng, Wong, and so on). The immigration process was

Chinese Funerals

Everyone, whether resident or tourist, pauses respectfully when a funeral passes. A brass band (sounding more like New Orleans than Nanking) follows a convertible automobile that displays a large photograph of the deceased. This journey allows friends to see the departed one last time, as he or she makes a final visit to favorite places in the neighborhood.

soon dominated by powerful merchants who established the Canton Company, or Sam Yup Association. They delivered peasant laborers to mines, railroads, and factories. In 1869, about 12,000 Chinese worked on the transcontinental railroad. Laborers formed an alliance of their own called the Sze Yup Association.

A third type of association was the Tong, or secret society. Some were organized for legitimate purposes, others for criminal. Tongs ran Chinatown's gambling, opium dens, and prostitution—understandable vices in a society of lonely men, who in early days outnumbered women by two thousand to one. Tongs also protected and avenged wrongs for members. Turf wars flared up, and Tong "hatchet men" (the source of this term) hacked and killed their rivals in illicit enterprises. Chinatown became a place of dark alleys and shadowy violence. To arbitrate disputes and promote civic activities, several district associations in the late 1850s united as the Chinese Six Companies, whose power dominated the community.

Chinese workers flooded the job market after the completion of the transcontinental railroad. American industrialists hired them at cheap wages, so white workers blamed the Chinese for taking away jobs. Resentment and xenophobia raged. Newspapers built hysteria over the "Yellow Peril." As it was, the Chinese were already isolated from American society. They kept to their own language, customs, and dress (including the long braided

queues that China's Manchu emperors required as a sign of loyalty). Increasing white hostility led to beatings and murders, and in 1877, a mob attempted to burn down Chinatown. In 1882, racism reached a peak in the Chinese Exclusion Act, which prevented Chinese laborers from immigrating to the United States. Another law barred Chinese women, thus condemning the working men of Chinatown to lifelong bachelorhood. No wives meant no families. Chinatown's population dwindled.

The 1906 earthquake and fire virtually erased Chinatown. But it also destroyed the citizenship records of the western United States, which meant the government couldn't dispute Chinese claims of citizenship. "Paper sons" from China, asserting dubious kinship with United States residents, began to immigrate.

The Old Chinese Telephone Exchange, which opened in 1909, now houses East West Bank.

After 1906, city officials talked about relocating Chinatown, but local merchants argued that it would be better to create a district that appealed to tourists. In the 1920s, an architectural style unique to San Francisco appeared, as American designers embellished plain Edwardian buildings with stylized pagoda roofs, painted balconies, and other bits of chinoiserie. Shops and restaurants proliferated, luring both tourists and Chinese, as they do to this day.

Grant Avenue

Chinatown Gate, the much photographed front door to Chinatown, is also known as the Dragon's Gate. It stands on Grant Avenue, Chinatown's main commercial strip.

A gift from the government of Taiwan, Chinatown Gate carries an inscription by Chinese revolutionary Dr. Sun Yat-sen that reads: "All under heaven is for the food of the people."

Chinatown Gate

Map p. 69

Grant Ave. at Bush St.

CC: California, Powell-Hyde, Powell-Mason; Bus: 1, 9X, 15, 30, 41, 45, 83

Chinatown Gate

The gateway was designed by architect Clayton Lee in 1970, with dragons and fish to imitate the ceremonial gates of Chinese villages. Traditionally, the central portal is reserved for persons of high rank to pass through. Two flanking portals are guarded by stone *fou* dogs (dragon-like dog figures); the female is on the right, while the male on the left watches over a pearl whose loss, it is said, would bring catastrophe to the village. The gate honors principles of feng shui, a system of Earth divination that aims to align structures in harmony with energy forces. The gate faces south, the direction most favorable for an entrance to a city.

Grant Avenue

This avenue is rich in history. Originally, it was Calle de la Fundación, the main street of the 1830s Mexican settlement of Yerba Buena. Later, as Chinatown's Dupont Street, it was a lair of gamblers and prostitutes.

The street's plain buildings add flair with Chinese architectural motifs and bright colors. Dragons twine around lampposts, their mouths gripping red lanterns. The streetlights were installed in 1925 as exotic touches when Chinatown began its tourism boom.

Between Bush and Broadway stand restaurants and shops selling fans, ceramic gods, chimes, silk robes, and other tourist items. ■

Waverly Place

Known as the Street of Painted Balconies—look up to see why—Waverly Place is sensually exotic. Iron balconies of red, yellow, and green evoke New Orleans' French Quarter . . . in psychedelic colors. The air is often redolent of temple incense, or the smoky tang of exploded firecrackers.

In early days this two-block street was known as "15 Cents Street"— the cost of a haircut from a Chinese barber. After the 1906 fire, functional brick Edwardian buildings were erected, then given Chinese trimmings. Commercial enterprises generally occupy a building's bottom floor, associations or dwellings fill the middle floors, and temples are on top, closest to heaven.

Color Symbolism

To the Chinese, colors have a symbolic meaning, which explains the bright red (happiness and vitality), green (longevity), and yellow (wealth) seen in Chinatown.

Tin How Temple
- Map p. 69
- 125 Waverly Pl.
- Bus: 1, 15, 30, 45

INSIDER TIP:

Visit a Chinese pharmacy to see how dried sea slug can boost virility and chrysanthemum leaves may improve eyesight.

—LARRY YEE
Retired director, University of California Hansen Agricultural Center

Tin How Temple

You must climb three flights of stairs to reach Tin How Temple, the oldest Chinese temple in the United States (founded 1852). This building dates from 1911. The ceiling is hung with lanterns, each dangling a red paper with black calligraphy that represents a member family of the temple. Incense sticks in bronze urns waft aromatic smoke. Folded papers with gold squares are offerings for the deceased.

On the altar resides Tin How, goddess of heaven and sea, who is worshipped by millions of Chinese. The golden figure is supposed to have come from China in 1848. Tin How was born in 960, began meditating at age 11, became a Taoist disciple, and was said to develop the transcendental power of riding the sea to rescue people in distress. As protector of sailors, Tin How has had an important role in San Francisco because Chinese immigrants had to cross the ocean. She also watches over travelers, actors, writers, and prostitutes—an eclectic group whose common traits make for interesting conjecture.

The carved main altar depicts the life of Confucius. Other temple figures include the three-eyed god Wah Kwong, as well as Madame Golden Lotus and the 18 guardian angels. Outside, more incense sticks waft perfume over Chinatown. ∎

Walk Through Chinatown

This walk winds through a warren of streets and back alleys that reveal Chinatown's public and private personalities.

Morning shopping in Chinatown provides fresh groceries and fulfills a social ritual for residents.

Begin at the iconic **Chinatown Gate ❶** (see p. 72) and walk up **Grant Avenue ❷**. Near the intersection of Grant and Pine, **St. Mary's Square ❸** features a 1938 statue by Beniamino Bufano depicting Sun Yat-sen (1866–1925), with face and hands of rose granite and a robe of stainless steel. Organizer of the Nationalist Party, Sun raised funds and started a newspaper in San Francisco to foster the 1911 overthrow of China's Manchu dynasty. He served as first president of the new republic.

Exit the park at California Street, pausing to enjoy a classic San Francisco view: Chinatown's pagoda roofs, cable cars climbing to Nob Hill, and the Financial District skyscrapers downhill. Across California, you'll see Dai Choong Low ("tower of the big bell"), better known as **Old**

NOT TO BE MISSED:

Grant Avenue • Portsmouth Square • Waverly Place • Tin How Temple

St. Mary's Church ❹ *(660 California St.)*. Dedicated in 1854, it was the city's first cathedral and California's largest building, modeled after a Gothic church in Vich, Spain. The foundation granite was quarried in China, and the bricks came around the Horn from New England as ships' ballast. As San Francisco grew, an ocean of sin began to lap against St. Mary's island of Catholic faith. Nearby were opium dens and a red-light district. (Note the

> ⛰ See also area map p. 69
> ▶ Chinatown Gate
> 🕐 2 hours
> ↔ less than 1 mile (1.6 km)
> ▶ Chinese Historical Society Museum

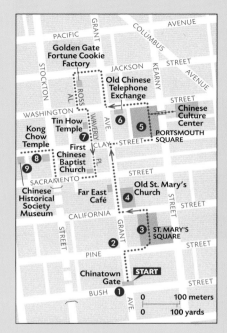

Victorian admonishment on the bell tower: "Son, Observe the Time and Fly from Evil.") In 1891, a new cathedral was erected in a less notorious area, and the original became Old St. Mary's. The church offers classical music concerts *(Tues., 12:30 p.m.)*.

Turn right on Grant and take a peek into the **Far East Café** *(631 Grant Ave., tel 415/982-3245)*, a 1920s Chinatown restaurant with tasseled lanterns and carved screens.

At Clay Street turn right to **Portsmouth Square ❺**, the community living room for crowded Chinatown. Children romp, while elderly men ponder card games. The square has had several historic roles. Laid out in 1839 as the plaza of Mexican Yerba Buena, it was located a block west of Yerba Buena Cove (whose shoreline reached today's Montgomery Street). An adobe customhouse processed ships' cargoes. On July 9, 1846, the American flag was first raised over San Francisco by Capt. John B. Montgomery of the U.S.S. *Portsmouth*, the warship for which the square was later named. A memorial marks the spot.

In May 1848, entrepreneur Sam Brannan displayed gold from the American River here and set off the California gold rush. In this wide-open era the square was lined with saloons and gambling houses. Oddly, in 1848, it also became the site of the city's first public school. In the 1860s, businesses moved to new commercial districts created as the cove was landfilled, and Chinese people moved in.

On the square's north side a small galleon sails atop a granite base. It is a model of the fictional *Hispaniola* from the novel *Treasure Island*, a monument to its Scottish author, Robert Louis Stevenson, who in 1879 lived nearby and came to the square to watch

the passing people and ships with his dark, thoughtful eyes. A statue of the Goddess of Democracy, commemorating the Tiananmen Square massacre, also stands in this park.

Detour to the incongruous gray cement tower of the Hilton hotel, erected without design review in 1971. The third floor displays contemporary art at the **Chinese Culture Center** *(750 Kearny St., 3rd fl., tel 415/986-1822, c-c-c.org, closed Sun.–Mon., Chinatown heritage walk $$$$$)*.

Exiting the square onto Washington Street, head left to the **Old Chinese Telephone Exchange ❻** *(743 Washington St.)*, a red-and-green pagoda with ornate roofs. Now a bank, it opened in 1909 as the Pacific Telephone and Telegraph exchange. Operators spoke English and five dialects of Chinese. They also had to memorize every customer's phone number, since callers asked for connections by name. (It wasn't polite to refer to a person as a number.)

At Grant Avenue, turn right to get to **The Ten Ren Tea Company of San Francisco**

Locals gather in Portsmouth Square to read, play Chinese chess, and visit with one another.

(949 Grant Ave., tel 415/362-0656), which sells more than 50 tea varieties. At Jackson Street, turn left to Ross Alley, part of a maze of Chinatown back streets with a colorful history from the bad old days. Nineteenth-century gamblers and prostitutes plied their trades here.

Turn left to the tiny **Golden Gate Fortune Cookie Factory** (56 Ross Alley, tel 415/781-3956), where women pour dough onto small griddles that revolve into an oven. Out come warm, flat cookies, which the ladies fold around paper fortunes. Bring your own messages for the factory to insert in cookies (great for birthdays and jokes). Follow the alley to Washington

and cross the street to **Waverly Place** ❼ (see p. 73), the "Street of Painted Balconies," the location of benevolent associations and temples such as the **Tin How Temple** and the **Norras Temple** (109 Waverly Pl., 3rd fl.), whose altar has gilded Buddhas.

Now continue on Waverly Place to the corner of Sacramento Street, where the **First Chinese Baptist Church** was built in 1908 of red clinker brick. Turn right on Sacramento, then right at Stockton to see Chinese grocery items (moon cakes, bins of bok choy), and other everyday items.

Across the street you'll see the **Chinese Six Companies** (843 Stockton St.), an umbrella group organized in the 1850s to unite district associations. The group is still a business power in Chinatown. The 1908 building is adorned with dragons and fish.

Proceed to the **Kong Chow Temple** ❽ (855 Stockton St., 4th fl.). With carved, gilded altars, the temple is devoted to Kuan Ti, a celebrated, third-century general who found solace in poetry. He watches over soldiers and poets, criminals and police alike. Turn left on Clay to the **Chinese Historical Society Museum** ❾ (965 Clay St., tel 415/391-1188, chsa.org, closed Sun.–Mon., $$), which occupies architect Julia Morgan's 1932 Chinatown YMCA, whose brick structure is beautifully integrated with three Chinese towers, decorative tiles, and painted ceiling panels. Exhibits look at Chinese life in the United States, and there are changing art shows.

EXPERIENCE: See Chinatown Behind the Scenes

To discover the *real* Chinatown—a place where people live, work, play, and struggle with social ills—join a young Chinese guide on a tour of the neighborhood's labyrinth of hidden alleyways (tel 415/984-1478, chinatownalleywaytours.org, $$$$$). The guides, some of whom grew up here, point out important sites (the former secret headquarters of revolutionary Sun Yat-sen) and discuss problems such as overcrowding (families often live, eat, and sleep in a single room). Stops include a barber shop that counted Frank Sinatra among its clients. The guides offer a peek behind the silk curtain of Chinatown, revealing the true life of the community.

North Beach, one of the city's most genial districts, and two hills discovered long ago by writers and artists

North Beach, Telegraph Hill, & Russian Hill

Eating well is easy in North Beach, the city's historic Italian neighborhood.

North Beach, Telegraph Hill, & Russian Hill

In a city of intriguing neighborhoods, North Beach is a favorite among San Franciscans themselves. In this sunny valley, you can let your gusto off the leash. Telegraph Hill and Russian Hill rise to either side, with steep streets, huge views, and beguiling houses.

Bakeries in North Beach, San Francisco's Little Italy, offer cannoli and other Italian favorites.

In North Beach the good things—music, art, talk, and especially food—are prized. For this zest for life, we owe the Old World Italians who brought an appreciation of food, wine, and good company. To pretend you're in Italy, just inhale the aromas from trattorias, bakeries, and coffeehouses. Bask in the warm Mediterranean mood at Caffé Trieste, where the family owners and locals sometimes sing opera on Saturday afternoons. To this Italian verve, North Beach adds a live-and-let-live philosophy inherited from the Beats, who hung out here in the 1950s. Stir in the Asian culture that has pushed in from adjacent Chinatown and the result is a remarkable melting pot of nationalities and lifestyles.

In Washington Square Park you might see an Italian baker sharing a bench with a bohemian poet. Meanwhile, on the lawn an elderly Chinese lady goes through the meditative movements of tai chi chuan.

Interestingly, earlier bohemian circles of writers and artists had lived nearby—in the 1890s on Russian Hill and in the 1920s on Telegraph Hill. Both places offered inspirational views and low rents. On Russian Hill, a group calling itself Les Jeunes (The Young) included architect Willis Polk and poet Gelett Burgess (of "I Never Saw a Purple Cow" fame, see p. 35). They met at the home of Catherine Atkinson, who also welcomed visiting writers Mark Twain and Robert Louis Stevenson. A similar salon

flourished in the home of poet, editor, and librarian Ina Coolbrith (see sidebar p. 97).

In 1952, Jack Kerouac stayed with his friend Neal Cassady on Russian Hill, while he finished *On The Road*. But today few bohemians live on these quiet hills. The houses, cottages, and apartments have largely been taken over by the city's elite. The views are still free and inspiring, though. Wander the atmospheric lanes and flights of steep steps on both hills. And don't miss the view from Coit Tower, a Telegraph Hill landmark donated by an eccentric lady who loved firefighters. ■

NOT TO BE MISSED:

City Lights, the celebrated bookstore of the Beat Generation 81

Washington Square Park, where the neighborhood's diverse cultures come together 82–83

Drinking at Vesuvio, a saloon that acts as a shrine to the Beats, jazz, and art 83–84

Eating legendary focaccia sandwiches at Mario's Bohemian Cigar Store Café 85

Admiring the city and bay from atop Coit Tower 90–92

Catching a performance of *Beach Blanket Babylon*, a wacky musical revue of San Francisco 96–97

Area of map detail

North Beach

Oddly, North Beach has no beach; by the 1870s the original shore was filled in for industrial use. Today's main street, Columbus Avenue, was laid out in 1872 by cutting a diagonal route between the Financial District and the northern waterfront. The street creates quirky triangular corners and buildings that lend North Beach a touch of Paris.

Family-run Caffé Trieste, a popular coffeehouse in North Beach, opened to customers in 1956.

The neighborhood gained its human character by being close to the port where 1850s immigrants poured in. Streets sang with the languages of Ireland, France, Germany, Chile, Peru, Spain, and Portugal. This was the Latin Quarter. By the early 1900s, an influx of Italians had transformed the neighborhood into Little Italy.

Beginning in the 1920s, Italians began moving out, either to the Marina District or to farms in rural areas. This left a vacuum in North Beach, creating low rents that attracted a now famous group of bohemians known as the Beats. They lived on poetry, red wine, bebop jazz, and motormouth conversation fueled by espresso coffee. The Beats scorned all authority and conformity, embraced racial and sexual variety, and idealized a vagabond lifestyle on the far-out fringe of society. San Francisco made a perfect roost for them, with its open attitudes and tolerance.

These days, North Beach, comes to life each evening with throngs of people, music, and the heady aromas of garlic, olive oil, and tomato sauce from eateries.

City Lights Bookstore

"A kind of library where books are sold," says a sign in the window of this pioneering bookstore, founded in 1953 by poet Lawrence Ferlinghetti and Peter Martin. The nation's first all-paperback bookshop (it now offers hardcovers, too), City Lights *(261 Columbus Ave., tel 415/362–8193, citylights.com)* is a literary landmark where the Beats used to hang out. You'll feel the presence of novelist Jack Kerouac and poets Gregory Corso, Zen-influenced Gary Snyder, and Allen Ginsberg. In the basement, simple shelves and a bare concrete floor seem to match the (involuntary) vow of poverty of the Beats.

Ferlinghetti named the store after a Charlie Chaplin film, as a symbol of the little fellow fighting the big, impersonal world. City Lights Publishers has nearly 200 titles in print, including the Pocket Poets Series; one work is Allen Ginsberg's "Howl" (see below). Ferlinghetti's own *A Coney Island of the Mind* is one of America's best-selling poetry books at more than a million copies.

Ferlinghetti—who has spent a lifetime thumbing his nose at officialdom—for a time served as poet laureate of San Francisco. As a send-up of corporate ritual, he handed out poet laureate business cards.

Broadway

The stretch of Broadway between Columbus Avenue and Montgomery Street is known as The Strip. (After all, this is where entertainers take their clothes off . . .) A series of nude bars and adult bookstores carry on, albeit mildly, the traditions of the sinful Barbary Coast of gold rush days, when brothels, gambling dens, and saloons filled neighboring Pacific Avenue. Bawdy entertainment spilled over to Broadway, especially after a cleanup of "Terrific Pacific" following the 1906 earthquake.

Carol Doda busted her way into history in 1964 as a topless

Columbus Avenue
- Map pp. 78–79
- Bus: 15, 30, 39, 45

Broadway
- Map pp. 78–79
- Bus: 15, 30, 39, 45

The "Howl" Heard 'Round the Nation

When New York poet Allen Ginsberg moved to North Beach (*1010 Montgomery St.*), he wrote an extended rant called "Howl" in early 1955. That October, at an old auto-repair shop converted into the Six Gallery (*3119 Fillmore St.*), he read the poem to a crowd of Beat writers and artists. His delivery was like a free-form jazz improvisation, all rhythm and risk: "I saw the best minds of my generation destroyed by madness, starving hysterical naked," he raved. Urged on by Jack Kerouac's shouts of "Go! Go!" Ginsberg made literary history—particularly when Lawrence Ferlinghetti published the poem in 1956, only to be arrested on obscenity charges. The poem was full of four-letter words, perversions, blasphemies, and generally unsettling or loathsome images. Ginsberg testified that his poem fell in the Hebrew tradition of Old Testament prophets howling in the wilderness. He claimed he was "howling against a crazy civilization." The First Amendment trial ended in acquittal and focused national attention on the Beats.

The **hungry I** (originally located at 599 Jackson St.) was a force in live entertainment in the late 1950s and early '60s, when its bare brick walls resounded with laughs for new acts like Lenny Bruce, Phyllis Diller, and the Smothers Brothers, not to mention Richard Pryor and Woody Allen. Singers performing at the club included Billie Holiday, Barbra Streisand, and the Kingston Trio, who recorded a live album at the hungry I. The club now presents seedy strip shows, like many others on the street. Barkers chant to entice tourists, sailors, and college boys in.

Washington Square Park

Often called the heart of North Beach, this park may also be its green soul. In the shade of cypress and sycamore trees, old Italian men sit on park benches and talk. Of them Lawrence Ferlinghetti wrote: "You have seen them/the ones who feed the pigeons/cutting the stale bread/with their thumbs and pen knives/the ones with old pocket watches/the old ones with gnarled hands and wild eyebrows." In early morning the sunny lawn attracts strollers and exercisers. At noontime picnickers appear. The park is a melting pot, arranged in a square.

Flanking the urban retreat are Edwardian buildings and the spires of the Church of Sts. Peter and Paul (which Ferlinghetti called the "marzipan church on the plaza"). The land was reserved as a park in 1847, but in 1872 the southwestern corner was cut off by

The Church of Sts. Peter and Paul borders the green expanse of Washington Square Park.

Condor Club
- Map p. 79
- 560 Broadway
- 415/781-8222

condorsf.com

hungry I
- 546 Broadway
- 415/362-7763

hungryisf.com

Washington Square Park
- Map p. 79
- Bus: 15, 30, 39, 45

dancer at the **Condor Club.** After various stints as a sports bar then seafood restaurant, the Condor is once again offering "exotic entertainment." Historically speaking, it preserves the piano on which Carol Doda descended, gyrating, from the ceiling, and photos and news stories about the club. The humorously philosophical Miss Doda once said: "Anyone can take off their clothes, but I made them laugh and then I took off my clothes." The Condor's bosomy advertising sign was taken down in 1991, but a plaque on the outside wall marks this historic spot.

Columbus Avenue. It now forms a separate triangle with statuary.

In the square's center stands a bronze Benjamin Franklin of 1879. Beneath it, a time capsule to be opened in 2079 contains a bottle of wine, a Ferlinghetti poem, and a pair of Levi's. Another sculpture (1933) depicts volunteer firemen and was funded by a bequest of Lillie Hitchcock Coit (see sidebar p. 90).

Church of Sts. Peter & Paul:

A cream-colored Romanesque confection constructed in 1924, the church is especially pretty when illuminated at night. On the facade a line from Dante's *Paradiso*, rendered in mosaic, translates: "The glory of Him who moves all things penetrates and glows throughout the universe." The four Gospel writers

INSIDER TIP:

A visit to City Lights Bookstore (see p. 81) is a must. Steeped in Beat history, the expansive collection breathes bygone times.

—ERIN STONE
National Geographic contributor

are represented by traditional statues: Matthew (winged man), Mark (lion), Luke (ox), and John (eagle).

On Saturdays, the church often buzzes with weddings. Stained-glass windows tint the warm interior, which is packed with statues.

EXPERIENCE:
Practice Tai Chi in Washington Square

In the pale morning light, elderly Chinese people move slowly and gracefully, like a gentle breeze through the leafy trees overhead. They are engaged in tai chi, a practice whose choreographed movements are based on Chinese martial arts but are now embraced for their health benefits: reduced stress and improved balance, posture, circulation, and flexibility. Find out for yourself how tai chi induces calm and mental clarity. Anyone is welcome to join the synchronized dance in Washington Square. Just show up and follow along.

A remarkable 40-foot-high (12 m) altar resembles an Italian Renaissance city, with spires, domes, and columns of marble and onyx. In October, a procession leaves the church for Fisherman's Wharf for the annual blessing of the fishing fleet.

North Beach Cafés

Coffee is the lifeblood and social lubricant of North Beach. Sample a few cafés; you'll not only catch up on cappuccino but begin to understand the soul of San Francisco.

Across Jack Kerouac Alley from City Lights Bookstore (see p. 81), **Vesuvio Café** is famous for its past as a favorite hangout of Ferlinghetti, Kerouac, Ginsberg, and other Beats. Opened in 1949, the café occupies a post-earthquake building with a fine pressed-metal facade. An outside wall is painted with a poem that reads "When the shadow of the grasshopper /

Church of Sts. Peter & Paul

🅰 Map p. 79
✉ 666 Filbert St.
☎ 415/421-0809
🚌 Bus: 15, 30, 41, 45

Vesuvio Café

✉ 255 Columbus Ave.
☎ 415/362-3370
vesuvio.com

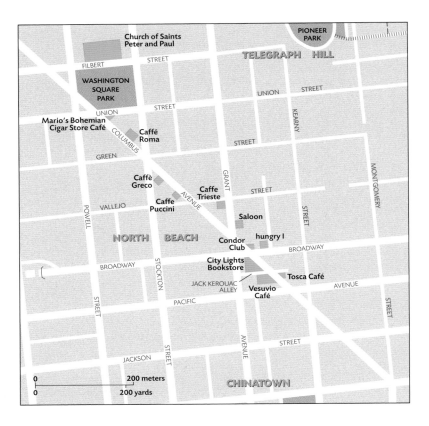

Tosca Café

✉ 242 Columbus Ave.

☎ 415/986-9651

toscacafesf.com

Caffè Greco

✉ 423 Columbus Ave.

☎ 415/397-6261

caffegreco.com

Falls across the trail of the field mouse/On green and slimey grass as a red sun rises/Above the western horizon silhouetting/A gaunt and tautly muscled Indian warrior/Perched with bow and arrow cocked and aimed/Straight at you, it's time for another martini." The Beats liked both wordplay and booze.

The café doesn't serve lunch, but you're welcome to bring your own to accompany your drink of choice. The decor includes photos of writers and paintings by local artists. Upstairs, one seating area is the "John Wilkes Booth," and another is intriguingly reserved for "Lady Psychiatrists."

Old & New: There's something about the booths of red leather, the murals of Roman landmarks, the four-foot-tall (1.2 m) espresso machine, and the jukebox with opera selections that makes you feel that the **Tosca Café** (see Travelwise p. 248) hasn't changed since it opened in 1919. It was later a Beat hangout. A New York chef has re-opened the kitchen, closed since the 1950s. You can order a cappuccino helpfully "corrected" with brandy and chocolate.

Coffee Primer

Espresso: Dark-roasted, brewed by forcing steam through powdered coffee; served black.
Cappuccino: Espresso topped with frothy steamed milk, or "foam," and powdered chocolate.
Caffé Latte: Espresso mixed with steamed milk.
Mocha Espresso: Espresso mixed with chocolate, topped with whipped cream.
Caffé Americano: American coffee.

Busy, busy **Caffè Greco** is a relative newcomer (1988), with calorie-bomb desserts and a variety of coffee drinks. There are tables inside among old European posters, as well as outside on the sidewalk. Next door is **Caffe Puccini,** whose big windows look onto North Beach street life.

A family-run place that opened in 1956, **Caffe Trieste** is a North Beach favorite and a feast for the senses, with steaming espresso, friendly chatter, old Italian murals, and, on occasional Saturday afternoons, live music played and sung by the owners and locals.

Caffé Roma roasts and sells its own coffee, which makes a good gift. **Mario's Bohemian Cigar Store Café** is a friendly little wedge of a café that lets you plug into the real North Beach. Mario's serves wonderful cappuccino and is legendary for its focaccia sandwiches (with meatball, eggplant, and other delicious fillings). ■

Caffe Puccini
✉ 411 Columbus Ave.
☎ 415/989-7033

Caffe Trieste
🅰 Map p. 79
✉ 601 Vallejo St.
☎ 415/392-6739
caffetrieste.com

Caffé Roma
✉ 526 Columbus Ave.
☎ 415/296-7942
cafferoma.com

Mario's Bohemian Cigar Store Café
✉ 566 Columbus Ave.
☎ 415/362-0536

Much of leisure life in North Beach revolves around drinking coffee, enjoying pastries, and reading.

The Beat Generation

The image is part of 1950s cultural history: a black-garbed beatnik wearing a beret, dark glasses, pointy beard, turtleneck, and sandals. He was allergic to work. Or so he appeared to mainstream America.

Gathering spot for 1950s Beat writers, City Lights Bookstore specializes in their work.

In the 1950s, most Americans were enjoying peace and prosperity, with new houses, jobs, and families. Along with this came a high level of social conformity. The Beats were disillusioned bohemians who found this conventional behavior intolerably stifling. They distrusted the "American Way of Life" and hated the prevailing complacency about racial problems and nuclear weapons. In North Beach, the Beats found a home.

The Beat movement in San Francisco was catalyzed by Allen Ginsberg's 1955 public reading of "Howl" (see sidebar p. 81). Jack Kerouac first used the term "Beat," meaning that his generation was beaten, weary, in their struggle for individual freedom. Beats wanted to "dig life" and remain in a high state of awareness—perhaps why some sources claim that Beat also relates to the word "beatific."

In 1958, local newspaper columnist Herb Caen invented the word "beatnik" by combining Beat with Sputnik, Russia's recently launched satellite. (Both were "far out," he wrote.) Caen didn't much like the Beats' lifestyle and meant the term to diminish them.

Hip Lingo

The Beats used a hip lingo derived mostly from blacks and jazz musicians. The terms slowly leaked out to the mainstream culture: cat (man), chick (woman), man (generic address for a cat), cool (good), dig (understand, appreciate), bug (annoy), drag (bore, disappointment), bread (money), blow (play an instrument), fuzz (police), hipster (person in the know), the most (greatest), pad (apartment), square (conformist), tea (marijuana), wig (mind, brain).

This lingo was staccato poetry, and poetry was paramount in Beat creativity. An older mentor, Kenneth Rexroth, was among the first to read poetry to the accompaniment of jazz. Beats soon gathered in bars and coffeehouses for poetry readings staged while musicians, or perhaps just a bongo drummer, played. Red wine and coffee were the intoxicants of choice, along with marijuana.

In no time the national news media caught on to the movement. Soon busloads of tourists were cruising North Beach, eager to see some genuine beatniks. The unwilling tourist attractions retaliated in 1958 by staging the "Squaresville Tour" through Union Square, marching in sandals and beards and gawking at the squares.

As Beat writers gained fame, wannabe beatniks poured into North Beach to "dig the scene." Suddenly teenagers all over America wanted to be goateed bongo players. As the tourist boom inflated rents in North Beach by the early 1960s, the Beats moved on—some to Haight-Ashbury, where their bohemianism inspired the emergent hippies. Beat icon Jack Kerouac died of alcoholism in 1969, while living in a Florida tract house.

INSIDER TIP:

You can see a first edition of Allen Ginsberg's legendary poem "Howl"—and the even more rare second edition confiscated by authorities—at the Beat Museum (see p. 96).

—JERRY CIMINO
Founder, the Beat Museum

The "best minds of my generation": Beat legends (left to right) Bob Donlin, Neal Cassady, Allen Ginsberg, painter Robert La Vigne, and Lawrence Ferlinghetti outside Ferlinghetti's City Lights Bookstore in 1956

Telegraph Hill

North Beach rises steeply to Telegraph Hill, where suddenly the vista expands to encompass the whole bay. The unobstructed view explains why the early San Franciscans climbed the 284-foot (86.5 m) hill to look for ships sailing into the Golden Gate. After 1850, arrivals were "telegraphed" to city merchants via a semaphore flag system that gave the hill its name.

Coit Tower rises 210 feet (64 m) above the top of Telegraph Hill, giving sweeping vistas of the bay.

Filbert Steps
🅜 Map p. 79
🚌 Bus: 39

The spectacular view also explains why Telegraph Hill accounts for some of today's most desirable real estate. But until the automobile made climbing the hill easier and opened it to the affluent, this was a blue-collar neighborhood housing a succession of immigrants from Chile, Peru, Ireland, and Italy. The 1906 fire torched most of Telegraph Hill's houses, but on the eastern slope Italian residents drenched blankets in red wine and spread them on their roofs to fight the flames.

Until 1914, part of the eastern slope was a rock quarry for ships' ballast, landfill, and street paving.

(Note the resulting cliff.) During the 1920s, bohemian writers and artists moved onto Telegraph Hill, attracted by the great views and the cheap rents. With the building of Coit Tower in 1933, the area became more popular and expensive, finally forcing out the artists.

At the foot of the hill, just before the Embarcadero, Levi's Plaza stands on gold rush landfill that includes at least one abandoned ship.

Filbert Steps

In San Francisco, steps work well where the terrain is too steep for a reasonable street. Few stairways anywhere have more charm than this one on the east side of Telegraph Hill.

The first section leads down Filbert Street from Telegraph Hill Boulevard to Montgomery Street. Here movie buffs may recognize the fine **1937 streamline moderne apartment house** *(1360 Montgomery St.)* as Humphrey Bogart's hideout with Lauren Bacall in *Dark Passage* (1947). Several striking reliefs adorn the building, including a Spanish mariner with a spyglass.

You can walk downhill on Montgomery to Alta Street, turning left to **Armistead Maupin's former house** *(60–62 Alta St., private).* The celebrated gay writer's 1978 novel *Tales of the City* started as a Bay Area newspaper

The Wild Parrots of Telegraph Hill

When homeless musician and truth seeker Mark Bittner moved into a cottage on Telegraph Hill in the 1990s, he began watching a flock of cherry-headed conures, most of them escaped pets, that regularly foraged near his house. In a book and 2005 documentary called "The Wild Parrots of Telegraph Hill," he introduces the parrots and reveals their relationships and his touching efforts to help them. His own search for companionship and purpose in life oddly parallels the lives of the birds. Today, the parrots are protected by San Francisco law, still wild and free, with the flock two hundred strong.

serial, an "alternative lifestyles" soap opera about various characters living on fictional Barbary Lane. Some say the setting was really Napier Lane; others claim it was Russian Hill's Macondray Lane (see p. 97).

The eventual nine novels in the *Tales* series sold more than six million copies, and several books were adapted as PBS

miniseries. Maupin was one of the first writers to tackle the topic of AIDS. He found most gay fiction "claustrophobic" and once noted, "I was allowing a little air into the situation by actually placing gay people in the context of the world at large."

The end of Alta Street has a vertiginous view. Below Montgomery, the wooden Filbert Steps take you through shady gardens of ferns, vines, and flowers edged with Victorian cottages. Among them, 224 Filbert dates from 1863, while 222 Filbert was once an unsanctioned bar. **Napier Lane** is simply a wooden plank sidewalk, one of the city's last, lined with cottages and apartments from the late 1800s, with lots of cats roaming. You wonder how residents move refrigerators and other heavy objects down the steps to their houses. At the bottom of Filbert, notice the old rock quarry; after the 1906

Coit Tower

🅰 Map p. 79

✉ Summit of Telegraph Hill, on Telegraph Hill Blvd.

☎ 415/249-0995

💲 $$ (elevator)

🚌 Bus: 39

earthquake, excavation went on here until a few houses slipped into the hole.

Coit Tower

One of San Francisco's most visible landmarks, Coit Tower rises above Pioneer Park on the summit of Telegraph Hill. In 1876, a group of public-spirited citizens bought the park land for $12,000 in gold coins to preserve it as open space. In the center of the parking plaza stands a 12-foot (3.6 m) bronze statue of Christopher Columbus, donated by the city's Italian community.

The 1933 tower also came about through a generous gift, a $125,000 bequest from Lillie Hitchcock Coit (see sidebar below). Arthur Brown, Jr., chief architect of City Hall and the Opera House, won the design competition for the memorial. Brown created a classical fluted column that stands 210 feet tall (64 m), with an observation loggia at the top. (Lillie Coit was devoted to the San Francisco's firefighters, but contrary to popular legend, the cylindrical tower is not meant to resemble the nozzle of a fire hose.)

An elevator and stairs take you to the top, where the view takes in an astounding panorama of city and bay—from Marin County and the Golden Gate to the Bay Bridge and downtown San Francisco. Don't miss this.

Murals: The tower lobby is lined with outstanding murals that capture life in California in 1934. They were a pilot program of the Public Works of Art

Lillie Hitchcock Coit

Lillie Coit wore men's clothes and smoked cigars in an era of petticoats and lace. A loyal supporter of firefighters, she loved to play poker and drink bourbon with them. She also attended every fire in town. (There were plenty in early San Francisco.) Lillie was a beloved San Francisco eccentric.

Lillie Coit was a little girl when her family came to San Francisco in 1851. One day when she was 15 years old, she saw the volunteers of Knickerbocker Engine Company No. 5 struggling up Telegraph Hill on the way to extinguish a fire. Impulsively, she tossed down her schoolbooks and ran to a vacant spot on the towrope, exhorting bystanders: "Come on you men! Everybody pull!" The engine was the first to reach the blaze.

The firefighters subsequently made Lillie an honorary member of Engine Company No. 5, and she embroidered a #5 on all her clothes (including her underwear, supposedly). The #5 pin that she wore was buried with her.

Lillie married Howard Coit, who held the influential position of caller at the Mining Exchange. Although wealthy, Lillie remained utterly free of snobbishness and was much loved for her wit and spirit. After being widowed, she lived in Europe for years, then returned to San Francisco. When she died in 1924 at age 87, Lillie bequeathed one-third of her wealth to San Francisco "for the purpose of adding to the beauty of the city which I have always loved."

That gift built Coit Tower.

In the Coit Tower lobby, 19 murals painted by a cadre of artists depict 1930s life in California.

Project (PWAP), a New Deal plan to employ artists during the Great Depression. Working for about $1 an hour, 25 painters and 19 assistants were turned loose on the tower's newly finished blank walls.

These artists and their work revived the art of fresco painting, in which a thin coat of wet plaster is painted with a brush dipped in dry pigments. The work is painstaking: An artist can cover only 2 square feet (0.18 sq m) a day, and mistakes have to be chipped out.

The frescoes are so similar in style that they appear to have been painted by one artist. The various painters achieved this unity by using a stock palette of earth tones and adhering to the style of Mexican muralist Diego Rivera, who liked to overlap two-dimensional figures.

Controversy swirled around the murals, for they depicted not only idealistic scenes of city, factory, and field, but also left-leaning political symbols. In one, a man was reading a Communist newspaper, the *Daily Worker*. Another mural showed a hammer and sickle. Such symbols caused particular tension at the time because a bloody strike of longshoremen was in progress, in which two union protesters

**Levi's Plaza &
Visitor Center**

⚠ Map p. 79

✉ Filbert St. at
Sansome St./
Battery St., 1155
Battery St.

🚌 Bus: 42, 82X

were shot down. Officials closed the tower until passions subsided. In the end, the hammer and sickle was removed.

Among the highlights of the murals are "City Life" (Victor Arnautoff), rich in detail: a newspaper stand selling leftist dailies, a banker reading stock market returns, a well-dressed man being robbed at gunpoint while indifferent citizens bustle past, and a cop orchestrating traffic; "California" (Maxine Albro) shows the state's agricultural bounty, with flower growers, a dairy, blossoming almond orchards, and vineyards; "Library" (Bernard Zakheim) depicts a reading room in which one man (modeled on fellow

INSIDER TIP:

**Ina Coolbrith Park
(Taylor St. & Vallejo St.,
see sidebar, p. 97) is a
gem with steep tree-
lined steps and a park
overlooking Alcatraz.**

—ERIN STONE
National Geographic contributor

artist John Langley Howard) is reaching for Karl Marx's *Das Kapital;* "Department Store" (Frede Vidar) shows a typical 1930s store with clothes, toys, salespeople, and two women in front of a menu that lists lunch for 25 cents; and "California Industrial Scenes" (John Langley Howard) depicts such enterprises as oil drilling and mining, but also bitterly contrasts the top and bottom levels

of technological society: Shabbily dressed migrants are regarded from a limousine by wealthy motorists out for amusement.

Levi's Plaza

This is the headquarters of Levi Strauss & Co., built in 1982 on gold rush landfill and landscaped as a reminder of the clothing company's links with the mining industry in California's canyons.

The staggered design of the complex harmonizes well with the stacked houses on Telegraph Hill behind it, and there is an appealing fountain of Sierra Nevada granite. On the Battery Street side, a 1903 wine warehouse built for the Italian Swiss Colony has been converted into a restaurant.

Levi's jeans were invented in San Francisco and have the city's initials right on their metal rivets. The use of rivets to strengthen points of strain such as pocket corners was patented by Levi Strauss and Jacob Davis in 1873. Their tough denim pants appealed to miners, who no doubt overloaded the pockets with promising rocks. The company created its first pair of Levi's 501 Jeans in the 1890s, a style that eventually became one of the best-selling clothing items in the world.

A **visitor center** in the headquarters lobby showcases the company's history, product innovations, and place in popular culture, reflected in changing displays such as jeans made for celebrities Elton John and Lady Gaga. ■

Russian Hill

At the summit of all residential neighborhoods in San Francisco, serene Russian Hill (294 feet/89.6 m) rises from the margins of North Beach and Fisherman's Wharf to overlook the waterfront, Coit Tower, and the cityscape. Actually, Russian Hill has two summits—Hyde Street at Lombard Street, and Vallejo Street between Taylor Street and Jones Street.

Many tourists visit crooked Lombard Street to navigate and document the street's hairpin turns.

Reportedly, the hill was named for early Russian otter hunters buried on top. Jasper O'Farrell's 1847 survey overlaid the hill with a street grid, including the steepest paved street in the city: Filbert between Leavenworth and Hyde, at a 31.5 percent grade. Other streets looked good on paper but were too steep to pave, so stairs were built, as on Vallejo Street.

The trudge uphill on routes such as Macondray Lane explains why few people lived here before cable car service came in 1880. But Russian Hill did not become an elite enclave. Residents with more taste than cash fashioned artistic houses and gardens. In 1890, Swedenborgian minister Joseph Worcester built a cottage of unfinished wood and

EXPERIENCE: Surviving the "Crookedest Street"

Want to try driving down San Francisco's crookedest (if not steepest) street? Herewith, tips for your ease and sanity:

Consider that San Francisco is busiest in summer, when weekends create a tourist traffic jam on Lombard Street: As many as 350 cars an hour descend this single block. (On a winter weekday, though, you might have it all to yourself.)

Watch for other drivers, each holding the steering wheel of an unfamiliar rental car with one hand and a camera with the other. Pedestrians often stand in the street, taking pictures and seemingly unaware of their surroundings. Be especially careful at the bottom of the block; it offers the best photo op, so throngs of

travelers pose here. (Tip: On this east-facing street, the best light for photography is in the morning.)

If you decide to avoid driving and walk, remember that the Powell-Hyde cable car stops at the top of the hill. Alight and stroll down Lombard at leisure, enjoying the flowers. And one last-ditch suggestion: When you get home, simply rent the Clint Eastwood crime flick *Magnum Force* and skip to the Lombard Street car-chase sequence.

Lombard is one of the few streets in the world that's famous in its own right, like Paris's Champs-Élysées. Maybe that's reason enough to make it a checkmark on your "life list" of traveler attractions.

Lombard Street

🅐 Map p. 78
🚋 CC: Powell-Hyde, Powell-Mason; Bus: 30, 41, 45

un-Victorian simplicity. Shingled houses followed, giving Russian Hill a distinctive look.

During the last half of the 1800s, Catherine Atkinson opened her house *(1032 Broadway)* as a literary salon for luminaries such as Mark Twain, Robert Louis Stevenson, and Ambrose Bierce. It was also headquarters for Les Jeunes, the coterie that included Gelett ("Purple Cow") Burgess and architect Willis Polk and poet Ina Coolbrith (see sidebar p. 97) hosted writers' gatherings at 1604 Taylor Street. In bohemian tradition, half a century later Jack Kerouac crashed at Neal Cassady's house at 29 Russell Street and wrote the Beat classic *On The Road,* in which he immortalized the kinetic Cassady as Dean Moriarty.

After the 1906 conflagration—during which one expressive Russian Hill resident sat somberly at a piano in the street playing "Danse

Macabre"—the neighborhood was rebuilt. Later, high-rises appeared and protests led to a 1974 moratorium on buildings taller than 40 feet (12 m). Nowadays, Russian Hill is quiet and well kept. Picturesque houses, sharply dropping streets, and bay views make it a popular movie location.

Lombard Street

A conga line of cars shimmies down the zigzags of the "crookedest street in the world," the 1000 block of Lombard. The street makes eight switchbacks as it drops from Hyde to Leavenworth.

The hairpin curves, added in 1922, adjusted the street's original 27 percent grade to 16 percent so cars could descend. In fact, here lies a problem: Every tourist in San Francisco feels a need to drive on this roller coaster, so cars stack up on the approach. About 750,000 cars make the descent each year.

You can walk down steps that edge the brick-paved street. They have no zigzags, and you'll have time to admire the flower gardens, houses, and apartments lining the street. The Hyde Street intersection at the top of Lombard offers a classic San Francisco view, looking along the cable car tracks to the waterfront and Alcatraz. Whip out your camera or cell phone; everyone does.

INSIDER TIP:

See San Francisco's *other* crooked street, steeper and more sinuous than famous Lombard—and less crowded. It's Vermont Street on Potrero Hill.

—LIZ EINBINDER
City guide, San Francisco Public Library

At this corner, the house at 1100 Lombard was built for Robert Louis Stevenson's widow, Fannie Osbourne Stevenson. It was designed in Mediterranean style by Willis Polk in 1900.

San Francisco Art Institute

Perched on a hillside, the West's oldest art school (founded 1871) occupies what appears to be a Spanish monastery, designed in 1926 by Bakewell & Brown, around a courtyard.

The **Diego Rivera Gallery** contains a 1931 mural in which the Mexican artist depicted himself painting a mural of American workers. The school café is open *(Mon.–Fri.)* to non-students, serving inexpensive food with a million-dollar view. There's also a fine view from the rooftop deck of a 1969 addition of brutalist concrete. ■

San Francisco Art Institute

🅰 Map p. 78
✉ 800 Chestnut St.
☎ 415/771-7020
🚋 CC: Powell-Hyde, Powell-Mason; Bus: 30

sfai.edu

At the San Francisco Art Institute, Diego Rivera's painting "Making of a Mural" depicts the artist on a scaffold.

More Places to Visit in North Beach & on Telegraph Hill & Russian Hill

Bustling Molinari's Deli, a fixture in North Beach, where locals buy everything from salami to basil

Beat Museum

A grace note on honky-tonk Broadway is this North Beach museum's small collection looking at Jack Kerouac *(On The Road)* and his literary pals, bohemians who became known as Beats. See displays on Beat writers, signed photos, and Allen Ginsberg's organ. *kerouac.com* Map p. 79 ✉ 540 Broadway ☎ 800/537-6822 💲 $$

Club Fugazi/*Beach Blanket Babylon*

John Fugazi was a Milanese who made his fortune in America selling hair oil, then went into banking. (His enterprise eventually became part of Transamerica.) He donated this 1912 building of brick and terra-cotta to the Italian community as a meeting hall. The Italian Heritage Room displays photos. But what draws crowds is the Club Fugazi theater, home of **Beach Blanket Babylon.** The high-energy, high-camp revue, which debuted in 1974, features characters who range from Snow White and Mr. Peanut to celebrities from pop culture and politics. All are spoofed in a fast-paced parade of sketches and solo turns. The longest-running musical revue in the world, the show is regularly updated to remain topical (e.g., a musical number called "Barack Around the Clock").

The show was founded by the late Steve Silver, who first created a company called Rent-A-Freak, which supplied parties with outlandishly costumed guests who arrived with props and even stage sets. Its success led to *Beach Blanket Babylon,* originally presented in a bar in North Beach that it quickly outgrew. The show moved to the 400-seat Club Fugazi, where Silver even staged a command performance for Queen Elizabeth. The show's costumes and comically oversize headdresses were exhibited at the de Young Museum. *beachblanketbabylon.com* Map p. 79

✉ 678 Green St. ☎ 415/421-4222
🚌 Bus: 8X, 30, 45

Green Street

The **Feusier Octagon House** (1067 Green St.), begun in 1858 as a single story, was designed according to the dictates of a popular phrenologist who claimed that octagonal houses promote good health. (See p. 148 for one you can visit.) Merchant Louis Feusier added the second story and mansard roof two decades later. The Tudor Revival former **Engine Company No. 31** (1088 Green St.), on Russian Hill, was built in 1908.
🅜 Map pp. 78–79 🚌 Bus: 30, 45

Macondray Lane

Trees, flowers, and ferns line Macondray Lane, a narrow street that only walkers can explore. Some San Franciscans say that this is the Barbary Lane of Armistead Maupin's *Tales of the City*. A number of houses date from the period after the San Francisco fire; the only pre-1906 survivor is 15–17 Macondray Lane.
🅜 Map pp. 78–79 ✉ Off Jones St., bet. Green St. & Union St. 🚋 CC: Powell-Hyde, Powell-Mason; Bus: 30, 41, 45

Molinari's Deli

Delectable whiffs of pesto and mozzarella, homemade ravioli, and air-dried salami fill this classic Italian deli in North Beach, which has been in business since 1896.
🅜 Map p. 79 ✉ 373 Columbus Ave.
☎ 415/421-2337 🚌 Bus: 15, 30, 39, 45

Sentinel Building (Columbus Tower)

This flatiron building (so named because its triangle shape resembles a clothes iron) is a beaux-arts jewel from 1907 with a storied history. Sheathed in green copper and white tile, it now houses American Zoetrope, the studio of the filmmaking Coppola family. Some colorful facts about Columbus Tower: One of the building's financiers, corrupt political boss Abraham Ruef, served time in San Quentin for graft. In the 1960s, the folk-singing Kingston Trio owned the building and had a recording studio in the basement.
🅜 Map p. 79 ✉ 373 Columbus Ave. at Kearny St.

St. Francis of Assisi

This pale Gothic church dates from 1860, but the congregation first met in an adobe

Ina Coolbrith

A beloved inspiration to two generations of California writers, Ina Coolbrith (1841–1928) attracted admirers such as Mark Twain and Bret Harte, who hinted he would leave his wife for her. Flamboyant poet Joaquin Miller described her as a "daughter of the gods, divinely tall and most divinely fair." Her literary correspondents included Henry Wadsworth Longfellow and Alfred, Lord Tennyson.

Friends called her the "virgin poetess," and none knew that she was once married to an actor. Born Josephine Smith, the niece of Mormon prophet Joseph Smith, she came west in a covered wagon in 1852,

the first child to enter California via the Beckwourth Pass. By age 11, she was a published poet, and in her late 20s, she helped Bret Harte edit the *Overland Monthly*.

In 1874, she took a job at the Oakland public library. One day she helped a poorly dressed 12-year-old boy find books. "I loved Ina Coolbrith above all womankind," said the boy, long afterward. "And what I am and what I have done that is good I owe to her." His name was Jack London. Another protégée was modern dancer Isadora Duncan. Ina's long-running literary salon drew many famous and talented writers.

chapel in 1849, the first American Roman Catholic parish on the West Coast. St. Francis (ca 1182–1226), the city's patron saint, renounced his father's wealth and adopted the ideal of poverty, leaving his hometown regularly to live as a hermit, and returning with illumination. He offers a good example for San Franciscans, who live within easy reach of silent places: redwood groves, mountains, and remote shores. *shrinest.org*

 Map p. 79 ✉ 610 Vallejo St. 🚌 Bus: 15, 30, 39, 45

Upper Grant Avenue

Heading north from Broadway, pubs and shops inhabit Edwardian buildings topped with apartments. The **Saloon** *(Map p. 84, 1232 Grant Ave.)* has served beer since 1861 and ranks as the city's oldest continuously operating purveyor of booze; a brothel once flourished upstairs. (Small wonder that firefighters saved the building during the 1906 blaze!) The bar at 1353 Grant Avenue was once a Beat hangout called the Coffee Gallery. A few steps off Grant, **101 Music** *(513 Green St.)* has 200,000 LP records (unsorted, so it's a treasure hunt), fine vintage stereo gear, and musical instruments. The eccentric

Aria *(1522 Grant Ave.)* sells eclectica, from architectural remnants to carved saints. Other shops sell upscale women's clothes.

Past Chestnut Street, on the east side of Grant Avenue, steps lead up to **Jack Early Park,** which offers a view from the Bay Bridge to the Golden Gate. Wharves are arrayed below. If Coit Tower is packed with cars and tourists, this makes a good alternative viewpoint.

 Map p. 79 🚌 Bus: 15, 30, 39, 45

Vallejo Street

On **Russian Hill Place** *(off 1000 block of Vallejo St.)* stands a row of Mediterranean cottages designed by Willis Polk in 1915 with red-tile roofs and wrought iron. At the top of the Vallejo Street stairs, the **Williams-Polk House** *(1013–1019 Vallejo St., private)* clings to a hillside, showing two stories on Vallejo, but six at the back. In 1892, Willis Polk designed this brown-shingled duplex for the widow of a founder of the San Francisco Art Institute.

The thin sliver of **Ina Coolbrith Park** *(Vallejo St. at Taylor St.)* honors Ina Donna Coolbrith (see sidebar p. 97), who in 1919 was named California's first poet laureate. The narrow, manicured park is shaded by pines.

 Map pp. 78–79 🚌 Bus: 30, 45

Macondray Lane, a shady refuge on Russian Hill, can only be explored on foot.

Fisherman's Wharf, with its historic ships, working docks, and tourist attractions—also the departure point for Alcatraz

Fisherman's Wharf & Alcatraz

A sign announces Fisherman's Wharf. Some 10 million visitors flock to the wharf each year.

Fisherman's Wharf & Alcatraz

Each year, 10 million people—that's nearly 30,000 a day—visit highly commercialized Fisherman's Wharf, a mile (1.6 km) stretch of the northern waterfront between Pier 39 and Aquatic Park. Across the water and accessible by ferry is Alcatraz Island, best known for the maximum security prison that occupied it between 1934 and 1963.

To avoid parking problems, it's best to take public transportation while visiting Fisherman's Wharf. The Powell-Mason cable car arrives on the wharf's east end at Bay Street.

The wharf's central section, along Jefferson Street, is a bedlam of shops peddling souvenirs, novelty museums, overpriced art galleries, and street vendors. Street performers work the passing crowd: A singer may compose a rap song about you as you walk by, or a human mannequin may stand frozen in position, hoping you'll toss a dollar in his hat. But if you look past the commercial hokum, you'll find the *real* Fisherman's Wharf: colorful fishing boats docked after unloading their catches, stalls where vendors steam Dungeness crabs, and a pier with historic sailing ships.

Boom Time

The waterfront's boom began in 1853 at the foot of Powell Street, where Harry Meiggs built 1,600-foot-long (490 m) Meiggs Wharf. As a city councilman deep in debt, "Honest Harry" embezzled $365,000 and fled to South America. He built a railroad across the Andes, made an astounding fortune of $100 million, and repaid his obligations in San Francisco.

Around Meiggs Wharf, a sawmill and other businesses grew up. Citizens came to enjoy bathhouses and saloons such as Abe Warner's Cobweb Palace, where customers ate crab chowder under a ceiling festooned with spiderwebs. (Superstitious Abe refused to harm spiders.) His menagerie included a

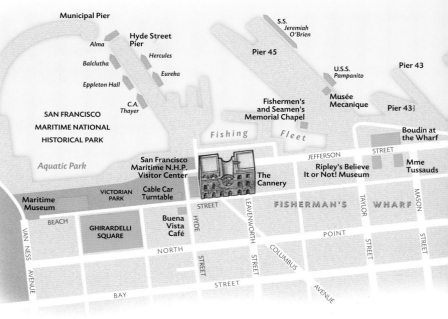

Municipal Pier

Hyde Street Pier

Alma

Hercules

Balclutha

Eureka

Eppleton Hall

C.A. Thayer

SAN FRANCISCO MARITIME NATIONAL HISTORICAL PARK

S.S. Jeremiah O'Brien

Pier 45

U.S.S. Pampanito

Pier 43

Musée Mecanique

Pier 43½

Fishermen's and Seamen's Memorial Chapel

Fishing Fleet

Boudin at the Wharf

Aquatic Park

San Francisco Maritime N.H.P. Visitor Center

JEFFERSON STREET

The Cannery

Ripley's Believe It or Not! Museum

Mme Tussauds

Maritime Museum

VICTORIAN PARK

Cable Car Turntable

STREET

LEAVENWORTH

FISHERMAN'S WHARF

TAYLOR

MASON

BEACH

GHIRARDELLI SQUARE

Buena Vista Café

HYDE STREET

POINT

STREET

STREET

VAN NESS AVENUE

NORTH

STREET

STREET

COLUMBUS

BAY

STREET

AVENUE

monkey that pestered patrons for peanuts and a famous parrot that spoke the nonsense line: "I'll have a rum and gum! What'll you have?"

The waterfront also saw nefarious characters such as Scabhouse Johnny and Three Finger Curtin abducting men for involuntary sea duty, usually by giving them knockout drops or a knock on the head. The victims awoke aboard a ship under sail. Captains were desperate because so many sailors arriving in San Francisco ran off to the gold country.

Fishing Fleets

The fishing fleet didn't take up permanent berth at Fisherman's Wharf until 1900.

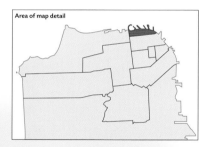

Area of map detail

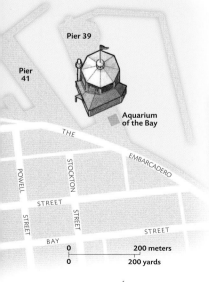

Pier 39

Pier 41

Aquarium of the Bay

THE EMBARCADERO

POWELL

STOCKTON STREET

STREET

STREET

STREET

BAY

STREET

| 0 | 200 meters |
| 0 | 200 yards |

NOT TO BE MISSED:

Sea lions barking on the sunny docks at Pier 39   102–103

A boat tour that takes you under the Golden Gate Bridge   103

Eating a crab cocktail with a great bay view   104

Seeing (and smelling) the boats of the real Fisherman's Wharf   104–105

Topping off a chilly day with hot Irish coffee at the Buena Vista Café   107

Exploring the island prison of Alcatraz   112–117

Previously, captains docked at more sheltered wharves jutting from Green, Union, and Filbert Streets. As the waterfront was developed for shipping, the fishing fleet moved to the foot of Taylor Street. Italian immigrants dominated the trade. First had come men from Genoa, who dotted the bay with their feluccas—narrow, 16-foot-long (5 m) boats with points at both ends. In the 1890s, Sicilians took over. As motorized boats and bigger nets became available, however, the bay and nearby ocean were nearly fished out. By the 1950s, San Francisco's fishing fleet was a vestige of what it had been.

But tourism held new promise. Outsiders had long come to the wharf to watch the picturesque scene. Fishermen in blue trousers with colorful sashes sat mending nets with wooden needles. Plump seagulls fluttered above the boats, whose decks were piled high with fish and crabs. Visitors dined at seafood houses such as Alioto's, founded by Sicilian immigrant Nunzio Alioto in 1938 as the wharf's first real restaurant. In 1964, the rehabilitation of the historic Ghirardelli chocolate factory as a complex of shops and restaurants drew more crowds, as did the creation of the similar Pier 39. ∎

Fisherman's Wharf & Around

Visitors flock to Fisherman's Wharf and nearby venues for three main reasons: (1) the water, (2) the lure of the tacky, and (3) seafood restaurants. Food, shopping, and family attractions make Fisherman's Wharf the most popular tourist spot in San Francisco.

Sea lions bask in the sun at Pier 39, one of many popular attractions at Fisherman's Wharf.

Pier 39

- 🅜 Map p. 101
- ✉ Beach St. at the Embarcadero
- ☎ 415/981-7437
- 🚌 Bus: 15, 39, 42; Streetcar: F

pier39.com

Aquarium of the Bay

- ✉ Pier 39
- ☎ 415/623-5300
- 💲 $$$$

aquariumofthebay .org

Pier 39

This development of shops, restaurants, and amusements is a little commercial world of its own. Situated just east of Fisherman's Wharf, Pier 39 showcases views of the bay and Golden Gate Bridge.

Built on a 1905 cargo pier, this imitation fishing village (1978, Walker and Moody) uses wood salvaged from other piers. Attractions include the **San Francisco Carousel** ($), with its horses, sea dragons,

and 1,800 twinkling lights.

At **Aquarium of the Bay** you're in the company of ocean creatures of the San Francisco Bay and northern California as you ride moving walkways through two clear acrylic tunnels surrounded by 700,000 gallons (more than 2.5 million L) of water. The aquarium's 30,000 creatures represent 200 species and include sharks, skates, jellies, and other undersea denizens from salmon to rock scallops. You can pat bat rays and tide-pool critters in

Ba-a-a-ark!

Follow the cacophony to the west side of Pier 39. The noise comes from a raucous colony of California sea lions (Zalophus californianus) that took up residence in the adjacent marina in 1990. They loll on docks, pile on top of one another, and generally show off.

Daily, staffers from the Sea Lion Center (located above K-Dock on Level 2) are on K-Dock to talk about California sea lions. Unlike seals, sea lions have external ear flaps. The blubbery creatures live along the Pacific coast and feed on fish and squid. To breed and give birth, they waddle ashore to form colonies. Males (which may be 8 feet/2 m long) assemble harems and maintain their territories with displays of barking and head shaking.

INSIDER TIP:

Street performers work an area they call the "circle pitch" just outside Pier 39 at Powell Street and the Embarcadero.

—BIG AL CATRAZ
Comedy magician at Pier 39

special "touch pools," and watch river otters at play.

Some Pier 39 attractions are free. At an outdoor stage, you can watch street performers juggle or do magic.

Bay Cruises & More

To see San Francisco from a fresh perspective, take a bay cruise. Out on the water you can look back at Fisherman's Wharf and the hilly city, observe the bustling port at work, and see the bay islands up close.

The **Blue & Gold Fleet's Bay Cruise Adventure** sails under the Golden Gate Bridge, around Alcatraz, and past Angel Island. An audio tour in nine languages plays on smartphones and tablets.

The company also provides ferry services to Sausalito, Tiburon, Alameda/Oakland, Vallejo, Angel Island, Harbor Bay, South San Francisco, and AT&T Park on game days.

The **Red & White Fleet's Golden Gate Bay Cruise** ventures under the Golden Gate Bridge and around Alcatraz, with audio narration in 16 languages focusing on landmarks of San Francisco history.

U.S.S. *Pampanito*

This 1943 submarine of the Balao class was designed for long-range cruises in the Pacific. During dangerous cat-and-mouse missions in World War II, it sank six Japanese ships and damaged four others, dodging torpedoes and surviving depth charges.

Another problem for the 80 crewmen must have been claustrophobia. The sub operated at a depth of 600 feet (183 m). It was so cramped that men slept in the torpedo room. (In addition, imagine 80 men at sea for two and a half months . . . without a shower.)

A self-guided audio tour, including sound effects, historic recordings, and accounts by *Pampanito* veterans, takes you through hatches

Blue & Gold Fleet
- Pier 39
- 415/773-1188
- $$$$$
- CC: Powell-Hyde, Powell-Mason; Bus: 30, 41, 45; Streetcar: F

blueandgoldfleet.com

Red & White Fleet
- Pier 43½
- 415/673-2900
- $$$$$
- CC: Powell-Hyde, Powell-Mason; Bus: 30, 41, 45; Streetcar: F

redandwhite.com

U.S.S. Pampanito
- Map p. 100
- Pier 45
- 415/775-1943
- $$$
- CC: Powell-Hyde, Powell-Mason; Bus: 30, 41, 45; Streetcar: F

maritime.org

S.S. Jeremiah O'Brien

🅰 Map p. 100

✉ Pier 45

☎ 415/544-0100

💲 $$$

🚋 CC: Powell-Hyde, Powell-Mason;
Bus: 30, 41, 45;
Streetcar: F

ssjeremiahobrien.org

Fishing Fleet

✉ Jefferson St. bet. Taylor & Hyde Sts.

🚋 CC: Powell-Hyde, Powell-Mason;
Bus: 30, 41, 45;
Streetcar: F

and down narrow companionways. Stops include the galley (look for the Betty Grable pinup picture that symbolized home for U.S. servicemen), engine and control rooms, officers' quarters, and torpedo tubes.

S.S. *Jeremiah O'Brien*

One of two remaining functional Liberty ships that carried cargo during World War II, she crossed the English Channel bringing personnel and supplies to the Normandy beaches during the D-Day invasion. Visitors can roam from the engine room to the flying bridge. The 2,500-horsepower engine gets fired up (third Sat.–Sun.), and the ship makes occasional cruises.

Jefferson & Taylor Streets

The hub of Fisherman's Wharf is Taylor and Jefferson Streets, where seafood restaurants overlook fishing boats tied up on the docks below. In a passageway of fish and chowder stalls, cauldrons steam Dungeness crabs, which will be cracked for sale by the colorful vendors. In the early days, fishermen and market laborers came to such stalls for chowder to eat on the run. Tomaso Castagnola gets credit for his idea of the "walk-away crab cocktail" in 1916.

Fishing Fleet: What remains of the city's historic fishing fleet is docked to the north of Jefferson Street. An open railing between Taylor and Jones looks onto the Jefferson Street Lagoon, with its Monterey-type fishing boats; these resemble the double-pointed feluccas used on the bay by Italian fishermen in the 1800s, but are enlarged and motorized.

The boats are laden with nets, coiled ropes, reels, plastic buckets, and other tackle, and there's definitely something fishy in the air. Most of the professional activity takes place around dawn, when fishermen unload their catches. The boats bring in squid, sand dabs, sole, sea bass, cod, mackerel, and halibut year-round. Crab, salmon, shrimp, and ocean perch are seasonal. The annual catch weighs 20 million pounds (more than 9 million kg).

Behind the Scenes: For a better view, walk to the end of Taylor and go left to the foot of Pier 45. Here you'll see the **Fishermen's and Seamen's Memorial Chapel,** a

---

Sourdough Bread

This crusty French bread with a sour tang and soft, chewy center was introduced in 1849 by Frenchman Isidore Boudin. Tours of his namesake bakery *(160 Jefferson St., tel 415/928-1849, boudinbakery.com, $)* include exhibits and bread tasting. More than 25,000 loaves of bread are baked here daily. Boudin created the city's first sourdough bread using unbleached flour, water, salt, and sourdough starter, or "mother dough." The starter used today dates back to his first loaf. San Franciscans say that sourdough microorganisms thrive only in their foggy city and therefore the true product must come from San Francisco. For SourFlour workshops at La Victoria Bakery in the Castro District, see p. 199.

simple brown wooden structure. Above the door a stained-glass panel depicts a ship's wheel. In addition to a Sunday Catholic Mass—most fishermen are of Italian descent—services are held

is **Fish Alley,** where catches used to be landed in the morning. Turn left up Richard Henry Dana Place to Jefferson Street and a reentry into the commercial hoopla.

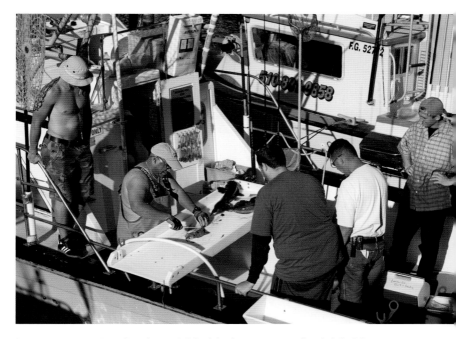

In contrast to its touristy side, Fisherman's Wharf also functions as a working hub for fishermen.

that reflect other nationalities and faiths. While you're nearby, have a look at **Pier 45,** where large fishing vessels tie up. You'll also see hungry sea lions and wheeling gulls.

To explore more of the working area of Fisherman's Wharf, go back to Jefferson Street and walk west; just past Castagnola's, turn right (opposite Jones Street); then turn left along the water, where you'll see more fishing boats. At the end of the block

Jefferson Street Museums

A strip along Jefferson Street has two museums designed to be "fun for the whole family." People who like this sort of thing will find this the sort of thing they like.

Ripley's Believe It or Not! Museum is an "odditorium" of peculiar-but-true displays, based on the famous newspaper cartoon feature begun in 1918 by Robert Ripley. Among the 400

Fishermen's and Seamen's Memorial Chapel

🅰 Map p. 100

✉ Pier 45

🚋 CC: Powell-Hyde, Powell-Mason; Bus: 30, 41, 45; Streetcar: F

Jefferson Street
- Map pp. 100–101
- Bus: 32; Streetcar: F

Ripley's Believe It or Not! Museum
- Map p. 100
- 175 Jefferson St.
- 415/202-9850
- $$$$

ripleys.com /sanfrancisco

Madame Tussauds
- Map p. 100
- 145 Jefferson St.
- 866/223-4240
- $$$$$

madametussauds .com

artifacts, re-creations, and interactive exhibits are a shrunken human head whose original owner lived in Ecuador, a Mona Lisa portrait assembled with Rubik's Cubes, a spinning tunnel to walk through and get dizzy, Lady Gaga made of candy, a mirror maze *(extra admission),* an African coffin shaped like a giant Coke bottle, a "vampire killing kit" (wooden stake, garlic, holy water, cross), a donkey made of wine corks (hey, why not?), a toilet-paper wedding dress, a walk-in kaleidoscope, and a cable car painstakingly made of 270,836 matchsticks (and 21 pints/10 L of glue) by a man with acute arthritis. Cartoonist Ripley himself was an oddity: He owned several luxury automobiles but didn't know how to drive. While drawing, he wore a Chinese bathrobe and

INSIDER TIP:

Take the ferry from Fisherman's Wharf to charming Sausalito *(oursausalito.com /sausalito-ferry.html)* for unparalleled views.

—MERYN CHIMES
National Geographic contributor

let squirrels scamper on his desk.

The famous folks on display at **Madame Tussauds**—Hollywood A-listers, music and sports stars, cultural icons—don't just stand there like, um, wax dummies. You can interact: Take a selfie with Leonardo DiCaprio or Steve Jobs, play drums for Lady Gaga, or sip Breakfast at Tiffany's tea with Audrey Hepburn.

One of many unusual-but-true re-creations at Ripley's Believe It or Not! Museum on Jefferson Street: An exhibit features a performer hanging by her teeth above the streets of New York.

Buena Vista Café

The Buena Vista is a classic—perhaps *the* classic—San Francisco saloon. The three-story Edwardian building (1911) was a boardinghouse for five years until the owner converted the ground floor into a bar.

The name Buena Vista means "good view" in Spanish—an accurate name, given the waterfront panorama outside the saloon's bay windows. Sardine cannery workers would pop in for whiskey while they waited for arriving boats. But this heritage isn't why San Franciscans regard the Buena Vista as a historical site.

It's because in 1952 this bar introduced Irish coffee to America. *San Francisco Chronicle* travel writer Stanton Delaplane returned home from Ireland, where he'd drunk Irish coffee at Shannon Airport, and encouraged Jack Koeppler, then owner of the Buena Vista, to add the concoction to the bar menu. In November the duo commenced experimentation. They just couldn't get it right, though, despite working into the wee hours one night—after which Delaplane nearly passed out across the cable car tracks outside the bar.

A whipped-cream dilemma had developed: The dollop wouldn't float atop the coffee. Eventually the city mayor, who owned a dairy, solved the problem: Age the cream for two days and whip it lightly.

The rest is warm, boozy history. Today, bartenders line up a dozen glasses at a time in assembly line fashion to make Irish coffees—as many as 2,000 each day. The elixir contains four essential food groups: caffeine, alcohol, sugar, and fat. What more could a traveler ask for on a cold, rainy day?

Hyde Street Pier

The romantic era of sail and steam comes to life through historic vessels docked at the wooden Hyde Street Pier. Once a ferry embarkation point, the pier is now part of **San Francisco Maritime National Historical Park.** The park also includes a visitor center and a maritime museum in the Aquatic Park Bathhouse building.

In the early days of San Francisco, almost everyone and everything came by sea. During the gold rush, sleek windjammers

---

EXPERIENCE: How to Make Perfect Irish Coffee

Making Irish coffee is an art at the Buena Vista, and you, too, can brew up a masterpiece with their time-tested recipe. Serve in a glass goblet. (Heat-treated ones are available on the bar's website.)

1) Fill glass with very hot water to preheat, then empty.

2) Pour hot coffee into hot glass until it is about three-quarters full. Drop in two cocktail sugar cubes.

3) Stir to thoroughly dissolve the sugar.

4) Add full jigger of Irish Whiskey for proper taste and body.

5) Top with a collar of lightly whipped whipping cream by pouring gently over a spoon.

6) Enjoy it piping hot. The coffee, not you . . . although you soon will be too. *Sláinte!*

Buena Vista Café
- Map p. 100
- 2765 Hyde St.
- 415/474-5044
- CC: Powell-Hyde, Powell-Mason; Bus: 15, 30, 41, 45; Streetcar: F

thebuenavista.com

Hyde Street Pier
- Map p. 100
- Foot of Hyde St.
- 415/447-5000
- $$ (to board historic vessels)
- CC: Powell-Hyde, Powell-Mason; Bus: 15, 30, 41, 45; Streetcar: F

nps.gov/safr

Hyde Street Pier is home to Scottish square-rigger *Balclutha,* one of five historic ships at the pier.

**San Francisco
Maritime
National
Historical Park
Visitor Center**

 Map p. 100

✉ 499 Jefferson St.
at Hyde St., in
Argonaut Hotel

☎ 415/447-5000

🚋 CC: Powell-
Hyde, Powell-
Mason; Bus:
15, 30, 41, 45;
Streetcar: F

nps.gov/safr

sailed through the Golden Gate
carrying hopeful argonauts from
the East Coast—a 17,000-mile
(27,360 km) journey around Cape
Horn. (The speed record for a
clipper from New York was 89
days, set in 1850.)

During the 1870s, cargo vessels left San Francisco with wheat
bound for Europe. To cross the
bay to points east and north,
travelers took ferries—the only
transport half a century before
the Golden Gate and Bay Bridges
were built.

The *Balclutha:* Among five
historical ships for visitors to
board, the pier's main attraction
is the *Balclutha*, a steel-hulled
square-rigger. The ship's proud
hull, three masts, and brass
fixtures evoke the glory days of
the sailing ship. Built in Scotland
in 1886, the 301-foot (91.7 m)

**The Bay Area is like a
theater in the round.
Circle the bay in a car
and view it from the
area's three bridges.**

—TOM ROCKWELL
*Director of Exhibits,
Exploratorium*

Balclutha was designed for cargo.
In 17 trips around the Horn, she
brought coal—and everything
from a piano to a shopkeeper's
display cabinet—from Europe
and returned with California
wheat. From 1902 to 1930, she
plied the Alaska salmon trade.

Later roles for the ship were
tragicomic. After the *Balclutha*
played a bit part in the 1934
movie *Mutiny on the Bounty*, a
promoter tarted her up as an

ersatz pirate ship to tour the West Coast. Ultimately, the *Balclutha* ended up on the mud flats in Sausalito, north of the Golden Gate Bridge. In 1954, the San Francisco Maritime Museum rescued her from the scrap heap, and with 13,000 hours of volunteer labor restored the ship.

Peek into the captain's Victorian cabin, with its maple cabinets, liquor bar (hung from the ceiling), and comfortable seating. In striking contrast, the boat's forecastle had hard wooden bunks for the weary common seamen. In the hold is the typical cargo: whiskey, wheat, cement, and Belgian glass.

Other Historic Ships: You can board the world's largest floating wooden structure—the *Eureka*—an 1890 side-wheel ferry 300 feet long (91.4 m). A steam engine four stories high was needed to propel the vessel, which carried up to 120 automobiles and 2,300 commuters between San Francisco and Sausalito. The lower deck displays autos from the 1920s and '30s, when ferries (not bridges) were the commuter's only way to the city.

You can also board the 1907 steam tugboat *Hercules.* On view too are the *Alma* (1891), the last San Francisco Bay scow schooner, which carried hay and lumber; and the *Eppleton Hall,* a 1914 English paddle tug, a steam side-wheeler that towed vessels that literally "carried coals to Newcastle."

The restored 1895 *C.A. Thayer,* a schooner, was the West Coast's last commercial sailing vessel.

Visitor Center & Maritime Museum: The visitor center, housed in a historic cannery warehouse, has information about the park and exhibits on maritime subjects, ranging from shipwrecks to the ocean routes from San Francisco to New York. There's a spectacular Fresnel lens of polished prisms from an 1855 island lighthouse located in treacherous waters beyond the Golden Gate. An extensive exhibit takes visitors

on a walk along the San Francisco waterfront, from the days of Native Americans through the early 1900s. Showcased are native marshlands, Yerba Buena Cove (showing how abandoned ships were used as landfill in the expanding city), Fisherman's Wharf, storefronts, and the requisite seafront saloon (where hapless sailors were shanghaied as crew on departing ships). Ranger-guided park tours and cell phone audio tours are available.

Maritime Museum

🅰 Map p. 100
✉ Aquatic Park, 900 Beach St. at Polk St.
☎ 415/447-5000
🚃 CC: Powell-Hyde, Powell-Mason; Bus: 15, 30, 41, 45; Streetcar: F

nps.gov/safr

Street Performers

Much of Fisherman's Wharf is a showcase for jugglers, street musicians, magicians, mimes, and other entertainers. One pavement pioneer of the 1970s was the "Human Jukebox"—basically a large carton that passersby encountered on the sidewalk. When you dropped a quarter in a slot, a disheveled guy holding a trumpet would pop out and play the requested song. It cost extra for "I Left My Heart in San Francisco," because the Human Jukebox was so sick of it.

The Ghirardelli sign radiates a greeting at dusk, luring visitors to Fisherman's Wharf.

Ghirardelli Square

- Map p. 100
- Bet. Polk & Larkin Sts., Beach St., & North Point
- 415/775-5500
- CC: Powell-Hyde; Bus: 10, 19, 41, 45; Streetcar: F

ghirardellisq.com

The Maritime Museum has limited temporary displays on West Coast seafaring, with plans for more permanent exhibits. The museum occupies the Aquatic Park Casino, built in 1939 by the New Deal's Works Projects Administration (WPA) as a public bathhouse on a man-made beach. With its streamline moderne design, the building resembles a 1930s ocean liner tied up at the shore. Works of the Federal Arts Project include carved slate decorations around the doorway by Sargent Johnson and interior murals by Hilaire Hiler of the submerged continents of Mu and Atlantis, with colorful fish and mythical sea creatures.

Ghirardelli Square

In 1964, Ghirardelli chocolate's historic factory was revamped as a festive marketplace of shops and restaurants—a design concept that would inspire many similar urban restoration projects (such as Boston's Faneuil Hall Marketplace). The multilevel complex offers visitors great views of the bay, and scattered plaques through the complex facilitate a self-guided walking tour.

The site's history began when Domingo Ghirardelli, son of a celebrated chocolatier in Rapallo, Italy, arrived in San Francisco in 1852 and began making chocolate. Most important, he learned how to remove cocoa butter from chocolate and grind the remains into a delicate powder called "broma," used in bakeries and dairies as well as for hot chocolate. By 1885, the company was selling 50,000 pounds (22,680 kg) of this powdered chocolate annually.

To accommodate the expanding business after Domingo's retirement, in 1893 his sons bought this city block, which included the 1864 Pioneer Woolen Mill, and converted it into a chocolate factory. Working with architect William Mooser II, they added the Mustard Building and others, all surrounding a courtyard where workers could eat lunch on sunny days.

The enormous Ghirardelli sign went up in 1915. Standing 25 feet high (7.6 m) and measuring 165 feet long (50 m), the sign has radiated a greeting to ships entering San Francisco ever since. (With the exception of the World War II blackout.)

The picturesque **Clock Tower** (1916) with four faces was inspired by the château at Blois in France. The renovation's landscape architect, Lawrence Halprin, outlined the tower in white lights, creating a delightful element of San Francisco's nighttime skyline.

In 1962, Ghirardelli Chocolate moved to a new factory, leaving its historic facility threatened with demolition to make room for an apartment development. William Matson Roth, heir to the Matson shipping empire, bought the factory with a vision in mind. Retaining the old brick walls and the wooden floors of the interior, Roth added buildings, fanciful pavilions, and landscaped terraces. The complex is filled with specialty shops and restaurants. ■

Fun Facts for Chocolate Lovers

The average American eats 12 pounds (5.4 kg) of chocolate a year.

The Maya discovered cacao in the Mesoamerican rain forest, burning seeds as offerings to the gods and grinding them into a paste they mixed with chili peppers. The Aztecs obtained cacao seeds by trade and tribute, and it's said that the ruler Moctezuma drank 50 cups of chocolate a day.

Spanish conquerors of the 1500s brought chocolate to Europe, where—sweetened with sugar—it swept through Europe's upper classes as a status symbol. In 1847, Britain's Fry & Sons developed the solid chocolate bar. Pennsylvania confectioner Milton Hershey later mechanized the process and became "the Henry Ford of chocolate makers."

Today, Halloween alone gobbles up 90 million pounds (almost 41 million kg) of chocolate. Two-thirds of all chocolate consumed is eaten between meals.

Popular on Valentine's Day, chocolate contains the same mood-elevating chemical (phenylethylamine, or PEA) our brain produces when we are in love.

Crusading nurse Florence Nightingale believed in chocolate for health. Indeed, chocolate contains antioxidants that reduce the risk of heart disease. Dark chocolate has twice as many antioxidants as milk chocolate—which Americans prefer by a ratio of nearly three to one.

Alcatraz

Alcatraz Island is "The Rock," home to the maximum-security federal penitentiary that held the superstars of crime—incorrigible bad guys such as Al Capone and George "Machine Gun" Kelly, as well as perverse killer Robert "Birdman" Stroud. From The Rock, prisoners had a heart-breaking view across the water to San Francisco and freedom, only a mile and a quarter (2 km) away. The penitentiary is chilling—and not only because of the harsh winds that blow here.

The penitentiary on Alcatraz Island, former home of more than 1,500 criminals, closed in 1963.

Alcatraz

⬛ See map on inside front cover

Alcatraz Tours

✉ Pier 33

☎ 415/981-7625

💲 $$$$$

alcatrazcruises.com

Alcatraz Island has had several lives: fortress, military prison, and federal penitentiary from 1934 to 1963. It was occupied by Native Americans during the 1960s. Today, the island is home not to jailbirds but seabirds, including thousands of western gulls. Hoards of visitors take the trip across the bay to experience the island's chilling past.

Early Days

In 1775, Spanish mariner Juan Manuel de Ayala became the first European to see the 22-acre (9 ha) island. He named it Isla de los Alcatraces, or Island of the Pelicans (although the birds he saw there may have been cormorants). The island's strategic position near the mouth of San Francisco Bay also made it ideal for a military fort, which was begun in 1853. The next year, the Pacific coast's first lighthouse was erected here.

Next, Alcatraz became a military prison, whose inmates included Confederate sympathizers during the Civil War and Native American captives from the 1870s Indian wars. After the 1906 earthquake flattened San Francisco's jails, civilian prisoners were lodged on the island.

Federal Pen

In 1934, the island was transferred to the new Federal Bureau of Prisons, which wanted to isolate the nation's worst criminal inmates in one maximum-security setting. The country was fighting back against a crime wave brought on by Prohibition, the Great Depression, and the rise of mobsters. The penitentiary's security measures included barbed wire, guard towers, lights, window bars of "tool-proof" steel, and remote door openers. The final insurance against escape was the surrounding bay, whose cold water and swift currents (51°F/10.5°C, up to 9 knots) were barriers no prisoner was likely to survive.

Alcatraz inmates did dream of escape, of course. But among the 1,545 men incarcerated over the years, only 36 attempted it. All were shot dead, recaptured, or presumed drowned in the frigid bay. In 1939, notorious "Doc" Barker and four other men sawed their way out of their cells. Surprised by guards on the beach, some surrendered, but Barker ran off into the fog and was cut down by bullets. In 1962, Frank Morris and brothers John and Clarence Anglin fooled guards into thinking they were asleep by placing

EXPERIENCE: A Walk in the Gardens of Alcatraz

It sounds crazy—the idea of growing flowers in a barren place called "The Rock." But prisoners and staff planted rose gardens, hillside terraces, flower beds, and lawns on this grim penitentiary island *(alcatrazgardens.org; for tours Fri. & Sun. a.m., take first two ferry departures to Alcatraz; Officer's Row garden viewings Wed.)*. Growing things raised not only flowers but also morale.

Your spirits will break free, too, as you take a docent or self-guided walk in the restored gardens. You'll learn that during the prison era, gardeners had to be creative; plants were nourished with scraps from the kitchen and water from the cell-house showers. Similarly, today's island gardeners nurture flowers and greenery with compost and a rainwater catchment system.

After the federal prison closed in 1963, its gardens slowly fell to ruin. Still, some hardy plants survived on rain and fog until Golden Gate National Parks Conservancy staffers and volunteers arrived in 2003 to reestablish the gardens. Now you'll see heirloom bearded irises, rare roses, fuchsias, and masses of succulents all over the island.

On the free docent tours, you'll also see areas where visitors usually aren't allowed. Be sure to peek over railings and behind walls to find hidden gems as you discover the softer side of The Rock.

It looks like Alcatraz
got me licked.
—"Scarface" Al Capone
(1899–1947)

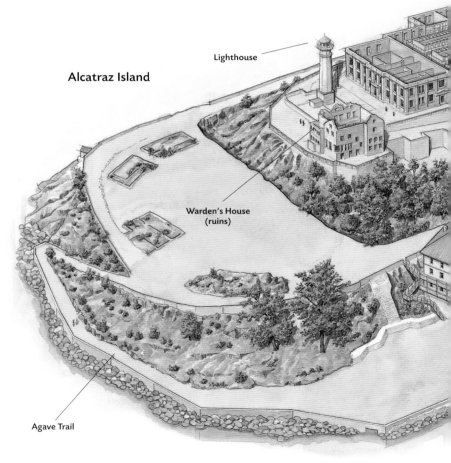

Alcatraz Island

Lighthouse

Warden's House
(ruins)

Agave Trail

dummy heads in their bunks. (The molded soap-and-concrete heads were thatched with hair pilfered from the prison barber shop.) The convicts broke out and set off across the bay using flimsy life jackets made of inflated raincoats. No trace was found except for Clarence Anglin's wallet, which washed up on nearby Angel Island. Most likely the men drowned—only to be immortalized in the 1979 Clint Eastwood movie, *Escape from Alcatraz*.

Post Exchange

Guardhouse

Barracks building

Alcatraz Jetty

A typical cell in Alcatraz maximum security penitentiary consisted of one bunk, one blanket, a foldout table, a chair, a toilet, and a small sink.

Notorious Prisoners at Alcatraz

"Scarface" Al Capone (1899–1947) The 1934 arrival of the notorious gangster made national headlines. Capone installed his family in a mainland hotel and through them ran his criminal organization in Chicago. Mentally disturbed from syphilis, he spent much of his four and a half years here in a hospital isolation cell.

Alvin "Creepy" Karpis (1907–1979) A partner of the notorious Ma Barker, Karpis laid waste to the Midwest in a flamboyant spree of robbery and kidnapping between 1931 and 1936. Declared Public Enemy Number One, he spent 26 years on Alcatraz.

George "Machine Gun" Kelly (1895–1954) Kelly was a bootlegger, bank robber, and kidnapper. His trial for abducting an Oklahoma oilman was the first under the Lindbergh Law, earning him a life sentence; he served 17 years.

Robert Stroud (1890–1963) Although called the Birdman of Alcatraz, Stroud was actually never allowed to keep birds during his 17-year stay. His avian studies took place earlier at Leavenworth penitentiary, where he killed a custodial officer in front of more than 2,000 other inmates.

James "Whitey" Bulger (1929–) The antihero of the 2015 film *Black Mass*, this Boston gangster passed through Alcatraz early in his criminal career, spending three years on The Rock from 1959 to 1962. Subsequently he became a long-time regular on the FBI's Ten Most Wanted Fugitives list and was eventually convicted in 2011 for his part in 11 murders, among numerous other crimes.

In the last escape attempt, two inmates inflated surgical gloves, filched from the prison hospital, and tried to float across the water. One actually reached San Francisco and collapsed; children summoned police.

In 1963, the high cost of transporting supplies and personnel to the island led to the penitentiary's closure. Six years later the unoccupied island was taken over for 19 months by the "Indians of All Tribes," who claimed ownership of Alcatraz for Native Americans under an 1868 treaty. The tribes finally abandoned the island in 1971, leaving graffiti—"Indian Power"—on the smokestack of the powerhouse.

INSIDER TIP:

Be sure to get tickets for an Alcatraz cruise and tour early, as they often sell out. Tickets are available up to 90 days in advance.

—CHARLES KOGOD
National Geographic contributor

Visiting Alcatraz

The cruise includes a recorded cell-block tour bringing history to life through the narration of former Alcatraz inmates and correctional officers. The recordings are available in 11 languages. Tickets for the cruise and tour can be purchased online *(alcatrazcruises.com).* Dress warmly and wear walking shoes. The first trip of the day is the least crowded. Partially guided, evening tours also offer special programs.

On-site interpretation includes National Park Service guided walks and an orientation video. For a nature outing, walk the **Agave Trail,** which leads past

(solitary confinement), an elevated gallery where armed guards kept watch, the mess hall (aka the "Gas Chamber"), and a typical 5-by-9-foot (1.5-by-2.7 m) unheated cell.

Inmates were locked up for 16 to 23 hours a day, with a "no talk-ing" rule. To communicate, they tapped out Morse code or put their heads in the toilet bowls, covered

Bleak and cold, D Block held Alcatraz's most dangerous prisoners in solitary confinement.

eucalyptus trees where black-crowned night-herons nest, across a hillside spiked with agaves, and down to views of tide pools and seabirds *(trail closed during nesting season, Feb. 1–mid-Sept.).*

Inside the Big House

In the cell-house you'll see bleak rows of cells, the D Block

them with blankets, and spoke through the pipes. Those who caused trouble were sent to the iso-lation cells, which they were allowed to leave only once a week to take a ten-minute shower. Passing time in the recreation yard was a privilege, easily revoked. Two of the prisoners' intramural baseball teams were the Safecrackers and the Bankrobbers. ■

More Places to Visit Around Fisherman's Wharf & Alcatraz

The Cannery

A pioneer effort in adapting old industrial buildings, this retail-restaurant complex began as a 1907 peach cannery. Del Monte developed it into the world's largest operation, turning out 200,000 hand-soldered cans a day until the Great Depression shut it down. In 1968, developers remodeled the brick shell for commercial use. Jack's Cannery Bar contains 17th-century elegant oak paneling from an English manor house. Newspaper mogul William Randolph Hearst purchased the paneling in the 1920s, and the bar bought it from his estate.

 Map p. 100 ✉ 2801 Leavenworth St. 🚋 CC: Powell-Hyde, Powell-Mason; Bus: 30, 47; Streetcar: F

Musée Mécanique

It's like an old-fashioned penny arcade—more than 200 antique games, strength testers, fortune-telling machines, peep shows, and orchestrions (automated orchestras). Also displayed: a rare steam-powered motorcycle. Among mechanized dioramas is a carnival so finely detailed it looks like a movie special-effects miniature. The games work and are coin operated. Bring quarters.
museemecaniquesf.com  Map p. 100 ✉ Pier 45, Shed A 🚋 415/346-2000 🚋 CC: Powell-Hyde, Powell-Mason; Bus: 30, 41, 45; Streetcar: F

Victorian Park

Encompassing more than 5 acres (2 ha) of tidiness and formality, Victorian Park has old-fashioned streetlights and benches. (You wouldn't dream that the park was created in 1960.) Rest your weary bones here after tramping through Fisherman's Wharf. Enjoy the flowers set against the backdrop of the San Francisco Bay.

 Map p. 100 ✉ Hyde St. & Beach St. 🚋 CC: Powell-Hyde; Bus: 15, 30, 41, 45

Tough enough? Test your strength or your skills at the Museé Mécanique, Fisherman's Wharf.

The San Francisco Headlands and west—showcasing historic buildings, cultural attractions, and rugged scenery

The Marina & Beyond

The Golden Gate Bridge, seen here from Fort Point, has cables weighing 11,000 tons (9,980 tonnes).

The Marina & Beyond

A gracious and remarkably uncitified part of San Francisco stretches along the bay from the Marina District westward to the Presidio, passing the Golden Gate, and hugging the shore of the Pacific Ocean.

Marina District

In the Marina District, a Mediterranean mood fills the air, with sea breezes, sailboats, and houses painted in pastel colors. The houses and apartments are mostly of Mediterranean revival style, with arches and red-tile roofs.

Unfortunately, these buildings stand on unstable ground—which became obvious during the 1989 earthquake, when a number of edifices sagged or collapsed. They were put up on landfill, originally brought in to prepare the vast site of the 1915 Panama-Pacific International Exposition.

Mudflats were filled with earth, sand, and, ironically, rubble from the 1906 earthquake. This gumbo virtually liquefied during the earthquake.

Highlights of the Marina include the historic Army post at Upper Fort Mason, as well as the museums and theaters at Fort Mason Center. Along Marina Green, dogs are walked, kites flown, and excess pounds jogged off. A jetty encloses the Marina Yacht Harbor. At the end is the wave organ, a scientific sculpture whose submerged pipes gurgle and hum a genuine sea chanty.

A lively neighborhood strip of shopping and dining runs along Chestnut Street, west of Fillmore. At the western edge of the Marina stands the last trace of the great 1915 exposition, the Palace of Fine Arts, a romantic classical rotunda and peristyle reflected in a pond.

The Presidio

The thickly wooded Presidio dates from the Spanish founders of San Francisco, who erected a fort in 1776. Later, it became an American military post. Now decommissioned, the Presidio constitutes an open-air gallery of American architecture from the mid-1800s on. Developments such as the recreation area at Crissy Field and the warmhearted Walt Disney Family Museum are revitalizing the historic area.

NOT TO BE MISSED:

Strolling in the sunshine on the grass at Marina Green   123–124

The Palace of Fine Arts, the last dreamy trace of a wondrous world's fair   124

Historic military buildings and bayside fun in the wooded Presidio   126–130

Admiring an American genius at the Walt Disney Family Museum   128

Looking at–and walking across–the Golden Gate Bridge   130, 131–134

Sculptures by Rodin at the California Palace of the Legion of Honor   135–136

Sunset cocktails overlooking the ocean at the Cliff House   137–139

Golden Gate Bridge & West

At the edge of the Presidio, the Golden Gate Bridge–an engineering marvel built in 1937–spans the opening to the bay. To the west lie the exclusive residential areas of Sea Cliff, China Beach, and Lands End, where the Coastal Trail loops across woodlands and bluffs, and down to secluded beaches. The Golden Gate is guarded by a lighthouse, Mile Rock.

The California Palace of the Legion of Honor stands in Lincoln Park. It displays European art and provides a fine backdrop for the Lincoln Park golf course. ∎

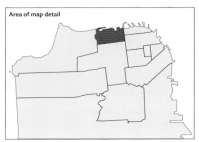

Area of map detail

The Marina

The Marina District—from Van Ness Avenue to the Presidio, between Lombard Street and the bay—sits on the site of the 1915 Panama–Pacific International Exposition, staged to celebrate the reemergence of San Francisco after the devastating 1906 earthquake.

Fort Mason

- 🏠 Map pp. 120–121
- ✉ Marina Blvd. at Laguna St.
- 🚌 Bus: 22, 28, 30, 42, 47, 49

Fort Mason

An outpost of history and culture, Fort Mason occupies 89 acres (36 ha) between Marina Green and Aquatic Park. It has two main areas, Upper Fort Mason and Lower Fort Mason.

Upper Fort Mason: This section *(enter at Bay & Franklin Sts.)* stands on a bluff above the bay. As a strategic military post, it dates back to the Spanish. In 1797, they installed five brass cannon to protect against invaders in the cove below, but the guns never fired at an enemy.

After California gained statehood in 1850, the site was declared a U.S. military reservation. But civilian squatters built houses, and bought and sold property they didn't own. Several Gothic Revival **squatters' houses** still stand on the east side of Franklin Street.

The area became known as Black Point for a dark cluster of laurel trees on the bluff. During the Civil War, the Union Army ejected the squatters and built Black Point Battery. A portion is now restored, with chest-high brick walls and a 10-inch (25.5 cm) cannon capable of lobbing a 124-pound (56 kg) shot more than 2 miles (3.2 km).

An old Civil War clinic is now a youth hostel *(tel 415/771-7277)*. The **General's Residence** (1866) housed Army generals and then became the officers' club. The fort was renamed for Col. Richard Mason, California's first military governor, in 1882. After the 1906 earthquake and fire, the point was crowded with the tents of refugees. Military buildings were razed to create the **Great Meadow,** a

A statue of Senator Phillip Burton, author of the National Parks and Recreation Act, stands on the Great Meadow.

pleasant open space now used for picnicking and sunbathing. In 1972, Fort Mason became part of Golden Gate National Recreation Area (see sidebar p. 130). The **GGNRA headquarters** is in the old military hospital; it has information on the GGNRA and western national parks.

You can walk the very scenic **Bay Trail** that leads about 5 miles (8 km) from Fort Mason through the Presidio to Fort Point.

Lower Fort Mason: On the waterfront *(enter from Marina Blvd. at Buchanan St.)*, this was the nerve center of wartime embarkation programs from 1910 to 1963. During World War II, its piers and warehouses operated 24 hours a day, shipping out an unending flow of troops and supplies to the

INSIDER TIP:

On Friday nights, eat "off the grid" at Fort Mason Center parking lot, where more than 30 food trucks circle their wagons with a variety of delicacies.

—KAY RABIN
City guide,
San Francisco Public Library

Pacific Theater—more than 1.6 million passengers and 23.5 million tons (21.3 million tonnes) of cargo.

Warehouses and piers have been transformed into a lively cultural complex, **Fort Mason**

Center. Home to varied organizations, it offers activities from music classes to festivals. Pick up a schedule at the Fort Mason Center office *(Bldg. A)*.

Marina Green

The community backyard of the Marina District is Marina Green, about 10 acres (4 ha) of waterfront promenade that stretches between Scott and Webster Streets.

Senator Phillip Burton

As chairman of the Subcommittee on National Parks, Phillip Burton set an unprecedented record for protecting parks, wilderness areas, trails, and wild and scenic rivers. His now famous National Parks and Recreation Act of 1978 has been called the most sweeping piece of environmental legislation ever to pass Congress. The national trails system was tripled with the addition of five new trails, including a new category of historic trails; the national wild and scenic rivers system was nearly doubled with eight new river designations and the addition of 17 new study rivers; wilderness acreage in the national park system more than doubled with the addition of nearly two million acres (809,400 ha) of wilderness.

Once a marsh (it was landfilled for the 1915 exposition), Marina Green is a "see-and-be-seen" zone, where affluent young San Franciscans walk their dogs, sunbathe, and jog. The bay views are dramatic, and people of all ages fly colorful kites in the steady breezes.

A jetty encloses the Marina Yacht Harbor, the home of the exclusive St. Francis Yacht Club, designed by Willis Polk. At the end

GGNRA Headquarters

✉ Upper Fort Mason, Bldg. 201

☎ 415/561-4700

nps.gov/goga

Fort Mason Center

☎ 415/345-7500

fortmason.org

Marina Green

🅰 Map p. 120

🚌 Bus: 22, 28, 30

The Palace of Fine Arts serves as a reminder of the 1915 Panama-Pacific International Exposition.

Palace of Fine Arts

🗺 Map p. 120

✉ 3301 Lyon St. at Bay St.

🚌 Bus: 22, 28, 30, 41, 43, 45

of the jetty is a scientific sculpture called the **wave organ,** whose underwater pipes make vaguely musical sounds as waves roll in.

Palace of Fine Arts

A remnant of the Panama-Pacific International Exposition of 1915 (see sidebar p. 125), the Palace of Fine Arts stands reflected in a lagoon. Architect Bernard Maybeck wanted the palace to evoke "the mortality of grandeur and the vanity of human wishes. A grand, classical ruin with a cloister enclosing nothing . . ." Influenced by the drawings of 18th-century Italian artist Giovanni Piranesi, he designed a rotunda with Roman arches and a dome 160 feet high (49 m). There were also a huge Corinthian colonnade and an exhibition gallery.

The palace was not meant to last. Its wood frame was covered with a mixture of burlap fiber and plaster called "staff," which wasn't enduring. San Franciscans loved the palace so much that when the exposition ended, they insisted that it not be razed. The rotunda

and colonnade were preserved, and the exhibition hall was used for art shows. Over time, the hall served a variety of purposes, starting in 1934 with the installation of 18 tennis courts. World War II vehicles were stored there, and later functions included parks department warehouse, telephone book distribution center, and temporary fire department headquarters.

With time, the palace began crumbling; its walls cracked and statues tumbled off their columns. A preservation movement arose with help from city groups and a $2 million donation from philanthropist Walter S. Johnson. In the mid-1960s, the derelict palace was demolished, then reproduced in concrete and steel. The exhibition hall became the original home of the pioneering Exploratorium science museum (see p. 193).

In 2011, a $21 million restoration project made the dome earthquake-safe. Statues of lions and griffins, diaphanously clad maidens, and angels were anchored to the building. The exhibition hall now houses a theater but may be changed to other uses.. ■

The Panama-Pacific International Exposition

The 1915 Panama-Pacific International Exposition ostensibly celebrated the opening of the Panama Canal, but it also trumpeted to the world that San Francisco had risen, glittering, from the rubble and ashes of 1906.

The grand fair was held in today's Marina District, where 635 acres (257 ha) of tidelands were landfilled so that architects and gardeners could create a fairy-tale city. Graceful beaux arts exhibition halls were designed on a grand scale. The Machinery Palace was so huge that pioneer aviator Lincoln Beachey flew an airplane through it. In the Palace of Transportation, an actual Ford assembly line manufactured six automobiles an hour. Visitors thronged the Joy Zone, a midway of rides and games with a 5-acre (2 ha) working model of the Panama Canal.

The fair's centerpiece was the 435-foot-tall (132 m) Tower of Jewels, covered with 100,000 colored glass jewels and dangling mirrors that shimmered in the breeze to produce light of ineffable beauty. At night, concealed spotlights shone on buildings and fountains to make them glow. In the sky a moving fan of rainbow colors was projected upon the city's fog banks, thanks to the "Scintillator," an array of searchlights mounted on a floating barge. (When there wasn't enough fog, an offstage locomotive produced great clouds of steam.)

Color served to unify the sprawling complex of pavilions and courtyards. Coordinating painter Jules Guerin chose hues that evoked the marble of ancient Rome, with accents of cerulean blue, pink, green, and gold creating a dreamlike aura around the exposition. Nearly

A vintage postcard advertised the exposition to encourage visitors to come to San Francisco to celebrate the city's return from the ashes.

19 million visitors from all over the world came to enjoy the fair's wonders. When the lights finally went out in December 1915, everything was demolished except for the Palace of Fine Arts—but the marvelous exposition will always be remembered.

The Presidio

In San Francisco's northeast corner lies a 1,500-acre (607 ha) haven of forests, grasslands, and sea cliffs—a miracle in the midst of a built-up city. You'll find hiking trails, beaches, and magnificent views. The Presidio is also an outdoor museum of 19th-century military architecture, a popular spot for dining and open-air gatherings, and home to fine small museums.

Presidio

- Map this page
- Off Lincoln Blvd.
- 415/561-4323
- Bus: 28, 29, 43, 82X

presidio.gov

The area was fortified in 1776, after Capt. Juan Bautista de Anza chose it for Spain's military base. A log palisade created a 275-foot (25 m) square, replaced two years later by solid adobe walls. So began an outpost of empire that never fired a shot in hostility. What remains of the glorious enterprise? Only some adobe walls from the circa 1810 residence of the *comandante,* on view inside the Presidio Officer's Club at the Main Post.

After the gold rush made San Francisco an important American city, the U.S. military reserved the Presidio for itself. A rich California was worth defending. The Army built Fort Point on the ruins of Castillo de San Joaquín, a 1794 Spanish gun battery overlooking the Golden Gate. During the Civil War, the fort guarded against Confederates (who never appeared).

In the late 1800s, a more developed Presidio housed soldiers of the Indian wars and the Spanish-American War. It sheltered 16,000 refugees after the 1906 earthquake and trained soldiers for World War I. During World War II, it was Western Defense Command headquarters. When decommissioned in 1994, it was home to the Sixth U.S. Army. Today, the Presidio is the world's largest national park in an urban area.

Main Post

The **Presidio Officer's Club**—which over time has housed living quarters for Spanish and Mexican soldiers, barracks for the U.S. Army, a mess room and kitchen, laundresses' quarters, post headquarters, an assembly hall, a ballroom, and a gathering spot for Army brass and their families—now contains exhibits and serves as the Presidio **visitor center**. A permanent center opens in 2018 in the post guardhouse.

The wall in the **Mesa Room** exposes adobe of the late 17th century. This and the Anza Room are the only features still standing from the Spanish era. In the hallway, exhibits show how Presidio history interwove with world

Visitor Center

Map this page

Montgomery St. barracks (Bldg. 105) on Main Post Parade Ground

415/561-4323

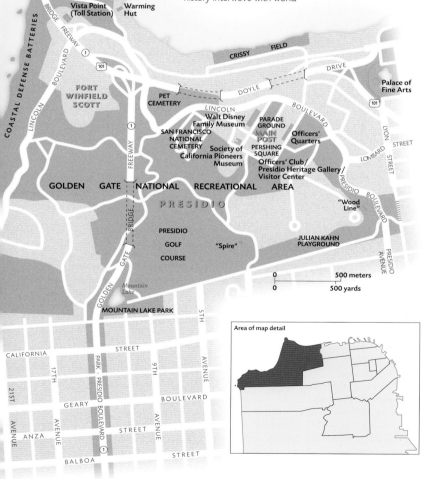

Marin Headlands

Fort Point

Fort Point National Historic Site

Vista Point (Toll Station)

Warming Hut

GOLDEN GATE BRIDGE

BOULEVARD

FREEWAY

COASTAL DEFENSE BATTERIES

LINCOLN

CRISSY FIELD

DRIVE

FORT WINFIELD SCOTT

PET CEMETERY

DOYLE

Palace of Fine Arts

LINCOLN

BOULEVARD

Walt Disney Family Museum

SAN FRANCISCO NATIONAL CEMETERY

Society of California Pioneers Museum

PARADE GROUND

PERSHING SQUARE

MAIN POST

Officers' Quarters

Officers' Club/ Presidio Heritage Gallery/ Visitor Center

LYON STREET

LOMBARD STREET

PRESIDIO BOULEVARD

FREEWAY

GOLDEN GATE NATIONAL RECREATIONAL AREA

PRESIDIO

"Wood Line"

PRESIDIO GOLF COURSE

"Spire"

JULIAN KAHN PLAYGROUND

PRESIDIO AVENUE

BRIDGE

GOLDEN GATE

Mountain Lake

MOUNTAIN LAKE PARK

5TH

0 ——— 500 meters
0 ——— 500 yards

CALIFORNIA

21ST AVENUE

17TH AVENUE

PARK - PRESIDIO BOULEVARD

STREET

9TH AVENUE

GEARY

STREET

ANZA

BALBOA

AVENUE

AVENUE

BOULEVARD

STREET

STREET

Area of map detail

events: Artifacts include the 1898 diary of a soldier in the Spanish-American War and a torn poker hand (soldiers ripped their last losing hands in half before shipping out, but kept winning hands for good luck).

The club's **Presidio Heritage Gallery** surveys 10,000 years of history, starting with the Ohlone people whose ancestral home included today's Presidio, through Spanish days to the present.

From the Officer's Club, it's an easy walk to explore the historical attractions around the heart of the Presidio. At the southeast corner of the Main Post, along Funston Avenue, stands a row of **officers' quarters**—Victorian houses built to a cookie-cutter plan during the Civil War. Originally they faced the other direction, but in 1878 the porches were moved to avoid the wind. At Funston Avenue and Presidio Boulevard stand several Victorians built in 1885 for higher ranking officers.

At **Pershing Square,** archaeologists discovered the foundations of the Spanish fort; plaques mark the northwest and northeast corners of the adobe quadrangle. Also here are two late 1600s bronze cannon with the Spanish royal shield. The flagstaff marks where Brig. Gen. John J. Pershing's house stood, until a fire in 1915. Pershing commanded the American Expeditionary Force in Europe during World War I.

Across the grassy green main parade ground stand a total of seven 1890s barracks that mark the first extensive use of brick among the Presidio's buildings, a symbol that the U.S. Army was there to stay. Each soldier had a bed, a footlocker, and zero privacy. But what a location!

At the Presidio, "living history" takes on new meaning. Today's

Walt Disney Family Museum

Walt Disney was to the 20th century what Mark Twain was to the 19th: America's storyteller. In entertainment technology, he was our Edison. But as "Disney" has swollen into a behemoth corporate brand, our picture of its creative founder has blurred—a big reason why his family opened this museum about Disney's life and accomplishments in animation, motion pictures, and theme-park design (104 Montgomery St., tel 415/345-6800, waltdisney.org, closed Tues., $$$$).

You'll see Walt's boyhood cartoon drawings and hear the story of how he arrived in Hollywood in 1923 with $40 and a coat and pants that didn't match. Within five years he had created Mickey Mouse,

and his own destiny. Exhibits look at milestones such as *Snow White and the Seven Dwarfs*, the first full-length animated film. To create lifelike depth in a cartoon, the studio invented a multiplane camera that could photograph seven layers of artwork painted on glass. This rarity is on display, along with the movie's Academy Award.

In the 1950s, Disney became a television pioneer, then built Disneyland, the world's first theme park. You'll see a detailed model and the park's first Autopia car. An artistic and marketing genius, Disney yet remained a wide-eyed little boy who never grew up. He managed to keep his creativity and enthusiasm alive—a good lesson for kids of all ages.

The grassy waterfront expanse of Crissy Field draws those seeking relaxation and recreation.

families and couples gather on the 7-acre (2.8 ha) lawn of the parade ground to picnic, enjoy the views and breezes off the bay, do yoga, fly kites, and generally goof off. On Sundays (March–Oct.), "Off the Grid" picnics include horseshoes and croquet, food trucks, and cocktails served blanket-side. Thursday evenings (April–Oct.) offer lantern-lit cabanas, fire pits, food, drinks, and live music.

Two former barracks nearby house the **Walt Disney Family Museum** (see sidebar p. 128) and the **Society of California Pioneers Museum,** whose exhibits of paintings, decorative objects, and manuscripts illuminate the experiences of California settlers.

You can stay at the park's only hostelry, the 22-room **Inn at the Presidio** (see Travelwise p. 250), the stylishly updated old officers' quarters. In 2017, a second hotel opens in an 1895 infantry barracks next to the parade ground.

National Cemetery

Graves at the San Francisco National Cemetery date back as far as the Civil War in what was originally the post burial ground; then in 1884, the site was declared a national cemetery.

The nearby **Pet Cemetery** interred dogs of the K-9 corps and later pets of families stationed at the Presidio.

Crissy Field

A former marsh that was landfilled for the 1915 Panama-Pacific International Exposition, this bayside stretch of land served as an Army airfield from 1919 to 1963. The National Park Service has transformed the asphalt expanse into a wild, open 100-acre (40 ha) shoreline park, with restored dunes, a tidal marsh, and a waterfront promenade that's popular with joggers and baby-strolling parents. Crissy's grass airfield has

Society of California Pioneers Museum
- 🅰 Map p. 127
- ✉ 101 Montgomery St., Suite 150
- ☎ 415/957-1849
- 🕐 Closed Sun.–Tues.

californiapioneers.org

San Francisco National Cemetery
- 🅰 Map p. 127
- ✉ Lincoln Blvd. at Sheridan Ave.

Pet Cemetery
- 🅰 Map p. 127
- ✉ Off Lincoln Blvd. on McDowell Ave.

Crissy Field
- 🅰 Map p. 127
- ☎ 415/561-4323

parksconservancy.org/visit

Golden Gate National Recreation Area

Extending in four directions from the Golden Gate Bridge, the Golden Gate National Recreation Area (GGNRA) is a group of parks that is overseen by the National Park Service covering some 80,000 acres (32,375 ha) and containing several natural and historical sites, from redwood groves to old forts. The area includes Alcatraz Island, the bay shore (Fort Mason, Crissy Field, Fort Point, the Presidio), the San Francisco Headlands (Baker and China Beaches, Lands End, the Cliff House), and the Pacific shore (Ocean Beach, Fort Funston).

Across the Golden Gate, the GGNRA takes in the Marin Headlands (Fort Baker; the Rodeo Valley, Lagoon, and Beach; Gerbode and Tennessee Valleys) and the west Marin coast (Muir Woods, Muir Beach, Stinson Beach, Bolinas Ridge, Olema Valley).

The recreation area embodies more than 200 years of history, from Native American culture, Spanish Empire frontier, California Gold Rush, the evolution of American coastal fortifications, and the growth of urban San Francisco; it includes 19 separate ecosystems and is home to 1,273 plant and animal species. You can find more information, including ways to plan your visit, and check ahead for weather forecasts at *nps.gov/goga.*

been restored, offering a huge lawn for recreation. Stop in for a hot drink or a sandwich at the **Warming Hut** *(Marine Dr., 415/561-3040),* enjoying them outdoors on the lawn or a small beach; both have views of bay, bridge, and boats.

A new 13-acre (5.2 ha) parkland is planned atop two tunnels that have replaced a highway through the Presidio. The project will integrate the Presidio's historic core with the San Francisco Bay waterfront. Besides spectacular views, it is likely to have pathways, vista points, events, and (of course, this being San Francisco) a range of food options.

Outdoor Recreation

A 24-mile (40 km) network of hiking and biking includes scenic and historic overlooks. The National Cemetery viewpoint is reached on a winding footpath, passing walls carved with poignant lines from "The Young Dead Soldiers" by poet Archibald MacLeish, who served as a World War I infantryman. The Presidio also has San Francisco's only campground, used for groups.

The **coastal defense batteries,** built in the 1890s to guard the Golden Gate, lie along the Coastal Trail between Fort Point and Baker Beach, with views of the Marin Headlands.

Natural Life

The urban forest of the Presidio numbers more than 200,000 pine, cypress, and eucalyptus trees. Woods and shoreline are home to more than 300 species of birds, from California quail to red-tailed hawks to brown pelicans. On the Pacific shore you might see anything from wee snails and brilliant sea stars in tide pools to a pod of dolphins passing offshore. ∎

From the Golden Gate Bridge to the Pacific Ocean

From the iconic Golden Gate Bridge, spanning San Francisco Bay, the coast curves westward and showcases a long ribbon of stunning scenery and historic sites. Offshore, sea lions loll on rocks in the sunset glow.

The Golden Gate Bridge spans the gap connecting San Francisco Bay to the Pacific Ocean.

Golden Gate Bridge

The Golden Gate Bridge spans the opening to the San Francisco Bay and links San Francisco with Marin County. Is it an embodiment of science or art? One can regard the bridge as a milestone of engineering, or as an art deco masterpiece, a reddish orange sculpture set against blue water and green headlands.

The Golden Gate is a suspension bridge. The basic design:

Towers at each end support cables, from which the roadway is suspended. This simple idea dates from before the Iron Age, when people used bamboo and vines as cables. As early as A.D. 65, the Chinese erected a 250-foot-long (76 m) iron chain suspension bridge over a river.

For sheer scale, the Golden Gate Bridge boggles the mind. Its length, including approaches, is 8,981 feet (2,737 m). The main

Golden Gate Bridge

📍 Map pp. 126–127

🚌 Bus: 28, 29, 76

goldengatebridge .org

span, at 4,200 feet (1,280 m), was the world's longest until 1964, when it was edged out by New York's Verrazano Narrows Bridge at 4,260 feet (1,298 m). The two side spans measure 1,125 feet (343 m) each.

Two art deco towers rise some 746 feet/227 m (191 feet/58 m taller than the Washington Monument), about 48 stories. Together, the towers weigh more than 88 million pounds (almost 40 million kg). The pier for the south tower had to be constructed a quarter-mile offshore, on a foundation 110 feet (33.5 m) below water level. Workmen built an oval concrete fender as long as a football field. Water was evacuated and the pier sunk inside. The fender, with conduits added to let sea water circulate, was left in place to cushion the pier against tides.

The bridge's two cables thread over the towers and anchor at each end to massive blocks of concrete. Each anchorage can withstand a pull of 63 million pounds (28.5 million kg) from the cables. The cables weigh 11,000 tons (9,980 tonnes) apiece. Each is 36.4 inches (92.5 cm) in diameter and contains 27,572 wires. The total length of wire adds up to 80,000 miles (almost 128,800 km), enough to twine around the Equator three times.

Chief engineer Joseph Strauss had to create a structure that could withstand 60-mile-an-hour (96.5 km/h) tidal surges, ocean waves, buffeting winds, fog, even earthquakes. He also had to overcome opposition by the Southern Pacific Railroad, whose ferries would lose profits. Construction (1933–1937) cost $35 million and provided jobs for thousands of workers during the Great Depression. Accidents killed 11 men, a number that might have been larger had not Strauss insisted on strict safety measures, including nets, during construction. Since the bridge opened, ironically, more than 1,000 suicides have jumped from it.

In a strong wind or earthquake, the bridge's center span is designed to handle 27.7 feet (8.4 m) of sway. The roadway has

(continued on p. 134)

The Bridge From Every Angle

For great views on the San Francisco side:
Bridge visitor center *(off Lincoln Blvd. or US 101, 415/426-5220)* At the toll plaza: Also café, exhibits, souvenirs, Strauss statue, cable cross section.
Fort Point *(off Lincoln Blvd.)* A view of the bridge from below, along the bay's seawall.
Lands End *(U.S.S. San Francisco Memorial parking lot, off El Camino Del Mar)* Views of the bridge from the west.

On the Marin side:
Vista Point *(off US 101 N)* Seen against the green Presidio.
East Fort Baker *(US 101 N to Alexander Ave. exit; at Bunker Rd. follow signs to Bay Area Discovery Museum)* Spectacular view from a cove below the bridge.
Conzelman Road *(US 101 N to Alexander Ave. exit; left at Bunker Rd., left on McCullough Rd., left on Conzelman Rd.)* Great prospect from the Marin Headlands.

EXPERIENCE: Get Up Close & Personal With the Golden Gate Bridge

Why be just another motorist driving one of the more than 2 billion cars that have crossed the Golden Gate Bridge since it opened in 1937? Instead, have an unforgettable personal encounter with San Francisco's famous landmark by venturing across on foot or a bicycle.

More than 200 feet (61 m) below, sailboats dart across the bay and great ships come and go from around the world. The breeze blows. The sun shines. (Well, except when it doesn't. Dress in layers for warmth, and bring a jacket.) Take time to gaze up at the bridge's towers soaring skyward. (And think about this remarkable fact: Building each of these towers took 600,000 rivets!)

The distance from the **San Francisco toll plaza** to the viewpoint on the Marin side is 1.7 miles (2.7 km). You can stop along the way to take pictures of **Alcatraz,** the city, the bay, and the **Marin Headlands.** If you're riding a bike, at the far end of the bridge simply coast downhill to the waterfront town of **Sausalito,** explore its shops and restaurants, and hop a ferry with your bike—the easy way back to San Francisco.

Visitors walk the 8,981 feet (2,737 m) of the Golden Gate Bridge, connecting the city of San Francisco to Marin County.

Sunrise to Sunset

The bridge is open to walkers and cyclists approximately from sunrise to sunset, but hours are adjusted seasonally, so double-check *(tel 415/921-5858, goldengatebridge.org)*. Pedestrians and cyclists share the east sidewalk (the city side); the west sidewalk is for bikes only. No skateboards, Rollerblades, or dogs are allowed. For the most serene trip across the bridge, choose a quiet traffic hour such as Sunday morning.

If you're not all that excited about hoofing it or pedaling across the whole bridge, even strolling out partway will give you a spectacular view. For an easier alternative take an electric-bike tour over the bridge to **Sausalito** *(baycitybike.com or blazingsaddles.com).*

Free Guided Walks

San Francisco City Guides *(sfcityguides.org)* offers walking tours with perspectives on the bridge that range from regional geology to sleazy politics. Walkers get both exercise and inside information—for example, that university professor Charles Alton Ellis was primarily responsible for the structural engineering of the bridge, but chief engineer Joseph Strauss fired him after a dispute and later denied him credit. This falsification was finally corrected in 2012, when a plaque commemorating Ellis was installed at the bridge entrance. Tours meet at the visitors plaza, on the San Francisco side of the bridge, on Sundays and Thursdays (check website for additional days).

San Francisco Headlands

⚠ Map pp. 126–127

🚌 Bus: 18

a mean clearance above the water of 220 feet (67 m).

The Golden Gate Bridge has been painted continuously since opening day in 1937. The first coat took 60,000 gallons (227,125 L) of paint. The bridge's distinctive color is International Orange but is more accurately described as vermilion, a vivid reddish orange.

Baker Beach

This beach *(off Lincoln Blvd. at Bowley St.)* offers picnic areas, dunes, and a view of the Golden Gate Bridge. Warning: Do not swim, due to riptides. On the northern stretch, you may spy the species *Homo sapiens* in its natural state. On the bluff stands **Battery Chamberlain** (1904), with its 6-inch (15 cm) "disappearing" gun that folds down behind a wall to vanish from view; rangers give demonstrations the first weekend of each month.

The hue was suggested by architect Irving Morrow as an alternative to the usual dull engineer's gray. It was also chosen for its high visibility to ships passing in fog. If the U.S. Navy had prevailed with its idea to make the bridge unmissable, it would be painted black with yellow stripes (!). Morrow's vision for lighting the bridge was finally realized on its 50th anniversary in 1987, with the mounting of 48 high-pressure sodium lamps. The desired effect was achieved—that the towers seem to fade gradually into the sky.

San Francisco Headlands

The San Francisco Headlands stretch west and south around the coast from Baker Beach. This is a rugged corner of ocean bluffs and tangled vegetation.

A civilized touch as you approach the headlands from the Presidio is the neighborhood of **Sea Cliff** *(off El Camino Del Mar at 25th–27th Aves.)*. It is unique among residential neighborhoods because it fronts the ocean. (Otherwise, the city's Pacific shoreline is devoted to parks and beaches.)

The sandy cove at **China Beach** *(end of Seacliff Ave.)* was named for Chinese fishermen who once anchored their junks and camped here. Sheltered from the wind, this is a good spot for sunbathing, a picnic, or a chilly swim. (Be wary of unpredictable surf conditions.) On clear days you can see Mount Tamalpais and Point Reyes in Marin County.

Lands End: Edging the coastline between Sea Cliff and the Cliff House, this wild swath contains a tame section, **Lincoln Park.** This was a cemetery area until John McLaren (of Golden Gate Park, see p. 155) laid out the plantings. It has a golf course (1909) with spectacular views. The Legion of Honor (see pp. 135–136) exhibits a treasure trove of European art.

The **Coastal Trail** *(accessible from palace or Merrie Way parking lot)* threads the headlands, among cypress trees, fields, and bluffs, with views of the strait. You can walk a rock labyrinth at **Eagles's Point.** The trail follows the old

roadbed of the 1880s Ferries *&
Cliff House Railroad.*

Walk the trail, or drive, to the
vista point and **U.S.S. *San Francisco* Memorial** *(off El Camino Del
Mar)*. This World War II cruiser
took 45 hits in the Battle of
Guadalcanal, and its shell-pierced
bridge wings serve as a monument. Offshore, treacherous rocks
have wrecked many ships. Parts of
some unlucky vessels can be spied
from the Coastal Trail. Farther
south are the Cliff House, Sutro
Heights, and Sutro Baths (see
pp. 137–139).

Lands End Lookout *(off Point
Lobos Ave.)* is a small visitor center
with artifacts from the Sutro
Baths and Cliff House, books, a
café, and an information desk.

Legion of Honor

The philanthropic Alma de
Bretteville Spreckels persuaded
her sugar-baron husband to
reproduce the French pavilion
from the 1915 Panama-Pacific
International Exposition as an
art museum. (The pavilion was
itself modeled on the 1782
Palais de la Légion d'Honneur in
Paris.) Then Mrs. Spreckels filled
the museum with treasures,
including more than 80 pieces
of Rodin sculpture. Many were
acquired directly from the artist
in his studio, including an early
cast of "The Thinker" (1904).

The museum, which honors
California's dead in World War I,
was designed in 1924 by architect
George Applegarth and expanded

Legion of Honor

- Map p. 126
- ✉ Lincoln Park,
  near 34th Ave. *&
  Clement St.*
- ☎ 415/750-3600
- 🕐 Closed Mon.
- 💲 $$, free 1st Tues.
- 🚌 Bus: 1, 18, 38

famsf.org

Rodin's early cast of "The Thinker" graces the entrance of the Legion of Honor.

INSIDER TIP:

The Legion of Honor is a thrillingly dramatic site. For breathtaking views of the Golden Gate, walk down the Lands End Trail. Also visit the galleries.

—FORREST McGILL
Chief curator, Asian Art Museum

belowground in 1994. To view the galleries in order, start to the left of the main entrance.

Medieval Art (Galleries 1, 2, & 3) opens a view into the Europe of monasteries and cathedrals during the thousand years after Rome fell in the fifth century. The art ranges from a French Limoges reliquary (ca 1200) to an alabaster carving of Jesus reprimanding Adam and Eve (Spain, 14th century). Styles include the flattened, stiff Romanesque (11–12th century) and more naturalistic Gothic (12–16th century). You'll also see early tapestries and a 15th-century Spanish ceiling.

During the **Renaissance** (Galleries 4 & 5), mankind took center stage. Look for early Renaissance works by Fra Angelico. High Renaissance art (Titian, Tintoretto) was realistic, but evolved into mannerism; an example is El Greco's "St. John the Baptist" (ca 1600), which elongates the gaunt figure to mystical effect.

Auguste Rodin (Galleries 8, 10, & 12) brought new psychological depth and sensual passion to renderings of the human figure. See "The Kiss" (1886) and reduced casts of figures from "The Burghers of Calais" (1886).

The **17th-century Dutch and Flemish** collection (Galleries 14 & 15) includes a portrait by a young Rembrandt, along with works by Van Dyck and Rubens.

In the **19th-century European** galleries (Galleries 17 & 18), rapid social change is reflected in the evolution from Romanticism—Gericault's equestrian portrait of Charles V (1814)—to Social Realism—Manet's "At the Milliner's" (1881)—and on to Impressionism and Pointillism—Seurat's "The Eiffel Tower" (1889).

New ideas emerged in **20th-century Europe** (Gallery 19). Don't miss Monet's "Waterlilies" (ca 1914–1917). ∎

Fort Point

Known as the "Gibraltar of the West," this four-tiered fort *(S anchorage of Golden Gate Bridge, at end of Marine Dr., tel 415/556-1693, nps.gov/fopo, check website for seasonal hours)* was erected between 1853 and 1861 to defend the Golden Gate. Granite and more than eight million bricks were used to create walls up to 7 feet (2 m) thick. By the mid-1880s, the fort's guns were outdated and it was soon abandoned. Today, it stands as a classic pre–Civil War fortress. Inside the ground floor are a visitor center and theater.

There's a memorable view of the bay from the seawall—not to mention the sight of surfers on huge waves that roll through the Golden Gate.

The Cliff House & Sutro Baths

In the 1880s the city's western shore was where San Franciscans regularly headed for a day at the beach. There, in a dramatic setting overlooking Seal Rocks and the Pacific, stood the Cliff House. Facing the setting sun, the Cliff House still purveys food and drink for weary travelers.

Built in 1863, the one-story wooden restaurant wasn't much to look at, but its location drew U.S. Presidents and the carriage trade, including Stanfords and Hearsts. Later the Cliff House fell on hard times, becoming a shady haunt for gambling and general debauchery.

Enter Adolph Sutro, a Prussia-born engineer who had gotten rich emptying Comstock mines (see p. 28) of water and noxious gas by digging tunnels. Now a millionaire, he owned one-twelfth of the land in San Francisco. Sutro purchased the Cliff House in 1883 and fell in love with the view from the bluff above it—land he promptly bought. There he built an estate called Sutro Heights, employing ten gardeners to transform the sandy acres with roses, parterre gardens, and exotic trees. He put in replicas of European statues "to educate and enlighten" the populace, who were free to visit. His guests ranged from President Benjamin Harrison to Oscar Wilde. To encourage the public to visit his seaside attractions, Sutro built a railroad whose egalitarian fare was just one nickel, bringing the ocean within reach of the working people of San Francisco.

After an 1894 fire destroyed the Cliff House, Sutro rebuilt in style. His eight-story Victorian château (known as the "Gingerbread Palace") had turrets, panoramic windows, and an observation tower. A much loved spot for dining, dancing, and entertainment, it too burned down in 1907. Two years later, Sutro's daughter erected a neoclassical Cliff House. This building survived the Great

Cliff House

▲ Map p. 126

✉ 1090 Point Lobos Ave.

☎ 415/386-3330

🚌 Bus: 18, 38

cliffhouse.com

The Camera Obscura near Cliff House

EXPERIENCE: See the World Through the Ancient Magic of the Camera Obscura

What do Leonardo da Vinci and the early Chinese philosopher Mozi have in common with Mr. Robert Tacchetto of San Francisco? They have all been fascinated by an optical trick that's as much magic as science: Shining through a pinhole, light rays from the bright outdoor world form a living picture on the inside wall of a darkened room. This "trick box" chamber is called a camera obscura, and Mr. Tacchetto operates one of the few such attractions in the world.

Mr. Tacchetto's enterprise is called the Giant Camera, for an obvious reason: The endearingly kitschy building looks like a huge 35mm camera turned on its side, with the lens pointing up at the sky. In one form or another, this camera obscura has been enchanting San Franciscans since 1948. It is located on a terrace below the Cliff House, facing out to Seal Rocks and the blue Pacific.

A camera obscura works like the human eye. Instead of a pupil, a small hole in one wall of the room lets light enter from outside. The rays crisscross as they pass through the pinhole, and the image formed on the opposite wall of the dark room is upside down—a phenomenon that Greek mathematician Euclid noted as long ago as 300 B.C. The colors and perspective, however, remain true to life.

To turn the image right side up, a lens was first inserted in the aperture of a camera obscura in the 16th century. Later, a mirror was added to reflect the image onto a viewing surface. At the Giant Camera, light enters through a window in

a slowly rotating pyramid on the roof, hits a mirror of high brilliance, is reflected down through two condensing lenses, and finally focuses

Stepping into Mr. Tacchetto's Camera Obscura is like viewing the natural world outside anew.

twelve feet (3.6 m) below on a gently curved cement table that forms a shallow basin.

Six Minutes of Magic

Every six minutes, the parabolic table inside the Giant Camera shows visitors a 360-degree rotating view of the waters offshore. People express amazement at the clarity and crispness of the image. Some think they must be viewing a film. The picture, though, is a real-time rendering of the living world outside. In a sense, a camera obscura is the earliest forerunner of a webcam.

The sunnier the day, the brighter and clearer the picture. The shimmering

image can seem like a canvas painted in pure light—and seeing it strikes many observers as a magical experience. Indeed, in the 5th century B.C., Mozi referred to the camera obscura as a "locked treasure room."

Mr. Tacchetto first encountered San Francisco's camera obscura as a boy of ten. "I used to sneak in here all the time!" he remembers fondly. Today, as its owner, he can enjoy its quiet magic every day. Atop the roof, he opens a small window in the pyramid to let in the light and get the show underway. The window panel is painted with a mysterious spiraling swirl of red and purple. "It's a symbol of the cosmic eye," he says, "seeing everything. Well, that's my interpretation!"

The Giant Camera ($) is open daily from 11 a.m. to 5 p.m., but closes during rain and heavy fog. The camera obscura is the last structure remaining from San Francisco's Playland amusement park at nearby Ocean Beach and was moved to the Cliff House in 1972. It was added to the National Register of Historic Places in 2001.

Depression of the 1930s and two world wars, and was later remodeled several times before the National Park Service acquired it in 1977.

In 2004, a total renovation created a new incarnation of the Cliff House. Terraces and two restaurants afford dramatic views of Ocean Beach, Seal Rock, and the hills of Marin County. The makeover was designed to bring back the character of the 1909 neoclassical structure and added a new wing inspired by the architecture of the old Sutro Baths.

The ruins of the **Sutro Baths** lie a short walk north of the Cliff House. In 1886 Sutro spent $250,000 to build the three-acre (1.2 ha) baths. The lavish public swimming house was a marvel of engineering and artistic detail. There were six saltwater "swimming ponds," ingeniously flushed by the tides to recycle 1.7 million gallons (6.4 million L) of water in just an hour. The pools, the largest 300 feet (91 m) long, were kept at varied temperatures by steam heat. Bathers frolicked on springboards, trapezes, and slides.

A freshwater pool was supplied by an ever flowing spring. There were 500 private dressing rooms. A laundry washed rental bathing suits (20,000 daily) and towels (40,000). Three restaurants seated 1,000 people at a time. Among other attractions were cabinets of ancient Egyptian artifacts and a theater for stage shows. The entire complex was elegantly sheltered under 100,000 square feet (9,290 sq m) of glass.

Guests paid only a dime to enter and 25 cents to swim. The baths' revenues didn't meet expenses, though, and in 1937 Sutro's heirs converted the large pool into a skating rink. A fire destroyed the baths in the 1960s. Today all that remains are the faded foundations. ∎

Sutro Heights Park

 Map p. 126

✉ Enter at 48th Ave. & Point Lobos Ave.

The Cliff House offers spectacular ocean vistas.

More Places to Visit in the Marina & Beyond

Fort Mason Center

For general information, phone the Lower Fort Mason office; the website has links to all facilities, including events and classes. Theaters housed at Fort Mason Center include the **Magic Theatre** *(Bldg. D, tel 415/441-8822, works by emerging playwrights);* **Young Performers Theatre** *(Bldg. C, tel 415/346-5550, kids performing plays for kids);* and **Bayfront Theater** *(Bldg. B, tel 415/474-6776, shows, workshops),* home to BATS Improv.

You can also visit the **Museo Italo-Americano** *(Bldg. C, tel 415/673-2200, Italian & Italian-American artists).* See Mexican and Latino art at the **Mexican Museum** *(Bldg. D, tel 415/202-9700).* **Greens** vegetarian restaurant *(see p. 250, Bldg. A)* is also located here. A bar/café, **The Interval** *(Bldg. A, tel 415/561-6582)* houses the Long Now Foundation, focused on creative long-term thinking. It has a never repeating digital painting by British artist Brian Eno, a machine that generates a unique bell sequence each day for 10,000 years, and Tuesday talks. *fortmason.org*

Map pp. 120–121 ✉ Lower Fort Mason, Marina Blvd. at Laguna St. ☎ 415/345-7500 🚌 Bus: 22, 28, 30, 42, 47, 49

Presidio Golf Course

This 6,477-yard (5,922 m), par 72 public golf course is located in a beautiful part of San Francisco. When it was built in 1895, on what was then a U.S. Army post, it was open to military personnel and members of a small private club only. The military post at the Presidio closed in 1995, and its ownership was transferred to the National Park Service, which opened the golf course to the public.

The only 18-hole golf course located on National Park Service land, it boasts century-old trees and fairways that roll past menacing bunkers. Presidents Teddy Roosevelt and Dwight Eisenhower played here. The Presidio Café is open to the non-golf-playing public. *presidiogolf.com* Map p. 127 ✉ 300 Finley Rd. ☎ 415/561-4661 (golf), 415/561-4600 (café), 🚌 Bus: 28, 29, 41, 43, 45

A beautiful San Francisco backdrop surrounds Presidio Golf Course, which is open to the public.

Mansions and luxury apartments in the elevated district of Pacific Heights, with Japantown on its southern fringe

Pacific Heights & Japantown

A young visitor at the Japan Center during the Cherry Blossom Festival

Pacific Heights & Japantown

San Francisco has no better address than Pacific Heights, which offers everything an elite residential neighborhood should: First, a preeminent perch on a high ridge. Second, beautifully designed and built houses and apartments. Third, multi-million-dollar views. Nearby Japantown is the cultural hub for the city's Japanese Americans.

The area developed as transit did. The advent of cable cars created the first wave of building in the 1870s. Mansions lined Van Ness Avenue, which was laid out as the city's widest street (125 feet/38 m) for this very purpose. In the 1880s, fine Victorians rose near two neighborhood parks, Lafayette and Alta Plaza, and others followed. Often rows of houses were constructed to similar plans by speculative builders. Owners chose decorative trim and gingerbread from millwork catalogs to individualize their homes. During the 1906 earthquake and fire, Brig. Gen. Frederick Funston had the houses on the

NOT TO BE MISSED:

east side of Van Ness dynamited to create a firebreak, successfully blocking the fire from marching westward across the city. Van Ness later became a commercial thoroughfare.

Pacific Heights' stock as an elite enclave rose higher after 1906, when wealthy families whose houses had burned on Nob Hill came to build lavish homes. You'll see everything from Italian villas to grand piles of brick and stone, often with well-tended gardens or landscaped terraces. In the 1920s and 1930s, apartment buildings replaced many old houses in the eastern section of Pacific Heights. Along the south side of the Presidio, more rows of magnificent houses fill Presidio Heights. A highlight of this neighborhood is the simple but profound Swedenborgian Church, a true retreat from city life.

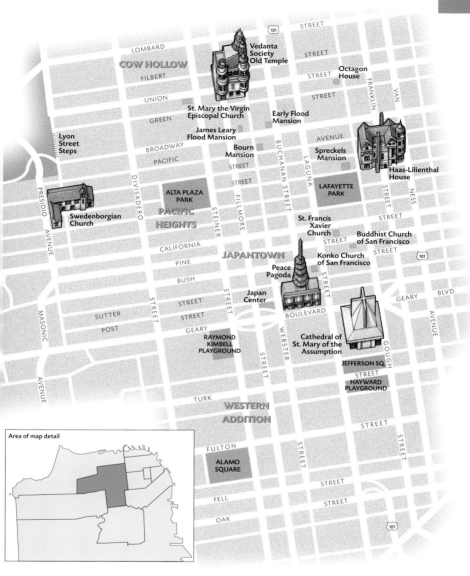

Between Pacific Heights and the Marina lies Cow Hollow, a former dairy-farm area that became a Victorian residential neighborhood. In the 1950s, shops and restaurants began to occupy many of the old-fashioned houses along the main thoroughfare.

South of Pacific Heights, the Japanese-American community of Nihonmachi (Japantown) occupies part of the city's Western Addition. It was once more expansive, but Japantown virtually emptied during World War II as Japanese residents were relocated to internment camps. In the 1960s, urban renewal razed many blocks of Victorians in what had become a slum, forcing 4,000 households to relocate. The Japan Center was constructed, as were temples and churches, making the district a cultural focus for Japanese Americans. ∎

Pacific Heights

The architectural extravagance of the magnificent houses in Pacific Heights—between Van Ness and the Presidio—makes them well worth a visit to the neighborhood.

The Haas-Lilienthal House, survivor of the 1906 earthquake, operates as a house museum showcasing Victorian style.

Pacific Heights
 Map p. 143

Grand Houses

In most cases, you can only gaze at the splendid homes of Pacific Heights from the outside. Only one is still open to the public.

Haas-Lilienthal House: The
Haas-Lilienthal House is the house you can visit. This stately gray residence of peaked gables, bay windows, and a corner tower blends Queen Anne and Stick styles. The 1886 house was lived in by two generations of the same family until 1972 and now serves as a Victorian house museum, worth seeing from its bed chambers to its paneled parlor. The house is a survivor: Many Victorians were lost in the 1906 fire, and of those that remained intact, most in this area of eastern Pacific Heights were demolished to erect apartments.

Designed by Peter Schmidt, the three-story house was built for William Haas, a German Jewish immigrant who started work as a wholesale grocer and ended as a director of Wells Fargo Bank. (His youngest daughter married Samuel Lilienthal.) The 24-room house, with 11,500 square feet (1,070 sq m), shows how an upper-middle-class mercantile family aspired to live. The interior glows with polished woods. The master bathroom boasts newfangled devices such as a gas jet to heat hair-curling irons. Parlors, the dining room, and bedrooms are furnished in varying styles of the half century after the house was built.

Spreckels Mansion: Do you mean to say that *your* house doesn't take up a whole city block, look like the Parthenon, and have 26 bathrooms? Few houses could match the palatial French baroque Spreckels mansion *(2080 Washington St., private)*

EXPERIENCE: Lookie-Loo Mansion Walk

To see some lovely houses, stroll Pacific Avenue between Steiner and Pierce. At **2516 Pacific** stands the British consul general's former home, an 1881 Tudor Revival mansion later expanded by Lewis Hobart, architect of Grace Cathedral. Queen Elizabeth II dined here, and in 2004 a local family bought it for more than $10 million. Across the street are

four **1880s Victorians,** three of them virtually the same design, like tract houses (but now worth millions). The late mayor Joe Alioto lived at **2510 Pacific,** a 1950s modern house set behind trees on a cobblestone courtyard, with an indoor pool, patios, and bay views. This quiet block offers a pleasant peek at the rarified life of Pacific Heights.

built in 1913 for Adolph Spreckels (son of sugar king Claus Spreckels) and his wife, Alma de Bretteville Spreckels. The architect was George Applegarth (designer of the California Palace of the Legion of Honor, which the couple donated to the city). Today, beyond the mansion's Ionic columns lies the sanctum of novelist Danielle Steel. Her dramatic, romantic novels, often about the rich and famous, have sold more than 800 million copies in 28 languages.

Flood Mansions: In 1915, the son of a Comstock silver king used his bottomless pockets to build the **James Leary Flood Mansion** (2222 Broadway, private), now part of the Schools of the Sacred Heart. Architects. Bliss & Faville designed the Italian Renaissance pile, sheathing it in Tennessee marble around a steel frame engineered to resist earthquakes. To imagine the Flood lifestyle, look through the front door, down a marble-clad hall that stretches nearly 150 feet (45 m) to a window at the end, which frames a grand piano.

Flood and his wife, Maud, lived with their two children in an earlier **Flood Mansion** (2120 Broadway, private) designed by Julius Krafft in 1901, after the 1906 earthquake gutted their mansion on Nob Hill (now the Pacific Union Club) and before they moved to the new mansion described above. Flood's sister, Cora Jane ("Miss Jennie"), remained in the stately house until 1924. Four years later it was converted into the Hamlin School for girls.

The 24-room Edwardian mansion has a classical symmetry imposed by Ionic columns, pilasters, and pedimented windows. Granite steps watched by gray marble lions lead to a mosaic-and-marble vestibule. Beyond that lies a two-story central hall paneled in oak and topped with an art-glass canopy measuring 26 feet (8 m) across. Among remarkable rooms are the solarium (now the student cafeteria) with its mosaic-tile floor and the Chinese Room with its bamboo ceiling, red lacquer, and green silk walls—one of the few remaining examples of a decorating conceit once popular among wealthy San Franciscans. ■

Haas-Lilienthal House

- 🅰 Map p. 143
- ✉ 2007 Franklin St.
- ☎ 415/441-3000
- 🕐 Tours Wed., Sat.–Sun. (call for times)
- 💲 $$
- 🚌 Bus: 1, 12, 19, 27, 47, 49

sfheritage.org

Presidio Heights

Just west of Pacific Heights, the neighborhood of Presidio Heights has rows of splendid houses built by the ultrarich, but its two striking and unusual religious buildings provide a pleasing contrast of style and mood.

Presidio Heights

Map pp. 142–143

Fine, large residences lie along Pacific, Jackson, and Washington Streets. Bernard Maybeck designed the **Roos House** (3500 Jackson St.), with dark half-timbering and large flower boxes. The elite **Presidio Terrace** neighborhood (off Arguello Blvd. near Washington St.) has residences by Bakewell & Brown (No. 15), George Applegarth (No. 34), and Julia Morgan (No. 36). The private street is gated and guarded. (Take a virtual look with Google Maps' "street view" function). The Presidio Heights community does its shopping, dining, and movie-going along a quiet, appealing section of Sacramento Street (bet. Lyon & Spruce Sts.).

Temple Emanu-El

Inspired by Hagia Sophia in Istanbul, Temple Emanu-El was designed in 1926 by Bakewell & Brown for a congregation of San Francisco's successful Jewish community. Jewish immigrants arrived with the gold rush and did well in the burgeoning city. This congregation dates from 1850. The temple's main designer, Arthur Brown, Jr., was also the architect of the War Memorial Opera House, City Hall, and Coit Tower. The most powerful feature of the temple, its Byzantine dome, soars to a height of 150 feet (45 m) and is sheathed in red terra-cotta tiles. Another major element, the cloistered courtyard, was inspired by the buildings of the 1915 Panama-Pacific International Exposition, which were

A walk up the Lyon Street Steps offers a million-dollar view.

joined by similar courtyards and covered walks with open colonnades. Plants named in the Bible have been put in the courtyard, including date and olive trees.

In the vestibule, the ceiling is painted to look like a star-studded sky. The 1,700-seat temple has no supporting columns, and the dome creates a lofty, uplifting feeling. The commanding Ark, which contains the Torah, lies in an ornate gilded cloisonné box under a green marble canopy. In 1973, stained-glass windows were added, designed by Mark Adams to represent the natural elements of fire (on the east, or bay, side) and water (to the west).

Swedenborgian Church

An architectural gem, the 1895 Swedenborgian Church has been called the "church of the simple life." The church's theological foundations come from Emanuel Swedenborg (1688–1772). A Swedish scientist turned mystic, he perceived that all life is spiritual and that all things in creation reveal the divine. His ideas influenced American transcendentalist Ralph Waldo Emerson. The twentieth-century Zen scholar D. T. Suzuki called Swedenborg the "Buddha of the North," and some of the Swede's meditative practices did resemble yoga.

The church was planned by theologian and architecture critic Joseph Worcester, who designed California's first full-fledged arts and crafts house in the 1870s. A. Page Brown guided the project, while Bernard Maybeck helped

Two Views & a Street

Three Pacific Heights experiences: Walking the Lyon Street Steps (Broadway to Green St.) gives a colorful view of the Palace of Fine Arts' red-orange dome, the blue bay, and green Marin County—just what you'd see from the window of a Pacific Heights mansion. Another fine view is the cityscape from the summit of Alta Plaza Park. To sample the neighborhood's tony but unstuffy public life, hit Fillmore Street (South from Jackson St.) for shopping and dining.

design the interior. The church is one of San Francisco's most popular wedding sites.

Visitors enter a walled garden to find what appears to be an Italian village church of simple stucco and oven-fired brick. Inside, the church evokes a rustic forest lodge, or perhaps a sacred grove. Beams of madrone wood are still covered in their natural bark. A fireplace fills the room with warmth and the scent of wood smoke. The congregation sits on comfortable maple chairs with rush seats, rather than hard pews. (These chairs inspired Gustav Stickley in creating his craftsman-style furniture.) Four pastoral murals by William Keith depict the seasons of northern California and reveal an appreciation of the subtleties and mystery of nature. ∎

Temple Emanu-El
- Map p. 142
- Arguello Blvd. at Lake St.
- 415/751-2535
- Bus: 3, 12, 22, 24

emanuelsf.org

Swedenborgian Church
- Map p. 143
- 2107 Lyon St. at Washington St.
- 415/346-6466
- Bus: 3, 12, 22, 24

sfswedenborgian .org

Cow Hollow

Dairy farms once dotted this hollow below the ridge of Pacific Heights, but it was the stink from the attendant slaughterhouses, meatpacking houses, and leather tanneries of the late 1800s that gave the valley its nickname. At last, neighboring citizens convinced the city to shut down these polluting businesses and landfill the hollow, which became a residential area.

Cow Hollow

⬛ Map p. 143

🚌 Bus: 22, 41, 45

St. Mary the Virgin Episcopal Church

⬛ Map p. 143

✉ 2325 Union St.

☎ 415/921-3665

smusf.org

Vedanta Society Old Temple

⬛ Map p. 143

✉ 2963 Webster St.

☎ 415/922-2323

🕐 Closed except during services

sfvedanta.org

Octagon House

⬛ Map p. 143

✉ 2645 Gough St.

☎ 415/441-7512

🕐 Open 2nd Sun., 2nd & 4th Thurs.

nscda-ca.org

In the 1950s, antiques dealers and interior designers moved into the Victorian houses on Union Street, and were followed by more shops, restaurants, and bars. Today, **Union Street** (Steiner St. to Van Ness Ave.) is a boutique boomtown. Designer clothes, expensive baubles for the home, fashion eyeglasses, jewelry—it's all here. Strolling down Union is a popular way to pass an early evening or weekend afternoon.

At Steiner and Union stands the redwood-shingled **St. Mary the Virgin Episcopal Church.** Resembling a church on a country lane, it has a garden courtyard that shelters an original spring where early dairy herds drank.

Look downhill from Union on Webster Street to see the **Vedanta Society Old Temple.** Built in 1905, it blends a basically Edwardian building with an East Indian balcony arcade, red onion domes, and other exotica. The eclectic mix of decorative elements is intended to reflect the Vedanta idea that all religions aim at realizing the same one god. Vedanta is a branch of Hinduism.

At **2040 Union Street,** the 1873 Victorian house and barn of Cow Hollow's first dairy farmer (the aptly named James

INSIDER TIP:

Intrigued by the Octagon House? Check out the courses at Golden Gate Feng Shui School (2323 Broadway, Oakland, tel 510/868-0489).

—JUSTIN KAVANAGH
National Geographic Travel Books editor

Cudworth) have now morphed into retail and restaurant space.

Are people healthier if they live in an eight-sided building? Some people believed so when the **Octagon House** was built in 1861. Perhaps the theory arose because a house with more sides lets in more fresh air and light. It turns out that when an octagonal house is divided into square rooms, it leaves triangles that make good closets (and bathrooms). The house, now home to the National Society of Colonial Dames of America in California, displays furniture and decorative arts of the colonial and federal periods, as well as the signatures of Thomas Jefferson, Benjamin Franklin, and others whose names appear on the Declaration of Independence. ∎

Japantown

A cultural center for the Japanese-American community (but not a residential hub like Chinatown), Japantown has two major sections: Japan Center and the Buchanan (or Nihon-machi) Mall.

Costumed performers celebrate their homeland at the annual Japantown Cherry Blossom Festival.

Anchored by the Hotel Kabuki and the Sundance Kabuki movie theaters, the **Japan Center Malls (East and West)** were built in 1968 during urban renewal. The 5-acre (2 ha) complex looks blandly modern, so don't expect anything like the gorgeous old Japanese city of Kyoto. However, it has all the sushi and tempura you can eat, shops filled with Japanese arts and household goods, and entertainment. The **Peace Pagoda** rises more than 100 feet (30 m), with five round, copper-clad roofs topped with a spire of nine rings supporting a golden ball that is an emblem of virtue.

Across the street is the **Buchanan Mall** a cobbled walking street lined with stucco-and-wood buildings scaled like a Japanese village. Sculptor Ruth Asawa created two origami-inspired fountains.

Japantown

Map p. 143

Bounded by Fillmore, Sutter, Geary, & Laguna Sts.

Bus: 2, 3, 4, 22, 38

sfjapantown.org

Japan Center

Map p. 143

Geary Blvd., Fillmore St. to Laguna St.

EXPERIENCE: Cherry Blossom Festival

Taiko drums thunder, and *kendo* swords-men perform mock combat. Women demonstrate the gentle art of *ikebana*, or flower arranging. The music of a plucked *koto* wafts through the air. You've landed in the middle of the Cherry Blossom Festival in Japantown *(April; sfcherryblossom.org)*.

Maybe you followed the big parade, with colorfully costumed folk dancers swirling along the route like butterflies. Or maybe you came to taste the goodies at the Japanese food bazaar. Whatever lured you, it doesn't matter: You've now joined the celebration of another culture, discovered another face of San Francisco.

Sokoji-Soto Zen Buddhist Temple

✉ 1691 Laguna St.

☎ 415/346-7540

Churches & Temples

The **Sokoji-Soto Zen Buddhist Temple** reflects Zen practice, with a simple interior and cushions for sitting *zazen*, or engaging in Zen meditation. The altar, though, is rich, with a golden

The Sokoji-Soto Zen Buddhist Temple combines a rich altar with a simple interior to enhance Zen meditation.

figure of Shakyamuni Buddha.

The beliefs of the **Konko Church of San Francisco** *(1909 Bush St., tel 415/931-0453)* revolve around the Principle Parent of the Universe, who combines aspects of mother earth and father heaven. The church, based on but independent from Shinto, has its roots in religious truths revealed to a Japanese farmer who survived a major illness in 1859. On the church's wooden altar offerings are placed that range from flowers to canned goods, soft drinks, and beer, in appreciation of the Principle Parent for the things that sustain human life. Above the altar a golden disk symbolizes divine light. (Konko means "golden light.")

Climb to the second floor of a plain building to reach the **Buddhist Church of San Francisco** *(1881 Pine St., tel 415/776-3158, call for appt.)*, whose rooftop stupa, or dome, holds reputed relics of the Buddha. In the worship hall are peacock screens and a gilded altar, combined with such western touches as pews and an organ.

Mission architecture melds with Japanese hallmarks (green-tile roof) at **St. Francis Xavier Church** *(1801 Octavia St.)*. ■

Cathedral of St. Mary of the Assumption

Just south of Japantown, the city's third Catholic cathedral (Belluschi, Nervi, McSweeney, Ryan, & Lee), built between 1967 and 1970, is like no other building in the city.

Italian marble covers the geometric facade of the Cathedral of St. Mary of the Assumption.

Following a geometric design known as a hyperbolic paraboloid, the reinforced concrete structure curves upward from the four corners, meeting in a cross 190 feet (58 m) above. Sheathed in Italian marble, the structure rests on corner pylons that can support ten million pounds (4.5 million kg) of pressure, yet are just 2 feet (60 cm) in circumference at their narrowest point. (They extend 90 feet/27 m into bedrock.) Huge corner windows open the church to the city.

Inside, four seams of stained glass, each 138 feet long (42 m) and 6 feet (1.8 m) wide, sweep to the top of the cupola. The colors represent the four elements of creation: earth (green), air (yellow), water (blue), and fire (red).

The altar is a massive, 10-ton (9 tonne) piece of Botticino marble. Hanging 75 feet (23 m) above it by golden wires, a baldachino of triangular aluminum rods reflects light, symbolizing the channel of love and grace from God. The 15-story-tall sculpture, created over three years (1967–1970) by Richard Lippold, weighs 1 ton (.9 tonne). Another remarkable feature is the 4,842-pipe organ, whose sound can fill the vast cathedral. Made by Ruffatti Brothers of Padua, Italy, it has a solid-state console installed high on a concrete pedestal. ■

Cathedral of St. Mary of the Assumption

Map p. 143

1111 Gough St.

415/567-2020

stmarycathedral sf.org

More Places to Visit in Pacific Heights & Japantown

Alta Plaza Park

This park is used mostly by nearby residents who come to play tennis or to give their kids and dogs some playtime. Alta Plaza gives you a chance to see how the other one percent live—the wealthy of Pacific Heights.

 Map p. 143 ✉ Bet. Clay, Steiner, Jackson, & Scott Sts. 🚌 Bus: 1, 3, 12, 22, 24

Kabuki Springs & Spa

One block west of Japantown is a traditional spa, equipped with sauna, steam room, and communal baths. Luxurious treatments such as shiatsu massage and body wraps are available by appointment.

kabukisprings.com ✉ 1750 Geary Blvd. ☎ 415/922-6000 🚌 Bus: 2, 3, 4, 22, 38

Lafayette Park

Join local dog walkers at this park, whose 12 acres (5 ha) climb from open lawns to a knoll shaded by trees. At 378 feet (115 m), this is the height of Pacific Heights and offers views of the city and bay. The hilltop was set aside for a park in 1855, but not improved with plantings until 1910.

Map p. 143 ✉ Enter at Sacramento & Octavia Sts. 🚌 Bus: 1, 12

Other Grand Houses

Grand residences can be seen all over the neighborhood, especially as you approach the Presidio along **Jackson Street, Pacific Avenue,** and **Broadway.** Across from terraced Alta Plaza Park stands the former **Music and Arts Institute** *(2622 Jackson St.).* Designed by Willis Polk as his first San Francisco project in 1894, the stone residence looks like a classical villa in Tuscany. Another Polk design, the baronial **Bourn Mansion** *(2550 Webster St.)* is an 1896 Georgian Revival town house with a restrained facade of rough, burned-looking (or "clinker") brick. Ornately carved stonework frames a central window, beneath which lies the unassuming entry.

Map pp. 142–143 🚌 Bus: 3, 12, 22, 24

Grand houses adorn the streets of Pacific Heights, one of the city's most elite neighborhoods.

Flower power at the fabled crossroads of Haight and Ashbury Streets, and real floral delights in nearby Golden Gate Park

Haight-Ashbury & Golden Gate Park

An unusual storefront greets visitors on Haight Street.

Haight-Ashbury & Golden Gate Park

Haight-Ashbury and Golden Gate Park were once bleak sand dunes occupied by squatters. In 1868, when the city acquired the land, a local newspaper hooted that the purchase was a white elephant, a sprawl of sand where constant winds would prevent anything from growing. Once the park was established, though, its environs became desirable, and Haight-Ashbury began its history as a respectable Victorian neighborhood.

It was the later decline of the neighborhood, and the cheap rents that resulted from it, that brought first the Beats and then the hippies (see pp. 160–161) to the area. "The Haight" remains the city's most countercultural neighborhood, packed with tattooed urban youth and wannabe hippies. Tourists dip into "head shops" to buy psychedelic posters and bong pipes as though they were sacred relics of the 1967 Summer of Love.

Golden Gate Park ranks as one of America's finest urban landscapes and its largest developed city park—1,017 acres (411 ha) in a

rectangle—stretching from Stanyan Street to Ocean Beach. Residents think of the park as their backyard, which makes sense in the West's most densely populated city.

Place for Renewal

In the park, residents soothe frayed city nerves with a balm of green leaves. They stroll through

NOT TO BE MISSED:

Flashing back to the psychedelic '60s on Haight Street **158–159**

Tiny orchids and gargantuan lilies at the Conservatory of Flowers **163–164**

A rarified world of American painting at the de Young Museum **164–167**

Exploring natural wonders at the California Academy of Sciences **167–169**

Tranquil ponds and blossoming cherry trees at the Japanese Tea Garden **169–171**

The Beach Chalet's murals of San Francisco life in the 1930s **175**

rhododendron dells and picnic in meadows, enjoy sports from Frisbee-tossing to tennis, and visit fine museums.

The park site was part of the "Outside Lands"—sand dunes the city obtained after a legal wrangle with squatters. In 1871, new park superintendent William Hammond Hall began planting beach grass, barley, and wild lupine to stabilize the soil against the wind. Within a

few years, trees and flowers flourished along an eight-block carriage approach to the park (the Panhandle) and in the park's eastern section.

In 1887, Hall's successor arrived at Golden Gate Park—John McLaren, a Scot who had worked at Edinburgh's Royal Botanical Gardens. Known as "Uncle John," he was determined, crusty, and beloved. He spent nearly 56 years creating groves, lakes, and flower gardens, meanwhile taming windy dunes and windier politicians who had designs on the park.

In 1894, the California Midwinter Fair was staged here to publicize San Francisco's Mediterranean climate. The fair site became the Music Concourse, hub of the park's museums. Today, about 13 million peole each year come to enjoy Golden Gate Park. ■

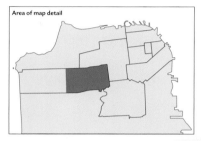

Area of map detail

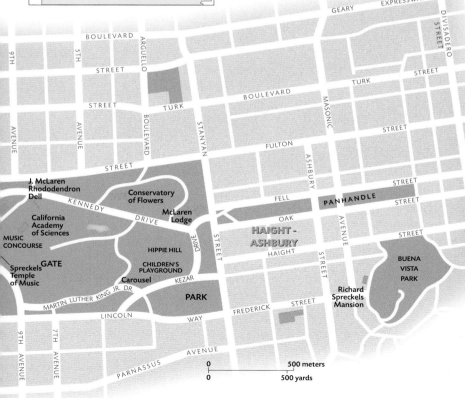

Haight-Ashbury

In the popular mind "Haight-Ashbury" means flower children, tripping along in tie-dyed clothes and flashing the peace sign through clouds of suspicious-smelling smoke. (Some nicknamed the neighborhood the "Hashbury.") Centered around Haight and Ashbury Streets, it was home to bands that invented psychedelic rock, including Jefferson Airplane and the Grateful Dead.

Laid-back cafés and rainbow mosaics in Haight-Ashbury reflect the area's counterculture heritage.

Haight-Ashbury

Map p. 155

Bus: 6, 7, 33, 37, 43, 66, 71; streetcar: N

It wasn't always this way. In the 1880s, the Haight was a resort district near Golden Gate Park. People rode the Haight Street cable car to an 1895 amusement park, the Chutes, to ride a gondola down a 300-foot (91 m) slide into a lake. Victorian houses rose on the flats near the Panhandle and on fancier Ashbury Heights. Growth boomed after the 1906 earthquake, as the neighborhood was undamaged.

With the Great Depression, the Haight declined and Victorian houses were divided into flats. By the 1950s, low rents attracted poor blacks and Beats driven from North Beach. The mid-'60s brought the flower children, mind-altering drugs, and "free love." By the end of

EXPERIENCE: Catch a Live Show at the Amoeba Music Store

San Francisco still showcases the music stars of tomorrow, as it did in the 1960s, and no place makes it easier (or cheaper) to discover them than Amoeba Music (1855 Haight St., tel 415/831-1200, amoeba.com).

This enormous store fills a converted bowling alley in Haight-Ashbury, on the eastern edge of Golden Gate Park. During free shows, you stand among bins that hold hundreds of thousands of music titles while performers play on stage. Artists have ranged from M.I.A.,

Sonic Youth, and Safe No More to the Preservation Hall Jazz Band.

Music in stock includes experimental rock, hip-hop, electronica, jazz, underground indie, garage, emo, art-punk, and "turntablism." For film fans, the store also stocks movie titles from every genre imaginable.

The original Amoeba Music opened in Berkeley in 1990 across the bay (2455 Telegraph Ave., tel 510/549-1125). The offshoot location in Haight-Ashbury debuted in 1997.

---

the decade, though, the love had gone out of the Haight with an influx of hard drugs, criminals, and the mentally unbalanced. The neighborhood became a psychedelic ghetto.

Remarkably, the neighborhood made a comeback as gays and young professionals restored Victorian houses with financial incentives from the city. More than 1,100 Victorians survive, mostly Queen Annes (see p. 43) with elaborate gingerbread and towers.

On Haight Street, visitors must adjust to the throng of panhandlers, skateboarders, neo-hippies, bikers, and gray-haired flower children. A few lines that young panhandlers have used on passersby:

(1) "Spare change for alcohol?"

(2) "Got any money so I can buy a sailboat?"

(3) Hand-lettered cardboard sign: "Need Change 4 Weed."

INSIDER TIP:

For city lights in a stunning 360-degree panorama, visit Twin Peaks lookout (501 Twin Peaks Blvd., S of Haight-Ashbury) on a clear night.

—FORREST McGILL
Chief curator, Asian Art Museum

(4) "Hey, how about a $15,000 loan for five years at 10 percent?"

(5) "I need a ticket to Indonesia so I can work for Nike for $33 a week."

(6) When turned down: "*@#! You're ruining my day, man! My whole *@#! life!"

But the street has interesting shops, good cheap restaurants, and blast-from-the-past encounters with black-light posters and scented candles to waft you back to the '60s. ∎

Haight-Ashbury Walk

This walk looks at the contemporary street scene of Haight-Ashbury and offers flashbacks to the hippie era. It also takes in fine Victorian houses from the turn of the 20th century.

Start at Haight and Stanyan Streets. Behind you in Golden Gate Park is **Hippie Hill,** where the "tribes" (see pp. 160–161) gathered in the '60s. A few decades later it became an encampment for aimless youth and street dwellers until they were moved. Today there are drum circles, and every April 20 at 4:20 p.m., a marijuana smoke-in. Walk east on **Haight Street,** and you'll meet the locals, including perhaps a rainbow-garbed, headband-wearing hippie born years after the Summer of Love; teenage girls with eyes far too streetwise; a couple with at least two dozen body piercings between them; a leftover 1960s flower child looking through pinwheel eyes at something the rest of us can't see; and panhandlers (see p. 157).

Haight Street is chockablock with shops. You can buy retro or trendy clothes, "healing crystals," books, hippie regalia, and psychedelic posters (especially of departed rock stars: Jimi Hendrix, Jerry Garcia, Jim Morrison). Along your way, look at **1779–1783 Haight,** the commercial zone's oldest building (1893); **1775 Haight,** site of the Diggers' free crash pad (see pp. 160–161); and **1677–1681 Haight,** a 1904 building in Parisian style.

The **Red Victorian ❶** is a 1904 hotel that for years ran as a shrine to the Summer of Love, with 1960s posters and beads. Reflecting the city's zeitgeist, it's now a "co-living hotel" and collaboration space for "creatives to connect and be in action around impactful projects." At **1660 Haight,** the art nouveau facade of the 1911 Superba Theater now fronts Wasteland, a vintage clothing store. The **Haight-Ashbury Free Medical Clinic ❷** (*Clayton St.*) opened in 1967 to provide no-cost help for bad LSD trips, venereal diseases, and other health problems of the hippie lifestyle.

On Haight between Cole and Clayton

NOT TO BE MISSED:

Street life on Haight Street • The Panhandle • Buena Vista Avenue West • Gabled houses on Waller Street

Streets, the Chutes amusement park once drew the public with a waterslide, zoo, theater, and other attractions. At **1535 Haight** stood the Psychedelic Shop, opened in 1966 as the world's first "head shop" (see pp. 160–161). At Haight and Ashbury, the intersection that gives its name to the neighborhood, turn left.

Walk two blocks to Oak Street and the **Panhandle ❸,** an eight-block swath of greenery laid out in the 1870s as a carriage entrance to Golden Gate Park. Here the elite of San Francisco rode and showed off their finest clothes. After the 1906 earthquake, 30,000 displaced people lived in the Panhandle in tents and refugee cottages. Today it's a park. Look past the seediness to see it as a living museum of trees, the earliest planted in the effort to fashion Golden Gate Park from windblown dunes. Look for eucalyptuses and cypresses, Chinese ginkgoes and Greek olives, Moroccan cedars and California sequoias. Avoid the area at night.

Turn right on Oak, and walk along the Panhandle to Masonic. Turn right and return to Haight. The building on the northeast corner housed the 1967 "Drogstore" café, a hippie gathering spot. A pharmacy previously occupied the building, but city officials wouldn't let the café keep the name "Drugstore" because of its counterculture connotations.

Turn left on Haight, noting **Bound Together** (*1369 Haight St.*), a longtime anarchist bookstore. At Lyon Street, you can detour left to **No. 122,** where rocker Janis Joplin once lived. (A renter, she was evicted—not for sex, drugs, or loud rock-and-roll, but for keeping a dog against the rules.)

At Haight and Lyon, go into **Buena Vista Park** 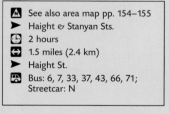 and climb the path to the right. The oldest park in the city, Buena Vista boasts a rarity—one of San Francisco's few remaining groves of California live oaks. Foresting of this 36-acre (15 ha) park began in the 1880s, when schoolchildren planted seedlings given by philanthropist Adolph Sutro. Around 1910, John McLaren (of Golden Gate Park) planted pines and cypresses, eucalyptuses, and a small redwood grove. Today, the trees partially screen the "good view" for which Buena Vista Park was given its name. In the 1930s, the WPA built retaining walls and drainage ditches of granite and marble salvaged from former cemeteries; look for faint inscriptions on headstone fragments.

Explore the park, then descend to the perimeter at **Buena Vista Avenue West** and head uphill. This street shows off residential styles from Tudor and Queen Anne to modernist. The 1897 **Richard Spreckels Mansion** 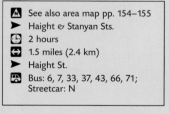 (*737 Buena Vista Ave. W.*) was built for a nephew of sugar king Claus Spreckels.

Grand marble stairs lead to a columned porch, and there are fanlights above the windows. Reputedly, tenants have included writers Jack London and Ambrose Bierce.

At Java Street, turn right and walk the short block to Masonic Avenue. You can detour uphill to see a shingled house designed by Bernard Maybeck (*1526 Masonic Ave.*). Walking downhill, you'll find a row of 1891 **Eastlake Victorians** 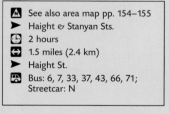 (*1322–1342 Masonic Ave.*). At Waller, see a row of 1896 **gabled houses** 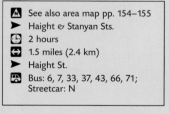 (*1315–1335 Waller St.*) that are among the most finely ornamented in San Francisco. Going west on Waller, detour south to a row of 1890s Queen Annes that include the old **Grateful Dead House** 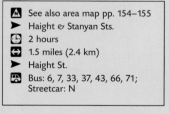 (*710 Ashbury St.*), where the band was busted for drugs in 1967. Or turn right on Ashbury and return to Haight.

- ▲ See also area map pp. 154–155
- ► Haight & Stanyan Sts.
- 🕐 2 hours
- ↔ 1.5 miles (2.4 km)
- ► Haight St.
- 🚌 Bus: 6, 7, 33, 37, 43, 66, 71; Streetcar: N

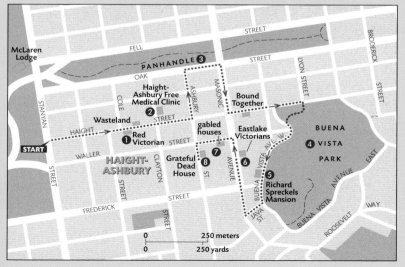

Hippies: The Love Generation

Before they shook all of America, the seismic social shocks of the hippie era took place in San Francisco. Repelled by established authority and the "system," hippies adopted ideals of community, peace, and love. Early on, theatrical anarchists called the Diggers espoused the idea that goods should be free, so they opened a store in Haight-Ashbury where no money changed hands and customers donated as well as took.

Hippies spread peace and love in Golden Gate Park during the so-called Summer of Love in 1967.

The Haight was already home to some relocated 1950s Beats, whose bohemianism was infectious. It was the Beats who coined the term "hippie," meaning junior-grade hipster. The word first hit print in a September 1965 story in the *San Francisco Examiner*.

In Haight-Ashbury, roomy Victorian houses were available at low rent. Some rock bands, like Jefferson Airplane, moved in together as communal "families." Men grew long hair, women donned Victorian lace and velvet from thrift shops. All wore "love beads" from India, perfumed themselves with patchouli

oil, and experimented with new lifestyles and art forms. Bands such as the Grateful Dead played freewheeling improvisations. To advertise rock concerts, posters vibrated with psychedelic colors (see sidebar p. 38).

Hippie life revolved around idealism and music, with a touch of Eastern mysticism—but also around marijuana, LSD, and other mind-altering drugs, as well as a new sexual liberation. In fact, "Sex, Dope, and Cheap Thrills" was the suppressed full title of a famous album by Janis Joplin. Its cover was drawn by San Francisco underground cartoonist

A peace sign stenciled onto a Haight Street café window reflects the area's hippie heritage.

R. Crumb, whose *Zap Comix* portrayed hippie lust and drugs with artistic glee.

Hippie Life

LSD (aka "acid") had come on the scene in 1965 via novelist Ken Kesey, who encountered it as a volunteer in experiments at Stanford University. With his Merry Pranksters, Kesey staged multimedia LSD happenings, whose handbills asked: "Can You Pass the Acid Test?" But by October 1966, California prohibited LSD, making hippies into outlaws. The same month, the Psychedelic Shop opened on Haight Street, selling various hippie accoutrements and pot-smoking paraphernalia. It was the world's first "head shop."

In January 1967, tens of thousands of flower children converged on the polo field at Golden Gate Park for the "Human Be-In/Gathering of the Tribes," an event featuring Jefferson Airplane, poet Allen Ginsberg, and Harvard professor turned acid guru Timothy Leary. This was probably the biggest event of the hippie subculture until Woodstock.

Strangely, it was San Francisco's police chief who first called hippies the "Love Generation." The national media took note, and the attention attracted hordes of footloose youth, who turned Haight-Ashbury into such a freak show that the Gray Line actually ran a bus tour there called the "Hippie Hop."

Summer of Love and Its Aftermath

The idea of the 1967 Summer of Love—an invitation to the world to share the good vibes—was popular with Haight-Ashbury merchants. Hippies objected to the commercialism of vendors who sold "Love Burgers" and the like.

The Summer of Love attracted sincere seekers and "plastic hippies" alike, along with drifters, the mentally disturbed, drug pushers, and violent criminals. Good vibes soon turned bad. In October, the Diggers held a "Death of Hippie" march to the Haight's Buena Vista Park. A 1969 free rock concert with the Rolling Stones at Altamont Speedway (east of the city) helped kill "peace and love." When Hells Angels—hired for security—faced a violent crowd, one fatally stabbed a concertgoer who brandished a gun. In the 1970s, cheap heroin poured into the neighborhood of Haight-Ashbury, bringing addiction, street crime, and death. The Love Generation was over.

Nonetheless, some good things survived: American society became more tolerant of nonconformity. (In San Francisco, this was reflected in open acceptance of gays.) Where there is acceptance, the original hippie spirit of "peace and love" lives on.

Golden Gate Park East

Not every city boasts a playground 3 miles (5 km) long and half a mile (0.8 km) wide. But that's Golden Gate Park. It has about 20 access points along its perimeter, while two main roads thread its length: John F. Kennedy Drive and Martin Luther King Jr. Drive. The eastern half of the park boasts some of the city's major museums.

An avenue of flowers leads to the Victorian-era Conservatory of Flowers and its tropical plants.

Golden Gate Park

Maps pp. 154–155 & 174–175

✉ Fell St. at Stanyan St.

☎ 415/831-2700

sfrecpark.org

goldengatepark.com

Get information and maps at park headquarters, inside the east entrance. The headquarters occupies **McLaren Lodge,** which was designed in 1897 by Edward R. Swain. This handsome Moorish-Gothic building with coarse sandstone walls and red-tile roofs was home to longtime superintendent John McLaren. A visitor center is located in the western section of the park (see pp. 173–175).

A free shuttle (*Sat.–Sun & holidays*) runs from McLaren Lodge to Ocean Beach at the park's west end, making stops along the way at 14 attractions. Route maps are available at the park.

Sights listed in the following pages run from east to west. The **Koret Children's Quarter,** formerly known as Children's Playground, was the nation's first public playground (1888). Nearby, you'll see the painted horses, camels, and dragons of the beautifully restored 1912 Herschell-Spillman carousel *($)*. The Conservatory of Flowers (see below) is a Victorian glass palace filled with 20,000 tropical plants. Farther west sprawls the **John McLaren Rhododendron Dell,** where spring blossoms set off a statue of superintendent McLaren—who, ironically, despised statues as intruders on nature and often screened them behind foliage.

The nearby Music Concourse is formally landscaped with English plane trees and fountains and bordered by museums: the de Young (see pp. 164–167) and the California Academy of Sciences (see pp. 167–169). At one end stands the **Spreckels Temple of Music** (1899), a bandstand of Italian Renaissance style donated by sugar king Claus Spreckels. Built of Colusa sandstone, with reliefs carved by Robert Aitken, it is home to the nation's oldest municipal band.

Conservatory of Flowers

The oldest existing wood-and-glass conservatory in the Western Hemisphere is a living museum of tropical plants, ranging from orchids to slightly unsettling carnivorous varieties.

One of the most visited places in Golden Gate Park, the greenhouse was put up in 1879 after being purchased as a kit from the heirs of wealthy businessman James Lick, who died before it could be erected at his Santa Clara Valley estate. Today, the conservatory displays 1,700 plant species from more than 50 countries, including a noted collection of Dracula orchids.

It was closed from 1995 to 2003 for a $25 million rehabilitation to repair damage from a 100-mile-an-hour (161 km/h) windstorm. Today, the conservatory envelops visitors in San Francisco "flower power"—a colorful, almost hallucinogenic trip to the cloud forests of Costa Rica, the steamy heart of the Congo, and the lush islands of the Philippines, under one huge glass roof.

Conservatory of Flowers

⧄ Map p. 155

✉ 100 JFK Dr., Golden Gate Park

☎ 415/831-2090

🕐 Closed Mon.

💲 $$, free admission 1st Tues. of month

🚌 Bus: 5, 7, 21, 33, 44, 71; Streetcar: N

conservatory offlowers.org

Where Can You Park in the Park?

Try the garage below the Music Concourse; enter from the north via Tenth Avenue at Fulton Street, or from the south via Concourse Drive at Martin Luther King Jr. Drive. There's limited parking on John F. Kennedy Drive, MLK Jr. Drive, and adjacent roads. On Sundays and holidays, Kennedy Drive is closed to cars, to the delight of bicyclists, from Kezar to Transverse Drive; on Saturdays *(April–Oct.)* it's closed from Tea Garden to Transverse Drive. On those days, a free shuttle runs to popular park stops every 15 minutes. Board at the Ocean Beach parking lot *(Kennedy Dr. at Great Hwy.);* leave your car there for free.

There are five galleries. Under the dome in the **Lowland Tropics gallery,** a light rain falls on a canopy of palms and the colossal leaves of a century-old imperial philodendron. Also on view are cycads, a type of plant that predated the dinosaurs, and modern commercial plants such as chocolate, coffee, and vanilla.

de Young Museum

🅰 Map pp. 154–155

✉ 50 Hagiwara Tea Garden Dr., Golden Gate Park

☎ 415/750-3600

🕐 Closed Mon.

💲 $$, free 1st Tues. of month

🚌 Bus: 5, 21, 38, 44, 71; Streetcar: N

famsf.org

The sweetest fragrances fill the air. The air cools in the east wing's **Highland Tropics section,** where orchids grow on the bark of gnarled trees among ferns and creeping vines. Cases resembling Victorian armoires hold valuable orchid specimens. The **Aquatic Plants gallery** enfolds you with the sound of water and the delightful sight of giant lilies and floating flowers. (One water lily variety has leaves that can grow to 6 feet/1.8 m across and support the weight of a small child.)

The west wing contains the **potted plant gallery,** with seasonal floral displays, and a gallery for special exhibits.

INSIDER TIP:

In summer, visit the dahlia garden just east of the Conservatory of Flowers. There's one of every kind of dahlia in a riot of colors.

—FORREST McGILL
Chief curator, Asian Art Museum

de Young Museum

The oldest public museum in San Francisco holds the West Coast's most comprehensive survey of American paintings. The original building, which was earthquake damaged, was replaced in 2005 by a dramatic, state-of-the-art structure (Herzog & de Meuron) sheathed in 475 tons (430 tonnes) of copper, perforated to suggest light filtering through a canopy

of trees, an effect that ties the building to its park setting. The museum is topped with a 144-foot (44 m) tower whose observation floor has wraparound windows looking out on Golden Gate Park, city neighborhoods, and all the way to the Pacific.

It started with M. H. de Young, the publisher of the *San Francisco Chronicle,* who helped the city acquire the Fine Arts building from the 1894 California Midwinter Fair as a museum. De Young established his own program of acquisitions—none too skillfully at first. His taste for the curious and ornamental was reflected in armor, paintings, objects from the South Pacific, an Egyptian mummy, birds' eggs, handcuffs, and even reproductions. One of his early acquisitions, John Vanderlyn's 1807 painting "Caius Marius Amid the Ruins of Carthage," which won a gold medal at the Paris Salon in 1808, formed the nucleus for the collection of American art.

The museum moved into a Spanish plateresque building in 1919. By the 1930s, it had refocused on fine and decorative art. In 1932, the museum held the "Group f/64" show of Bay Area photographers—among them Edward Weston, Imogen Cunningham, and Ansel Adams. In 1979, John D. Rockefeller III donated more than a hundred works of American art, propelling the de Young into the big leagues. Other donations included the H. McCoy Jones collection of rugs, carpets, and embroideries from the Near East and Central Asia, and the Wagner collection of

The boldly modern de Young Museum, sheathed in copper, houses exhibits from around the world.

Teotihuacán murals from Mexico. The major focuses are as follows:

American Painting: More than a thousand paintings in the collection offer a survey of American art from colonial days through the mid-20th century. The museum's earliest painting is "The Mason Children" (1670), which depicts three upper-class Boston youngsters. (Note the numbers above their heads, indicating their ages.)

Noteworthy portrait artists include self-taught John Singleton Copley ("Mary Turner Sargent," 1763), Gilbert Stuart (famous for his portrait of George Washington), John Singer Sargent, the most sought-after portrait artist at the turn of the 20th century

("A Dinner Table at Night," ca 1880), Robert Henri ("O in Black With Scarf," 1910), and Mary Cassatt, associated with the French Impressionists and here represented by an 1889 portrait of her mother in beige and black.

The museum hangs landscapes by Albert Bierstadt ("California Spring," 1875), the Hudson River school's Frederic Edwin Church ("Rainy Season in the Tropics," 1866), and William Keith, who painted the western out-of-doors.

Less purposefully majestic, genre paintings portray daily life. A highlight is George Caleb Bingham's "Boatmen on the Missouri" (1846), which depicts three raftsmen, one wearing a broken top hat, who sell wood to passing steamboats. The men are painted in bold patches of color, with the misty landscape subtly painted behind. This was one of the first views of frontier life to appeal to viewers on the East Coast. Other genre works include Winslow Homer's "The Bright Side" (1865) and Thomas Anschutz's master-work, "The Ironworkers' Noon-time" (1880).

EXPERIENCE:
Lindy in the Park

We've all heard of dancing in the dark—but dancing in the park? On Sundays from 11 a.m. to 2 p.m., a group gets together in Golden Gate Park for a free swing dance party in the fresh air—and you can join in *(near Music Concourse on the S side of John F. Kennedy Dr., lindyinthepark.com)*. Meet the locals, practice your social dancing, and have fun swinging and swaying to big band music of the 1930s and '40s and jazz. If you're a newbie dancer, come to the begin-ners' lesson at noon; no partner is required.

Regionalist art is represented by Grant Wood in "Dinner for Threshers" (1934), which pre-sents a farmhouse at mealtime in a cutaway view of multiple rooms. The panoramic painting looks strikingly modern, yet also harks back to Italian Renaissance triptychs. John Langley Howard's "Embarcadero and Clay" (1935) gives a view of San Francisco with vintage cars and a hotel.

Raphaelle Peale's small "Black-berries" (1813) is one of the earli-est American still lifes. A gallery of trompe l'oeil still lifes presents the uncannily realistic "The Trumpeter Swan" (1900) by Alexander Pope,

and William M. Harnett's "After the Hunt" (1885), depicting an iron-hinged door hung with a rifle, pow-der horn, and game. John Frederick Peto's "The Cup We All Race 4" (1900) is almost holographic in its representation of reality . . . or surreality.

Early 20th-century paintings include the immense purple blossoms of Georgia O'Keeffe's "Petunias" (1925). Look also for mid-20th-century works by Rich-ard Diebenkorn ("Seated Woman," 1965) and Bay Area artists such as Wayne Thiebaud, whose "Three Machines" (1963) pictures colorful gum ball machines.

The sculpture collection includes William Wetmore Story's "King Saul" (1882) and Frederic Reming-ton's "The Bronco Buster" (1895), a bronze with details characteristic of the artist's paintings.

Decorative Arts: An Adams-style George III dining room, a federal parlor from an 1805 Massachusetts home, Joseph Dufour wallpaper, a 1780 high chest made in Philadelphia, silverwork by Paul Revere, and Shaker chairs all trace early work in America.

The arts and crafts movement of the early 20th century is repre-sented by a Stickley oak sideboard with hammered metal fixtures, and by Frank Lloyd Wright's "Tree of Life Window" (1904), his finest from the prairie school period, with a stylized tree motif in clear, colored, and iridescent glass. Also on view is a Greene and Greene side chair of mahogany with ebony, copper, pewter, coral, and mother-of-pearl.

Textiles: Pieces are rotated from a collection of rugs, carpets, and embroideries from the Near East and Central Asia, including the finest holdings of Anatolian kilims outside Turkey. Kilims are flat-woven wool textiles used as floor coverings, wall hangings, and bed coverings, with geometric designs in rich, brilliant colors. Other highlights are *suzanis,* dowry embroideries from Samarkand, Bokhara, and Tashkent.

Oceanic Art: Oceanic art pieces from the 1894 California Midwinter Fair became part of the museum's charter collection. Among them is a Maori canoe prow from New Zealand (19th century), made of wood and shell. Also notable: a roll of feather money from the Nindu island of Santa Cruz, a rare navigation figure from the Caroline Islands of Micronesia, and a 10-foot (3 m) house post from the Iatmul culture of Papua New Guinea.

African Art: Sub-Saharan Africa is represented in such pieces as a power figure from the Congo and carved granary doors from Mali. A helmet mask made by the Fang people of Gabon, painted with white kaolin, was used to initiate members of the Ngil society, a sort of tribal "police." Luba figures from Zaire were among the earliest African sculptures to inspire modern artists.

Art of the Americas: Fine pieces cover the period from 1200 B.C. to the 16th century. These include several stunning Teotihuacán murals and a mouth mask (ca A.D. 200–600) of hammered gold with red cinnabar, made by the Nazca culture of Peru. Northern Peru's Moche civilization (400 B.C.–A.D. 600) produced ceramic vessels decorated with surprisingly naturalistic and expressive figures. From Mexico, Colima ceramic animals and figures were funerary objects meant to escort the dead into the afterlife. Aztec, Olmec, and Maya works are also on view. From British Columbia comes a cedar Tsimshian totem pole (late 19th century), carved and painted to represent a bald eagle, killer whale, bear, and fish.

There's an App for That

San Francisco is app happy—and a useful iPhone application for Golden Gate Park is Guidekick (available in the iTunes store). Created by the park's unofficial historian, the app focuses on notable sites through text, new and historic photos, music, and video (e.g., a 1918 film of a handyman riding the spars of the Dutch Windmill). Use the app at home for advance learning or as an intelligent navigation tool with your phone's GPS and the app's 3-D map, which orients you and alerts you to nearby points of interest in the park.

California Academy of Sciences

The oldest scientific institution in the West (1853), the California Academy of Sciences has grown into one of the world's most advanced facilities. It is the world's only combined natural

California Academy of Sciences

 Map p. 155

✉ 55 Music Concourse Dr., Golden Gate Park

☎ 415/379-8000

$ $$$$$

🚌 Bus: 5, 21, 38, 44, 71; Streetcar: N

calacademy.org

history museum, planetarium, and aquarium, and was designed by Pritzker Prize–winning architect Renzo Piano to immerse visitors in the natural world.

In fact, the academy makes nature part of its very structure with a colorful "living roof," a 2.5-acre (1 ha) expanse planted with 1.7 million native California plants and wildflowers. The roof's undulations mimic the natural landscape nearby. The academy is green in other ways too, using energy-saving materials. (The roof, is bordered by a glass canopy with 60,000 photovoltaic cells to supply part of the facility's energy.)

In contrast to the dark, segregated halls and "cabinet of curiosities" displays of traditional natural history museums, here exhibits

flow together in open galleries. Inside a four-story glass sphere, a **living rain forest**—representing Borneo, Madagascar, Costa Rica, and the Amazon—teems with creatures. As visitors climb a spiral ramp, they wander among free-flying butterflies and birds (and meet flying snakes and flying frogs). They see chameleons and golden silk orb-weaver spiders. After descending by elevator to the Amazonian Flooded Forest, they walk through an underwater tunnel and see armored catfish, river turtles, and angelfish.

At the **Kimball Natural History Museum,** some of the dioramas in the **African Hall** showcase live animals, including African penguins that dip and dive

An open-air terrace lets visitors see the green canopy of the California Academy of Sciences' roof.

A Living Rooftop Pays Homage to the City's Hills

The California Academy of Sciences' 197,000-square-foot (118,300 sq m) rooftop features seven green undulating hills, an homage to the seven hills upon which San Francisco is built. These are Telegraph Hill, Nob Hill, Russian Hill, Mount Sutro, Twin Peaks, Mount Davidson, and Rincon Hill.

Constructing such a green rooftop to accommodate a living canopy presented many challenges. Primarily, how do you keep the plants and soil from sliding off the roof's extreme dips and slopes? A solution called the Bio Tray was developed and patented to do the job. Some 50,000 porous, biodegradable trays made from tree sap and coconut husks were used as containers for the vegetation.

The trays, which line the rooftop like tile, allow the roots of the plants to grow and interlock. In this way, the trays are bound together like patchwork, and the boundary between building and plant life is blurred.

in a tank complete with simulated waves. The **Color of Life** exhibit reveals nature's secret language of color through interactive displays and live animals. In an aviary, for example, Gouldian finches show how varied color patterns affect female birds when choosing a mate. The **California area** focuses on the destructive power of earthquakes—a subject quite relevant to San Francisco—and how societies handle them. An earthquake simulator gives visitors a high-magnitude jolt, and a planetarium show brings seismic science to life.

Coral reefs have been called the rain forests of the sea, and the **Steinhart Aquarium** boasts the world's deepest living coral reef display. Visitors gaze into an aquarium tank 25 feet (7.6 m) tall with corals, sharks, and a rainbow of more than 2,000 reef fish. Also on view are a discovery tide pool, a two-story swamp, and hundreds of aquarium tanks revealing the amazing diversity of aquatic life—including sea horses, a giant clam, and lungfish (a species that can breathe air).

Visit Mars, explore the galaxies—inside the **Morrison Planetarium dome** almost anything is possible. It employs the latest technologies, from a digital projector to tricks borrowed from video games, to immerse you in a cosmic experience. The 90-foot-diameter (27 m) dome is tilted at a 30-degree angle (like the tilt of the Earth), making it seem that you're not just looking up at the sky but sitting among the stars.

Japanese Tea Garden

On an uncrowded day in this garden of cherry trees, ponds, and bonsai trees, you might feel

Meandering paths and stylized gardens at the Japanese Tea Garden encourage contemplation.

Japanese Tea Garden

🅰 Map p. 154

✉ 75 Hagiwara Tea Garden Dr., Golden Gate Park

☎ 415/752-1171

💲 $$, free admission Mon., Wed., Fri. 9–10 a.m.

🚌 Bus: 5, 44, 71; Streetcar: N

japaneseteagardensf.com

you've been wafted to a quiet corner of the old Japanese city of Kyoto. In Japanese tradition, the garden captures the spirit of nature in a limited space. Its serenity is stylized, an expression of high art.

The nation's oldest Japanese garden began as part of the 1894 California Midwinter Fair. It was proposed by Asian art dealer George Turner Marsh, who admired gardens in Japan, and it was overseen for decades by gardener Makoto Hagiwara. From 1895 until 1942, his family lived in the garden, caring for its plantings and features. Visit in March, when the cherries blossom, or autumn, when

ginkgo trees blaze yellow.

In Japanese gardens, many plants have symbolic meanings: Pines, often twisted and sculpted with time, represent dignified old age. (Black pines are considered masculine, red pines feminine.) The chrysanthemum is the symbol of Japan's Imperial House.

You enter the 5-acre (2 ha) garden through a ceremonial gate of Japanese Hinoki cypress, traditionally used for temples. Winding paths give changing views of the foliage. The **Moon Bridge** arches high over a pond, its reflection completing a circle, like a full moon. The garden's five-roofed **pagoda** was built for the 1915 Panama-Pacific International

Exposition. Nearby is the green bronze **Peace Lantern,** a 9,000-pound (4,082 kg) symbol of friendship funded by schoolchildren in Japan to mark the 1951 U.S.–Japanese peace treaty.

At the **tea pavilion,** waitresses in silk kimonos serve fragrant tea, Japanese snacks, and fortune cookies. The cookies were introduced here by Makoto Hagiwara in 1909 and were later taken over by Chinese restaurateurs. Nearby sits a bronze **Buddha** that weighs a ton and a half (1.36 tonnes). Cast in Japan in 1790, it is called Amazarashi-No-Hotoke (The Buddha That Sits Throughout Sunny and Rainy Weather Without a Shelter).

There is also a small **Zen garden,** a meditative space originally designed to aid monks in their search for enlightenment. Japanese landscape architect Nagao Sakurai designed this example in 1953.

San Francisco Botanical Garden

As an urban oasis or an outdoor classroom for plant lovers, this spot can't be beat. Here the gardening possibilities of San Francisco's climate are gloriously displayed across 55 acres (22 ha) planted with more than 8,000 different kinds of rare and unusual plants from around the world. The garden opened in 1940 through a bequest from philanthropist Helene Strybing. Tours are available daily.

Arranged around a central lawn are geographic and specialized collections from places as varied as a California meadow and an Asian cloud forest. Among the highlights is the **South Africa garden,** representing a rich area for botanical species. Among them are proteas (which look like science-fiction plants from Venus) and brilliant orange aloe flowers. The **Australian garden** shows

**San Francisco
Botanical Garden**

🅰 Map pp. 154–155

✉ 9th Ave. at Lincoln Way, Golden Gate Park

☎ 415/661-1316

💲 $$, free 7:30–9 a.m. daily, and 2nd Tues. of each month

🚌 Bus: 44, 71; Streetcar: N

sfbotanicalgarden.org

EXPERIENCE: National AIDS Memorial Grove

Take a quiet, reflective walk in this grove, which defines itself as "a dedicated space in the national landscape where millions of Americans touched directly or indirectly by AIDS can gather to heal, hope, and remember."

Or you can pitch in as a volunteer to maintain the grove by weeding, mulching, and planting.

Begun in 1991, the project succeeded in rehabilitating the wildly overgrown de Laveaga Dell at the east end of Golden Gate Park. It brought together professional landscape architects and designers with volunteer workers, who

have donated more than 60,000 hours in clearing overgrowth and planting new trees and shrubs, as well as creating six gathering spots paved in flagstone.

Free 20-minute tours of the grove are offered from March through October on the third Saturday of the month. On the same days, visitors can take part in volunteer workdays. For more information, go to *aidsmemorial.org* or phone 415/765-0497.

Donors of $1,000 or more can engrave a name in the Circle of Friends to honor someone they love and/or miss, and to help maintain the grove.

off such unusual plants as the kangaroo paw, with its clusters of yellow, green, and red blossoms. Plants from **Chile** include rhubarb with giant leaves that look like dinosaur food and winter's bark, a sacred tree used for healing.

In the **California area** stands a grove of redwood trees more than a hundred years old. At the Japanese **Moon-Viewing Garden,** a pond reflects maple trees by day and the moon by night. In the **Mesoamerican Cloud Forest** are colorful passion vines and tree daisies with large leaves.

Inhale deeply at the **Garden of Fragrance,** whose aromatic plants include rosemary, salvia, and lavender. The garden was designed for blind and visually impaired visitors, with plants chosen for their scents or textures. Birds flock to this warm area of the gardens, so the bronze statue

INSIDER TIP:

Golden Gate Park's botanical garden is another world in winter, with huge pink and white magnolia blossoms hanging on bare branches in the cool, misty air.

—TRULY HERBERT
National Geographic contributor

of St. Francis is appropriate. Planting beds are edged with stones from a 12th-century monastery purchased in Spain by William Randolph Hearst.

The garden's 28,000-volume **Helen Crocker Russell Library of Horticulture** provides help with plant research and presents botanical art exhibits. ■

Flowers thrive in the 55-acre (22 ha) San Francisco Botanical Garden, a green oasis amid city life.

Golden Gate Park West

The rest of Golden Gate Park stretches west toward the ocean. The carefully reclaimed and landscaped area devotes itself to outdoor recreation and enjoyment, with man-made features simulating idyllic rural settings.

Boaters row near the Chinese Moon Pavilion, a popular spot to meditate and appreciate nature.

A pleasant place to stroll or go boating is **Stow Lake,** created in 1893 as a reservoir. It holds 15 million gallons (56.7 million L) of water and feeds directly into the park's irrigation system. The lake encircles **Strawberry Hill,** a woodsy island that rises 425 feet (130 m) and is the park's highest point. (When the park was first being planted, the hill was known as "The Island" because it was the only area of vegetation in a sea of sand. These days it's a true island, surrounded by water.) You can rent rowboats and pedal boats (some with electric power) at the boathouse *(stowlakeboathouse.com).* Two bridges take you to the hill's nearly 1-mile (1.6 km)

perimeter path, to stroll and talk back to quacking ducks. You'll come upon the **Chinese Moon Pavilion,** donated by San Francisco's sister city, Taipei. Octagonal, with red columns and a green-tile roof, the pavilion is intended for people to rest and contemplate nature (including the moon). Nearby **Huntington Falls,** financed by railroad baron Collis P. Huntington in the 1890s, cascades 100 feet (30 m).

If you decide to walk up Strawberry Hill, you'll find California quail running across your path. Look for New Zealand tea trees, which have white flowers in spring; this species is widely used to reclaim sandy areas. The hilltop is usually peaceful and quiet, a place

**Golden Gate
Park West**

▲ Map pp.
174–175

to get above it all, with wonderful views of the park, city, and bay.

North of the lake, the carved sandstone **Prayer Book Cross** was modeled on a Celtic cross on the Scottish island of Iona. Below it, **Rainbow Falls** tumbles down a cliff. When the falls were created in the 1930s, hidden colored lights made rainbows appear in the spray.

Alongside tranquil Lloyd Lake, the **Portals of the Past** is a neoclassical colonnade that once was the entry to the Nob Hill mansion of railroad tycoon Alban Towne. Damaged in the 1906 earthquake, it was moved here as a remembrance. Nearby

Spreckels Lake is popular with model-boat enthusiasts. The park's recreational areas also include fly-casting pools, archery fields, and a Frisbee golf course.

Don't miss the **Buffalo Paddock,** home to shaggy American bison. The park's first bison were brought from Montana in 1890. At the western edge, the **Queen Wilhelmina Tulip Garden** blooms with tulips and Icelandic poppies in March and April. The **Dutch Windmill** once pumped 30,000 gallons (113,000 L) of water hourly to irrigate the park. Built in 1903, the shingled windmill has spars of 102 feet (31 m).

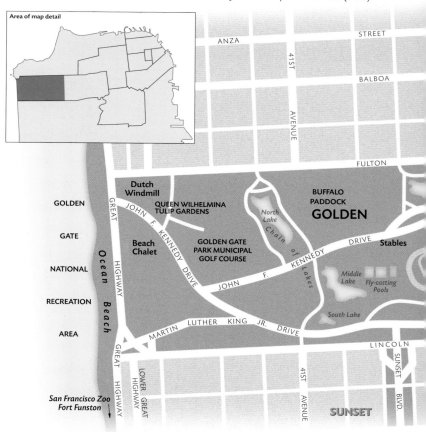

Area of map detail

The **Beach Chalet** is located on the Great Highway that fronts the park and the ocean. Inside, a visitor center has park information and maps. The Spanish colonial building was the last design (1925) of architect Willis Polk, with a restaurant on the upper floor and changing rooms downstairs. In the early 1930s, two sisters opened a tearoom on the first floor, carefully screening off their Oriental carpets from the sandy-footed bathers.

Then in 1936, French artist Lucien Labaudt—a fashion designer who costumed San Francisco's high society—began painting the walls of the first floor with murals depicting life in San Francisco. At painted Baker Beach, children play on the sand, a woman uses a newspaper for a sun hat, and hot dogs grill over a fire. The artist often painted his wife and friends into such scenes. During World War II, the Army occupied the building, which afterward became a bar and social hall. Today, there are two restaurants, one with an ocean view, the other in a garden, sharing their own brewery (*tel 415/386-8439*). ■

Beach Chalet Visitor Center

🅰 Map p. 174
✉ 1000 Great Hwy.
☎ 415/386-8439
🚌 Bus: 5

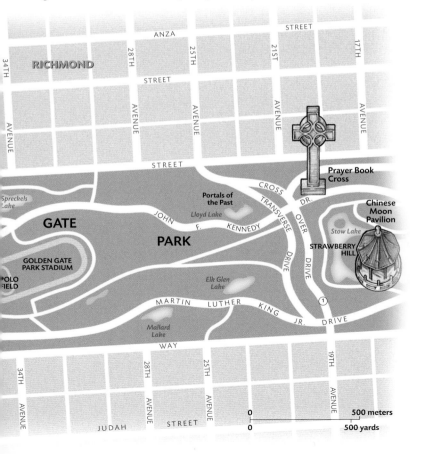

More Places to Visit South of the Park

Fort Funston

Fort Funston, a coastal parkland of bluffs and sand at the south end of Ocean Beach, is part of Golden Gate National Recreation Area (see sidebar p. 130). Among hang gliders, this ranks as one of the nation's top spots for ridge soaring (best March–Oct.), thanks to steady ocean winds and dunes as high as 200 feet (61 m). A hillside deck gives a great view. Bank swallows nest on the northern cliffs (April–July). On the beach, look for sand dollars and shells.

The fort is named for Frederick Funston, the general in charge of relief efforts after the 1906 earthquake. The Battery Davis (1938) housed two 16-inch (40 cm) guns capable of shooting shells 25 miles (40 km). It was the first coastal gun battery to be protected in a fortified enclosure. (With advances in military aircraft, batteries on open ground became easy targets.) Nike missiles guarded the coast from the 1950s until the fort closed in 1963. ⚠ Map p. 174 ✉ Off Skyline Blvd. 0.25 mile (0.4 km) S of John Muir Dr. 🚌 Bus: 18

Ocean Beach

San Francisco's longest beach runs 3.5 miles (5.6 km) south from the Cliff House (see pp. 137–139) along the edge of the **Sunset District,** a residential neighborhood that was once a sand-dune wilderness. The beach is part of the Golden Gate National Recreation Area (see sidebar p. 130) and makes for good strolling, but the water is dangerous; rip currents have swept people away even in shallow water. Many ships foundered along Ocean Beach, and for residents, scavenging was a recreation. At a wreck near the Cliff House in 1887, about 50,000 people came to pick up souvenirs. ⚠ Map p. 174 🚌 Bus: 5, 18, 23, 31, 38, 48, 71; Streetcar: L, N

San Francisco Zoo

Located near the south end of Ocean Beach, the zoo devotes itself to conservation. Lemurs frolic in a forest where visitors observe them at treetop level. Penguins play in the water around their own island, while koalas snooze in a eucalyptus grove. Kids can see meerkats through a low glass wall, nose to nose. Grizzly bears live in a meadow with a stream. An African savanna is home to giraffes, zebras, and ostriches—all viewable from platforms and, via a tunnel, from the middle of the habitat itself. The savanna is linked to the expansive lowland gorilla habitat. Endangered primates housed here include François' langurs, howler monkeys, siamangs, pied tamarins, and macaques. Other zoo denizens range from tarantulas and colorful toucans to anteaters and rhinos. *sfzoo.org* ⚠ Map p. 174 ✉ Great Hwy. near Sloat Blvd. ☎ 415/753-7080 💲 $$$$ 🚌 Bus: 18, 23; Streetcar: L

EXPERIENCE:
Ride the Wild Surf!

The waters of the Pacific Ocean to the west of San Francisco may be frigid, but, as long as you are appropriately insulated in a wet suit, they offer great surfing and kitesurfing. Go out with local outfitters to learn the skills.

Surfing: In Pacifica, 15 miles (24 km) south of the city, NorCal Surf Shop *(tel 650/738-9823, norcalsurfshop.com)* offers lessons that cover technique, surfing etiquette, and ocean safety. Surfboards and wet suits are provided.

Kitesurfing: Programs at Kite the Bay *(tel 415/295-5483, kitethebay.com)* range from three-hour introductory lessons, designed to develop skills and confident handling of wind and tides, to jet-boat–supported excursions under the Golden Gate Bridge.

Civic Center, seat of government and home of arts venues. To the south, SoMa—a lively arts scene with major development projects

Civic Center, SoMa, & the Embarcadero

The Embarcadero and the Ferry Building give San Franciscans a cool setting for ice-skating in winter.

Civic Center, SoMa, & the Embarcadero

These districts show different aspects of the city. The Civic Center assembles what may be the nation's finest collection of beaux arts buildings. In contrast, neighboring South of Market, or SoMa, was designated an industrial zone but has become a focus of culture and tech. The Embarcadero, on the eastern waterfront, draws outdoor enthusiasts.

When the 1906 earthquake and fire smudged out much of San Francisco, it offered a golden opportunity to institute the Burnham Plan (see p. 31), a design for a lovelier city. Only the City Hall was achieved at first. Later, the Civic Center was built up more, but the overall plan for the city was not realized.

The original City Hall, built with shoddy materials under an earlier corrupt city government, tumbled in the earthquake like a house of cards. In 1915, the productive administration of Mayor James "Sunny Jim" Rolph, Jr., built a new City Hall, and the opera house, symphony hall, and other public buildings followed. Today, the Civic Center is an active government hub, a beacon of culture, and a focal point for the arts, as the immense and impressive Asian Art Museum demonstrates.

Surprisingly, the wealthy lived in industrial SoMa, sipping their tea in mansions on Rincon Hill and town houses around South Park. But the development of the cable car in the 1870s lured the rich away to Nob Hill. This left the district to workers' families and to warehouses, factories, and wharves.

After the 1906 earthquake and fire, cheap hotels and rooming houses appeared, mostly occupied by old-age pensioners and day laborers, and by the vagrants and alcoholics of skid row. In 1936, houses on Rincon Hill were removed for the approach to the Bay Bridge. By the mid-1950s, the city made plans to demolish some of the district for urban renewal projects. When developers tried to

move hundreds of residents out of the area in 1967, however, an injunction and lawsuits tied up the development for a decade. Finally, low-cost housing was included as part of the vast Yerba Buena Gardens plan. The Moscone Center opened for conventions in 1981.

In the 1980s, an alternative art scene thrived in SoMa as painters and musicians converted warehouse spaces into studios and homes. When Yerba Buena Gardens and the San Francisco Museum of Modern Art opened in the 1990s, the cultural die was cast. Now this area has upscale hotels, restaurants, museums,

and nightlife. It is home to tech giants, from LinkedIn and Pinterest to Uber. South Park has several small Internet companies.

Meanwhile, the Embarcadero—a curving, breezy thoroughfare running from Fisherman's Wharf past the Ferry Building to Pier 45 at SoMa's eastern edge—lures people eager to breathe fresh salt air, walk dogs, or take a jog. ■

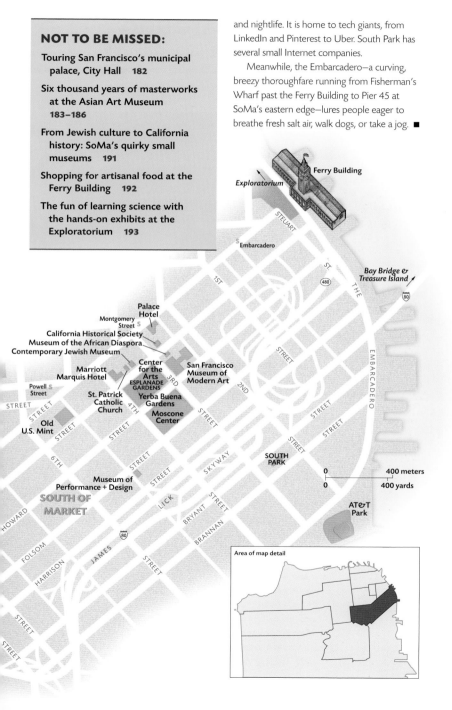

Civic Center & Around

Civic Center Plaza, which stretches east of City Hall, has been restored to its original appearance with a long lawn and rows of English plane trees. The plaza serves as a platform for political protests, as it holds tens of thousands of people.

The Sunday outdoor market at the Civic Center attracts a brisk business each week.

Bill Graham Civic Auditorium

- Map p. 178
- 99 Grove St.
- Bus: 5, 19, 21, 26, 42, 47; Streetcar: J, K, L, M, N; BART: Civic Center

On the south side of the Civic Center Plaza, **Bill Graham Civic Auditorium,** designed by Arthur Brown, Jr., in 1915, was built for the Panama-Pacific International Exposition. It occupies a full city block and is now a top performance venue.

To the east of the plaza are the **Asian Art Museum** (occupying the redesigned beaux arts Old Library Building; see pp. 183–186) and the stunning **San Francisco Main Public Library** by Pei Cobb Freed & Partners, completed in 1995. The library's plaza facade gives a postmodern twist to beaux arts architectural conventions, yet relates to the nearby historic structures by using granite from the same quarry. The back of the public library, though, is contemporary, deconstructionist, and angular.

Between the library buildings, on Fulton Street, stands the 1894 **Pioneer Monument** by Frank Happersberger. The sculptures depict a Spanish friar with an Indian convert, and gold miners striking pay dirt, while bronze panels portray California figures

INSIDER TIP:

The bar on the 39th story of the Marriott Marquis Hotel *(4th St. bet. Market & Mission)* is great for watching the sunset.

—LIZ EINBINDER
City guide,
San Francisco Public Library

such as Padre Junípero Serra and John Sutter.

Just to the east, the rather non-descript **United Nations Plaza** commemorates the 1945 drafting of the United Nations Charter at the War Memorial Opera House and its signing at the Veterans Building. Columns carry the names of United Nations member nations. An **outdoor market** on Sundays and Wednesdays brings affordable produce from local farms to the urban community.

To the west of City Hall, across Van Ness, stand two practically identical beaux arts buildings designed in 1932 by Arthur Brown, Jr. Both buildings honor World War I soldiers. On the right, the **Veterans Building** plays host to small concerts and lectures in the Herbst Theatre.

On the left is the **War Memorial Opera House** (see Travelwise p. 262), whose 3,100 seats fill up for San Francisco's celebrated opera and ballet companies. This was the nation's first opera house to be financed by a municipality.

Just south on Van Ness Street at Grove Street is the curving

glass and granite of the 1980 **Louise M. Davies Symphony Hall** (see Travelwise p. 262), by Skidmore, Owings & Merrill. In addition to housing the city's symphony orchestra, this modern but warm space boasts a computer-assisted organ with 9,235 pipes.

Located in the performing arts district, the $64 million **SFJAZZ Center** bills itself as the nation's first stand-alone building designed for jazz. In the 700-seat auditorium, no listener is more than 50 feet (15 m) from the stage. Some 300 events a year focus on jazz (Wayne Shorter, Chick Corea), but also include world music (Zakir Hussain) and classical (Kronos Quartet).

The **Tenderloin Museum** looks at a notorious area that has also been a fertile artistic ground, where Miles Davis played at a jazz club and the Grateful Dead recorded albums. Immigrants, bar-tenders, and prostitutes tell their stories in audio and video. Walking tours visit single-room-occupancy hotels to meet residents in this very real neighborhood. ∎

The Tenderloin

An unsavory district with sex and drugs for sale, a high crime rate, and home-lessness, the Tenderloin spreads through this area and is bounded roughly by Polk, Mason, O'Farrell Golden Gate, and Market. Use caution when visiting the area. In general, it's not a good place to ven-ture and is best avoided at night.

San Francisco Main Public Library
- 🗺 Map p. 178
- ✉ 100 Larkin St.
- ☎ 415/557-4400
- 🕐 Tours 1st Tues. noon
- 🚌 Bus: 5, 19, 21, 26, 42, 47; Streetcar: J, K, L, M, N; BART: Civic Center

sfpl.org

Veterans Building
- ✉ 401 Van Ness Ave.
- ☎ 415/621-6600
- 🕐 Closed Sat.–Sun.; bldg. tours (also opera house, symphony hall) Mon., 301 Van Ness Ave., 415/552-8338
- 🚌 Bus: 5, 19, 21, 42, 47; Streetcar: J, K, L, M, N

SFJAZZ Center
- 🗺 Map p. 178
- ✉ 201 Franklin St.
- ☎ 866/920-5299
- 🚌 Bus: 5, 6, 16X, 21, 47, 71, 71L, 90; BART: Civic Center

sfjazz.org

Tenderloin Museum
- ✉ 398 Eddy St.
- ☎ 415/351-1912
- 🕐 Closed Mon.
- 🚌 Bus: 27, 31, 38 BART: Powell, Civic Center

tenderloinmuseum .org

City Hall

When the 1989 earthquake damaged City Hall, San Francisco spent some $300 million on seismic retrofitting and refurbishing. Once again, the building gleams like a municipal temple, all granite and marble and gilded ironwork. Filling two city blocks, this is the world's largest building that doesn't touch the ground: Its foundations rest on "base isolators," huge metal and rubber discs designed to absorb the shock of an earthquake.

City Hall

- Map p. 178
- Polk St. bet. Grove St. & McAllister St. Go to Goodlett Pl. kiosk for tours.
- 415/554-6023
- Closed Sat.–Sun.; tours Mon.–Fri. 10 a.m., noon, & 2 p.m.
- Bus: 5, 9, 19, 21, 47, 49; BART: Civic Center

Built in 1915, the City Hall edifice has two colonnaded wings linked by a copper-domed rotunda. The dome resembles that of St. Peter's in the Vatican and soars 307 feet 6 inches (93.7 m), which is taller than the U.S. Capitol in Washington, D.C., by about 40 feet (12 m)—a fact that Mayor Rolph (see p. 178) delighted in pointing out. With the advent of such a building, San Francisco announced that it was no longer a mere frontier town, but the great port of the West Coast and a capital of the Pacific Rim.

The City Hall's French Renaissance Revival design by Arthur Brown, Jr., was influenced by his studies in Paris at the École des Beaux-Arts. It incorporates classical elements such as Doric columns and sculptured pediments; the figures above the Polk Street entrance, carved by Henri Crenier, represent California's agriculture and riches (on the left) and navigational skills (right). They also symbolize San Francisco's role as a link between the riches of California and the mercantile needs of the rest of the world.

Inside the central rotunda gleams a marble floor, while glass lanterns glow in ornate iron fixtures. Fancy plasterwork abounds. The rotunda rises through all four stories to a ring of Corinthian columns and the lofty dome (which is in fact three nesting domes). Ceremonial occasions (such as inaugurations, vote announcements, and lyings-in-state) are staged on the landing of the monumental staircase.

Up the stairs, the Board of Supervisors' chamber is so fine that you almost want to be a politician. Oak-paneled walls glow under an ornate Spanish ceiling of blue-green and gold. Computer terminals at the supervisors' seats look anachronistic, but installing modern electronics was a big part of the building's refurbishment.

In the upstairs mayor's offices in 1978, ex-supervisor Dan White shot and killed Mayor George Moscone and Supervisor Harvey Milk, the nation's first openly gay official. ■

San Francisco's City Hall is specially designed to survive the impact of an earthquake.

Asian Art Museum

With 18,000 objects spanning 6,000 years of history and more than 40 Asian countries, this is the largest museum in the United States devoted exclusively to Asian art and culture. The museum began in 1966 as a means of displaying a vast collection donated by Chicago industrialist Avery Brundage. Its mission is to "spark connections across cultures and through time, igniting curiosity, conversation, and creativity."

The museum's galleries, which display more than 2,000 objects from the collection and introduce all of Asia's major cultures, emphasize three themes: the development of Buddhism; trade and cultural exchange by pilgrims, travelers, and armies; and local beliefs and practices:

India

India is represented by works of art that range from temple sculptures to miniature paintings, from wood carvings to calligraphic scrolls.

Religious statuary in many media (bronze, wood, stone, clay) highlight the collection. A carved schist Bodhisattva Maitreya (2nd–3rd century) represents an enlightened being, called a bodhisattva; this example came from Gandhara, an area influenced by Greco-Roman styles through foreign contact dating to Alexander the Great. A south Indian carved stone Ganesha (13th century) depicts the Hindus' elephant-headed god of wisdom and wealth. A gallery is devoted to Sikh art, the only such exhibit in the Western Hemisphere.

Persian World/West Asia

Art on display from this region (Iran, Iraq, Afghanistan, Turkmenistan, Uzbekistan) begins with Neolithic ceramics (stags, mythical creatures) and ranges through intensely colored Islamic ceramics, jewelry, architectural adornments, bronzes, miniature paintings, jade vessels, and illuminated manuscripts.

Southeast Asia

These galleries hold objects from Thailand, Cambodia, Burma, Laos, Vietnam, Indonesia, Malaysia, and the Philippines. From Thailand come ceramics and a notable collection of paintings, as well as a large collection of Thai and island-nation *krises* (daggers), many elaborately decorated or jeweled, so

Avery Brundage

Avery Brundage's interest in Asian art came from a visit he made to an exhibition of Chinese art at the Royal Academy in London in 1936, after the Winter Olympics in Garmisch-Partenkirchen. The Chicago industrialist was quoted as saying, "We spent a week at the exhibition and I came away so enamored with Chinese art that I've been broke ever since."

Born in Detroit in 1887, Brundage competed in the 1912 Olympics pentathlon and decathlon, placing sixth and sixteenth respectively. He went on to become a successful sports administrator, dying in 1975.

Asian Art Museum

- 🅰 Map p. 178
- ✉ 200 Larkin St.
- ☎ 415/581-3500
- 🕐 Closed Mon.
- 💲 $$$, free 1st Sun.
- 🚍 Bus: 5, 19, 21, 26, 47; Streetcar: J, K, L, M, N, T; BART: Civic Center

asianart.org

they are at once lovely and menacing. One particularly beautiful object in the collection is a gold repoussé dedicatory plaque (perhaps eighth or ninth century) from a Cambodian Hindu temple—a place thought to be the gods' domain on Earth. Angkor Wat is represented by many stone and bronze objects. Shiva and Uma (11th century) are examples of the refined sculptures that the Khmer people of the kingdom of Angkor created to decorate temples.

INSIDER TIP:

Make sure to see the museum's collection of bamboo baskets. It's the largest and finest collection outside of Japan.

—FORREST McGILL
Chief curator,
Asian Art Museum

Himalaya/Tibetan Buddhist World

From Tibet come rare scrolls from the Shalu and Ngor Monasteries. A thunderbolt and bell of gilt metal (15th century) are objects used in Tibetan Buddhist prayers and rituals. A lacquered wood figure, "Simhavaktra Dakini" (18th century), depicts a dancing, lion-faced female guardian of Vajrayana Buddhism who guides mortals on the proper path and can clear away obstacles such as pride and ego. In Tibet's Tantric Buddhism, ritual objects of human bone

are used as reminders that life is brief, death inevitable.

Works from Nepal include colorful cotton mandalas (mystical diagrams to aid meditation) and Buddhist sculptures.

China

As the principal focus of the museum's founding donor, Avery Brundage, the Chinese arts are strongly represented with bronzes, ceramics, calligraphy, sculpture, and painting. Of historical importance are Neolithic oracle bones that record ritual events and represent China's first written language. Also significant is China's oldest lacquer vessel that has a maker's mark (A.D. 1).

A collection of nearly 300 Chinese ritual bronzes, some nearly 3,000 years old, is considered the best outside Asia. The earliest known Chinese Buddha (A.D. 338), a highlight of the collection, is a seated figure of gilt bronze, with eyes and nose that look quite Chinese, indicating an evolution of the Indian style that dominated China's early Buddhist art. Buddhism spread at the close of the Han dynasty (A.D. 220), penetrating a 2,000-year-old Chinese culture that considered itself superior to foreign ideas and that had a state religious cult based on Confucianism. Buddhism was attractive during the era's warfare and famine because it offered all people an end to the cycle of suffering.

Bronze ritual vessels from the Shang dynasty (1122–1028 B.C.) include an appealing rhinoceros whose naturalistic shape cleverly

The Asian Art Museum houses 18,000 objects of art, including this 18th-century representation of the Buddhist deity Simhavaktra Dakini in the Himalaya and Tibetan Buddhist World Gallery.

suits its function as a wine container. Ceramics range from a Neolithic earthenware jug with a roof-shaped top (2500–1500 B.C.) to pieces from the Song dynasty (A.D. 960–1279) glazed in green celadon. A tomb figurine from the Tang dynasty (A.D. 618–907) depicts a camel in three-color *sancai* glaze. The Tang dynasty developed porcelain, a hard white translucent ceramic made by firing a pure clay and then glazing it. China's first blue-and-white porcelain appeared early in the Ming dynasty (A.D. 1368–1644).

The collection also includes fan painting, and calligraphy on paper from the Ming dynasty. Hanging scrolls use varied textures and tones of ink to evoke exquisite landscapes of mist-shrouded mountains, foliage, and water.

Among the collection's more than 200 jade pieces, one standout is a late Neolithic *cong* (3100–2200 B.C.), a short tube that is square on the outside and round on the inside; it was probably used in rituals to worship the Earth. A rare *bi* disk (2500 B.C.) has a round shape with a central hole and symbolizes the sky.

The collection is rich in Qing dynasty (1644–1911) jades with auspicious meanings. These include a 19th-century openwork carving of the "Three Plenties" represented as fruits: a Buddha's-hand *citron* (blessings), a peach (longevity), and a pomegranate (fertility, symbolized by its seeds). A modern tour de force is an incense burner with ten musicians intricately carved in translucent white jade.

Korea

The oldest objects in the collection, which is the finest outside Korea, are two Bronze Age slate daggers (600 and 500 B.C.). Other important pieces include bronze Buddhas, earthenware and stoneware vessels, and hanging scrolls. A duck-shaped earthenware vessel, probably made for ritual purposes, represents the Three Kingdoms (57 B.C.–A.D. 668), a period famous for earthenware and stoneware in imaginative forms.

The Unified Silla Kingdom (A.D. 668–935) presided over the golden age of Buddhist art. Its capital, Kyongju, was described as having Buddhist temples as numerous as the stars and pagodas lined up like flying geese. A large eighth-century gilt bronze figure of Amitabha Buddha—the Buddha of eternal life and boundless light—is notably fine.

The Buddhist Goryeo dynasty (A.D. 935–1392) produced many rich paintings, such as the 14th-century "Buddha Amitabha With the Eight Great Bodhisattvas," while the ensuing Joseon dynasty (A.D. 1392–1910) embraced stern neo-Confucianism. The "Portrait of Sosan Taesa" (late 16th century), painted in ink and colors on silk, depicts an elegantly dressed monk who taught the unity of Confucianism, Buddhism, and Taoism.

Japan

No U.S. museum offers a broader survey of Japanese art, including bronze ritual bells, gilded wood Buddhas, dry lacquer figures, glazed stoneware, porcelain, hanging scrolls, and rare painted screens.

The earthenware "Standing Warrior" (6th century), wearing a tunic, puffy pantaloons, and a helmet, was a burial object meant to show off the high economic and social position of the deceased. Among glazed stoneware, look for the tea bowl with dragon medallions (mid-17th century) by Nonomura Ninsei, one of the first potters to mark his works with his own seal. This large bowl would keep tea warm longer for guests in winter, and it is partly glazed black like a winter night.

Notable among the museum's screens is "The Path Through Mount Utsu" (18th century), portraying a scene from *The Tales of Ise,* a 10th-century poetic narrative that unfolds around a romantic journey. ∎

Confucius & Jade

Popular with visitors to the Asian Art Museum are objects made of jade, a mineral whose qualities Chinese philosopher Confucius (551–479 B.C.) likened to those of a true gentleman: "Its polish and brilliancy represent the white of purity. Its perfect compactness and extreme hardness represent the sureness of intelligence. Its angles, which do not cut although they seem sharp, represent justice . . . Its interior flaws, always revealing themselves through its transparency, call to mind sincerity. Its iridescent brightness represents heaven."

Yerba Buena & Around

Yerba Buena is a dynamic SoMa neighborhood. A $2-billion-dollar redevelopment project was overlaid on an existing neighborhood whose residents ranged from blue collar to skid row. Now increasingly white collar, Yerba Buena includes the San Francisco Museum of Modern Art, Moscone Center, Center for the Arts, luxury hotels, residential units, restaurants, and stores.

Fronting Mission between Third and Fourth, **Yerba Buena Gardens** is built (although the casual visitor wouldn't know it) atop the underground Moscone Center. Nearly 750,000 square feet (69,700 sq m) of convention exhibit space are covered with a five-acre (2 ha) oval of grass, trees, and flowers called the Esplanade. (Fun fact: The center's roof couldn't support heavy soil, so under the lawn are blocks of Styrofoam.) Locals and visitors come here to chill out, have lunch, and perhaps hear a free concert.

A **memorial to Rev. Martin Luther King, Jr.,** consists of an artificial waterfall and grotto, where quotations from the civil rights leader are chiseled into granite and glass: "We will not be satisfied until justice rolls down like water and righteousness like a mighty stream." A promenade and cafés line the terrace.

On the northeastern side of the complex, the **Yerba Buena Center for the Arts** (YBCA; 701 Mission St., tel 415/978-2787, ybca .org) offers adventurous contemporary work: visual arts at the **Galleries** (closed Mon.–Tues., $$, free first Tues. and 3rd Thurs. eve.), performances at the **Forum,** and film/video at the **Screening Room.** Fumihiko Maki's design for

the YBCA building (1993) evokes a sleek factory sheathed in aluminum and glass. Inside, windows frame carefully chosen views, in the manner of "borrowed scenery" in Japanese architecture. At the adjacent **Yerba Buena Center for the Arts Theater** (700 Howard St., tel 415/978-2787), designed in 1993 by James Stewart Polshek, industrial-looking exposed beams and lighting hardware make it seem as if you're sitting backstage.

Yerba Buena Gardens

 Map p. 179

✉ Bounded by Market, Harrison, 2nd, & 5th Sts.

🚌 Bus: 9, 12, 14, 15, 30, 38, 45, 76; BART: Embarcadero, Montgomery, Powell St.

yerbabuenagardens .org

Modern buildings dwarf 1909 St. Patrick Catholic Church.

San Francisco Museum of Modern Art

- Map p. 179
- 151 3rd St.
- 415/357-4000
- Museum reopens in 2016. Check website for opening hours.
- Check website for admission prices.

sfmoma.org

Also on top of Moscone Center, the **Yerba Buena Ice Skating & Bowling Center** (tel 415/820-3532, skatebowl.com) has an NHL-size rink and 12 lanes. A multimedia art and tech studio, the **Children's Creativity Center** (tel 415/820-3320, creativity.org) lets kids try stop-motion clay animation or make a music video. On the 1906 **Looff Carousel** (4th St. at Howard St., $$), originally from Playland-at-the-Beach, 62 brightly painted wooden giraffes, bejeweled horses, and other animals whirl in a glass pavilion illuminated at night.

INSIDER TIP:

A favorite brewery is 21st Amendment (563 2nd St.). Its Hell or High Watermelon Wheat beer is great.

—RYAN GADDUANG
Supervisor, Sir Francis Drake Hotel

San Francisco Museum of Modern Art (SFMoMA)

The museum dates to 1935 and was first housed in the War Memorial Veterans Building. In the 1940s, it gave Jackson Pollock his first major solo show and acquired his early masterpiece, "Guardians of the Secret" (1943). The museum also exhibited work by other charter members of the abstract expressionist movement—Arshile Gorky, Clyfford Still, Mark Rothko, and Robert Motherwell—back when they were art-world nobodies.

Over the years, the museum continued to expand its holdings, in 1995 moving to a new building designed by Swiss architect Mario Botta, whose powerful design is a mass of geometric forms. A brick facade steps back from the street in three huge, windowless blocks. On top rises a central cylinder finished in bands of black and silvery gray granite.

The tower is sliced off at an angle to create a skylight, larger than the western rose window of Paris's Notre Dame Cathedral. (Although widely praised, the design wasn't popular with everyone. The late newspaper columnist Herb Caen wrote that the skylight looked like the funnel on an ocean liner. Later he apologized, making this correction: "The building looks more like a giant toaster extruding a cheese Danish.")

The museum's 2016 expansion rises ten stories—a rippling white slab that added 235,000 square feet (21,830 sq m) of space and cost $555 million. One of its purposes is to house the Fisher Collection of 1,100 works by 185 major artists, donated by the founders of the Gap.

Its design, by the architectural firm Snøhetta, aims to connect the museum to the city around it. A glass-walled gallery faces the street and puts art on free view to passersby.

One of two new outdoor terraces has expansive city views from the seventh floor.

For performance art, multiscreen projections, and special installations, there's a "white box" space with advanced lighting and acoustics. The expansion also created of vivid colors and strong, often distorted, forms. Also represented are modernist Mexican painting (Rivera, Tamayo), abstract expressionism, Bay Area figurative art (Joan Brown's 1964 "Noel in the Kitchen"), funk, and contemporary art (Warhol, Polke, Koons).

Wenda Gu's "United Nations—Babel of the Millennium" installation is a wall of words.

the nation's largest exhibition space for photography.

Highlights of the SFMoMA Collections:

Among the museum's vast collections of painting and sculpture, early modernism is represented by Cézanne, Brancusi, Gris, Picasso, and Matisse, whose "Femme au Chapeau" ("Woman With a Hat," 1905) is the museum's most renowned picture. It is a classic example of fauvism, an early 20th-century French style

Noteworthy examples include Robert Rauschenberg's "Erased de Kooning Drawing" (1953), in which he tried to expunge the other artist's drawing—and, symbolically, the practices of abstract expressionism. Rauschenberg's conceptual "Automobile Tire Print" (1953) was produced by having his friend, composer John Cage, drive a Model A Ford over art paper as he continually re-inked one of the tires; the 22-foot-long (6.7 m) tire print is shown unrolled like a Japanese scroll.

The museum owns René Magritte's "Les Valeurs Personelles" ("Personal Values," 1952), one of the artist's masterpieces, and Piet Mondrian's unfinished "New York City III" (1942–1944), which still shows the strips of colored tape the artist employed to refine the placement of his vertical and horizontal lines before painting them in oil. Andy Warhol's "Red Liz" (1963) is an early portrait of Elizabeth Taylor in lavender, black, and turquoise set against a red background.

Other areas of the collection focus on architecture, furniture, and product and graphic design, with pieces by Bernard Maybeck, Willis Polk, Frank Lloyd Wright, and Frank Gehry. Highlights include an entire conference room designed by the revolutionary Charles and Ray Eames, as well as more than 400 rock-and-roll posters.

The museum's photography collection begins with the 1840s and represents each of the major developments and movements from 19th-century photographers to contemporary artists. There are images by Alfred Stieglitz, Edward Weston, Ansel Adams, and European avant-gardists of the 1920s and 1930s, as well as conceptual work by Duane Michaels and manipulated images by Ray Metzker. A collection of films, videos, and computer work represents electronic media.

The Fisher Collection brings new depth to the museum's holdings of Pop Art, figurative art, minimalism, abstraction, photo-realism, and color-field painting. It includes seminal works by Alexander Calder, Chuck Close, Roy Lichtenstein, Richard Serra, Andy Warhol, and more.

In the Area

Several museums are located in the neighborhood, including the **California Historical Society** *(678 Mission St., tel 415/357-1848, calhist.org, closed Mon., $$),* which mounts exhibitions from its collections, including paintings by Albert Bierstadt and William Keith; furniture, silver, and costumes; and photographs documenting California history.

"Femme au Chapeau" ("Woman With a Hat," 1905), by Matisse, is a SFMoMA highlight.

Art-chitecture: Contemporary Jewish Museum

At this museum wedged into a courtyard, the visual pyrotechnics are typical of architect Daniel Liebeskind, who also won the competition to plan the new World Trade Center. The design adapts a 1907 redbrick power substation into which collides a new, 85-foot-tall (26 m) tumbling cube (2008)—together neatly conveying the $47.5 million museum's mission to blend tradition and innovation.

Liebeskind's off-kilter cube is sheathed with more than 3,000 blue steel panels that subtly change shade according to the weather, time of day, and viewer's location. A second jagged shape emerges from the roof. The two forms symbolize Hebrew letters (*chet* and *yud*), part of the traditional phrase L'Chaim, meaning "To Life!" In fact, the power substation brought energy back to San Francisco after the 1906 earthquake and fire—and today's museum adds a dynamic charge to the city as a place to engage with Jewish culture.

The **Museum of the African Diaspora** (*685 Mission St., tel 415/358-7200, moadsf.org, closed Mon.–Tues., $$*) looks at the journeys and achievements of Africa-descended people. With subjects that range from slavery to culinary traditions, the museum explores the culture, art, and history of these scattered groups.

INSIDER TIP:

SFMoMA's Museum Store offers the West Coast's finest selection of modern and contemporary art books, as well as exceptional design objects.

—KAY HANKINS
National Geographic contributor

The **Contemporary Jewish Museum** (*736 Mission St., tel 415/655-7800, thecjm.org, closed Wed., $$$*) presents modern perspectives on Jewish culture and history. With no permanent collection, it relies on exhibits, live music, film screenings, and lectures. For intellectual sustenance, Wise Sons deli serves Jewish comfort food, ranging from matzo ball soup to pastrami sandwiches.

Redbrick **St. Patrick Catholic Church** (*756 Mission St.*) dates from 1909; the interior glows with stained-glass windows on Celtic themes and marble from Ireland. In the background looms the **Marriott Marquis Hotel** (1989), a controversial, glitzy building that apparently got lost on the way to Las Vegas.

Rotating exhibits at the **Museum of Performance + Design** are drawn from archives of 3.5 million performance-related materials ranging from the Gold Rush to the present day: vintage playbills, photos, posters, sheet music, radio interviews, musical theater recordings, and more. Exhibit themes have ranged from ballet as a form of resistance in Soviet Russia to rare lobby cards from the early days of the San Francisco Opera. ∎

Museum of Performance + Design

- Map p. 179
- 893 B Folsom St.
- 415/255-4800
- Closed Sun.–Tues.; open for research Wed.–Thurs.
- Bus: 12, 27, 30, 45; BART: Powell

mpdsf.org

Ferry Building

The Ferry Building centers around a 660-foot-long (201 m) skylit nave that evokes the market halls of Europe and is lined with food shops, cafés, and restaurants. Still, with its restored brick arches and marble floors, it is easy to picture the days when the Ferry Building was the world's second busiest transit terminal.

Ferry Building

 Map p. 179

✉ Foot of Market St.

🕐 Tours Tues., Thurs., Sat. through City Guides, sfcityguides.org

🚌 Bus: 1, 14, 32; Streetcar: F, J, K, L, M, N; BART: Embarcadero

ferrybuilding marketplace.com

The 1898 Ferry Building by Arthur Page Brown is a beautiful sight, especially when illuminated at night. Its 235-foot (71.5 m) clock tower, designed by Willis Polk, survived the 1906 and 1989 earthquakes. But ferry service couldn't survive the building of the bay's bridges in the 1930s. Today, though, ferry use is on the rise again, with 11,000 commuters every weekday traveling from Marin and the East Bay. Behind the Ferry Building is a 1988 bronze **sculpture of Mahatma Gandhi.**

Since its 2003 renovation as a public market, food lovers throng here every day to shop for wine, meats, oysters, herbs, tea, and gourmet cookware. Items prefaced with the word "artisanal," including cheese, olive oil, bread, and chocolate, also draw a brisk business. Occasional events range from celebrity-chef book signings to a "fungus festival." Three times a week there's an outdoor **farmers market** *(tel 415/291-3276, cuesa.org, Tues. & Thurs. 10 a.m.– 2 p.m., Sat. 8 a.m.–2 p.m.).* Among the restaurants and cafés, the acclaimed Slanted Door (see Travelwise p. 255) serves Vietnamese cuisine in a modern space with windows overlooking the bay. ■

EXPERIENCE: Top Chef Cooking Demos

Want to polish your skills in the kitchen? Top San Francisco chefs show you their special secrets at cooking demonstrations at the Ferry Plaza farmers market. You can taste their delectable creations and even take home the recipes. Culinary coaching might focus on a one-pot meal one day and a gourmet dessert the next. The chefs use seasonal, sustainable ingredients bought that morning at the farmers market. The demonstrations are sponsored by **CUESA**, the Center for Urban Education about Sustainable Agriculture *(tel 415/291-3276, cuesa.org, Feb.–Dec.).*

CUESA also organizes free seasonal events, each centered around a product

or agricultural theme—for instance, the Stone Fruit Celebration or the Goat Festival. In addition, CUESA arranges all-day tours, departing from the Ferry Building, to visit area farms. You eat a meal prepared with fresh produce from the farm, a great way to "take in" what you learn.

Are you more of a do-it-yourself type? Gather your own vittles in San Francisco's parks during wild food walks with **Forage SF** *(foragesf.com/wild-food -walks, $$$$$).* The natural noshes you discover may be anything from wild currants to nasturtium flowers for accenting salads. Take them home, along with your new skill at urban foraging.

Exploratorium

The original hands-on science museum has moved from the Palace of Fine Arts to Pier 15, with triple the exhibition space. This fun house of learning, great for kids and adults alike, explores science, art, and human perception.

At the Exploratorium, visitors learn through hands-on exhibits like this soap film experiment.

You'll hear amazed laughter and many a "Wow!" Among the wonders are magnetic sand and the **Tornado,** which lets you dance with an ever changing column of fog. In one exhibit, the air is painted with brushstrokes of color from the sun. In another, people seem to shrink and grow in a distorted room. The pitch black **Tactile Dome** has you crawling through textured chambers using only your sense of touch. In the **Life gallery,** a research-grade video microscope lets you see stem cells that have been turned into beating heart cells—cutting-edge research that's rare to see at any museum.

Focusing on the museum's natural and man-made surroundings, the all-glass **Bay Observatory** is crowned by a circular opening in the ceiling that turns the entire gallery into a timepiece tracking the sun's movement. Want to create or invent something? Head for the **Tinkering Studio** to dismantle teddy bears or build yourself the world's largest marble machine—all in the spirit of learning.

Outside, changing exhibits include a 27-foot-tall (8 m) "harp" strummed by the wind, a cylindrical mirror that creates a Renaissance-era visual illusion, and a 60-yard-long (55 m) "echo tube." ■

Exploratorium

Map p. 179

Pier 15/17 on the Embarcadero

415/528-4444

Closed Mon.

$$$$$

Bus: 1, 10, 12, 31, 38, 39; Streetcar: F; BART: Embarcadero

exploratorium.edu

More Places to Visit in Civic Center, SoMa, & the Embarcadero

The Embarcadero

This breezy curve of road was built atop a seawall along the eastern waterfront. People stroll, ride bikes, walk dogs, jog, and eat at the Ferry Building or Red's Java House, a funky breakfast-and-burger joint perched by Pier 30 since 1923. Public artwork includes "Cupid's Span" (Claes Oldenburg, Coosje van Bruggen), a 60-foot-high (18 m) bow and arrow made of steel and painted fiberglass, and set into the grass at Rincon Park as a symbol of love; the bowstring and arrow correspond to the Bay Bridge's cables and towers. ▲ Map p. 179 ✉ On bay bet. AT&T Park & Fisherman's Wharf

Old U.S. Mint

The old mint was built in 1874, when the city's original mint couldn't process all the wealth of Nevada's Comstock Lode. The mint is a neoclassical building with a solid granite foundation and Doric columns. The mint stamped out vast numbers of silver dollars that bore the "S" mint mark (for San Francisco). The mint building survived the 1906 fire, thanks to employees who helped wield a fire hose, thus rescuing $200 million in silver and gold from a meltdown. The mint went out of service in 1937. ▲ Map p. 179 ✉ 88 5th St. 🕐 Closed to the public 🚌 Bus: 14, 26, 27; Streetcar: J, K, L, N

San Francisco–Oakland Bay Bridge

Forever playing second banana to the graceful span across the Golden Gate, the San Francisco–Oakland Bay Bridge opened in 1936 as the world's longest steel structure. The $70 million bridge extends some 8.4 miles (13.5 km)—an impressive seven times longer than its golden rival.

Its two sections meet at Yerba Buena Island, where cars pass through a tunnel. The spans join at an immense concrete anchorage reaching 220 feet (67 m) below the bay. In the 1989 earthquake, part of the upper deck collapsed onto the lower, killing one person. A new eastern span opened in 2013 but has had problems, including cracked anchor rods. On a happier note, artist Leo Villareal placed 25,000 white lights on the western span's vertical cables. Flashing in patterns, they create the world's largest LED light sculpture. ▲ Map p. 179

South Park

Established by Englishman George Gordon in 1855, South Park was modeled on parkside developments in London; each resident of the original town houses set around the long oval park had a key to the gate. After the neighborhood lost its cachet in the early 1870s, cheap rooming houses and machine shops moved in. In 1876, writer Jack London was born at Third and Brannan, an event commemorated by a plaque on the corner bank building.

Still industrial, the neighborhood has seen an influx of designers and tech companies, restaurants and bars. Much new energy has come as fans throng **AT&T Park,** the San Francisco Giants' state-of-the-art baseball stadium on the bay at the Embarcadero's south margin. *sanfrancisco.giants.mlb.com* ▲ Map p. 179 ✉ King & 3rd Sts., by China Basin ☎ 415/972-2000 (Giants tickets)

Districts with a zest that makes each worth visiting: the Mission, the main Hispanic quarter, and the Castro, the city's gay capital

The Mission & Castro Districts

Padre Junípero Serra, founder of the mission system

The Mission & Castro Districts

Located neither close to the bay's blue waters nor high on panoramic hills, these southern districts of San Francisco have been a sort of backwater, largely bypassed by tourism. Genuine, vital, down to earth, they feel like neighborhoods and are worth checking out.

The colorful, diverse Mission District (bounded approximately by Potrero Avenue and 14th, 25th, and Church Streets) has the city's greatest concentration of Hispanic residents, most from Mexico and Central America. You'll smell south-of-the-border foods at taquerías (taco shops) and hear salsa music. Hispanic roots date to 1776, when Padre Francisco Palou celebrated Mass under a brush shelter in this wide valley. In 1791, Franciscan fathers built Mission Dolores, the district's namesake.

By 1990, Latinos made up more than half the Mission's population. Next came women opening stores and bars, and more recently hipsters and tech workers, many commuting to Silicon Valley. Gentrification had begun.

Gays started flocking to the Castro District in the 1970s. Somewhat isolated

NOT TO BE MISSED:

Learning about the city's early history at Mission Dolores   198–199

Full immersion in multiculturalism along Valencia or 24th Street   199

Enjoying the range of Chicano/ Latino art on display at Galeria de la Raza   199

Catching the San Francisco spirit with the colorful array of characters at play in Mission Dolores Park   199

Getting close to the Mission District's wildly colorful murals and taking some eye-catching photos to send home or post on social media   200–201

A trip through the city's gay community via the Cruisin' the Castro Walking Tours   203

Stepping into another era at the Castro Theatre, a 1920s movie palace   203

without major transit, the Castro made a perfect separate world. Men restored Victorian houses, barhopped, and opened businesses. Today, San Francisco has 125,000 LGBT (lesbian, gay, bisexual, transgender) residents, fifteen percent of the population, and is the nation's top gay-friendly destination. ■

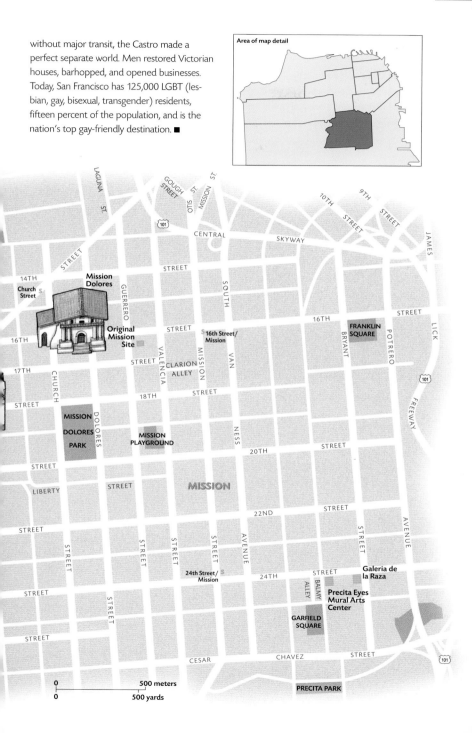

Area of map detail

Mission Dolores

San Francisco's oldest building, finished in 1791, Mission Dolores exudes an air of the past. Swing open the wooden door to the chapel. Adobe walls damp the noise of the outside world. Incense rises toward a beamed ceiling painted in zigzag stripes of gray, white, red, and ocher, a design taken from the baskets of the Ohlone Indians who lived here before the Spanish came.

Mission Dolores's 3-foot-thick (0.9 m) adobe walls house the chapel and its redwood beams.

Mission Dolores

- Map p. 197
- 16th St. & Dolores St.
- 415/621-8203
- $$
- Bus: 14, 22, 33, 49; Streetcar: J; BART: 16th St. or 24th St.

missiondolores.org

The sixth of the 21 California missions founded by Franciscan padres between San Diego and Sonoma, it is officially called Mission San Francisco de Asís. The mission was originally established in 1776 about two blocks east, near a small stream the Spanish named Nuestra Señora de los Dolores (Our Lady of Sorrows). Hence the mission's popular name, Mission Dolores. Padre Francisco Palou designed the adobe chapel. The roof is supported by the original redwood logs, lashed together with rawhide (and later reinforced with steel). At the front of the chapel, the baroque *reredos*

(decorative altar) was brought from Mexico in 1796, the two gilded side altars in 1810.

Outside the north door, a **diorama,** made for the 1939 Golden Gate International Exposition, depicts the mission quadrangle in 1799 in its original pastoral setting. In the **mission museum,** a patch of the wall's cement overlay has been removed to reveal the actual adobe, a mixture of clay and straw. Religious articles from the mission era are on view, with a book listing people buried in the cemetery. Some 5,500 Native Americans lie in unmarked graves. Buried in places of honor are the first Mexican governor of Alta California, Capt. Luis Antonio Arguello, and Padre Palou. A statue depicts Padre Junípero Serra, founder of the mission system.

Mission Neighborhood

A mix of residents makes for a lively area. For Latin street life, head to 24th Street (Mission Street to Potrero Avenue), where restaurants cater to locals from Mexico and Guatemala, the air is scented with fresh churros (fried donuts), and grocery stores carry nopales (cactus leaves). Near Bryant Street stands **Galeria de la Raza,** a gallery of Chicano and other Latino art. Residents also like to celebrate with gusto: Cinco de Mayo (first weekend in May), Festival de Carnaval (Memorial Day weekend), and Día de los Muertos (Day of the Dead, November 1).

Valencia Street (16th to 24th Streets) reveals changes in the neighborhood, as new groups have joined the Hispanic community—feminist/lesbian, hipster, techie. When cool young San Franciscans say "I live in the Mission," this is the part they mean. Many tech employees reside here but ride to work at Google and other Silicon Valley companies on private company buses. Businesses along Valencia range from thrift stores to coffeehouses, bars, and music shops.

La Victoria Bakery embodies the Mission's changing character. It still makes *pan dulce* with a 60-year-old recipe, but has added vegan items and organic coffee. La Victoria offers classes (cookies, cupcakes), and a guest baker teaches sourdough bread making *(sourflour.org).*

For Anglo heritage, visit Liberty Street *(part of Liberty Hill Historic District bet. Dolores, Mission, 20th, & 23rd Sts.)* to see Victorian architecture styles: No. 159 (Italianate, 1878), No. 123 (Queen Anne, 1890s), and Nos. 111–121 (Stick, 1880s). ∎

Galeria de la Raza

⬛ Map p. 197
✉ 2857 24th St.
☎ 415/826-8009
galeriadelaraza.org

La Victoria Bakery

✉ 2937 24th St.
☎ 415/642-7120
lavictoriabakery.com

EXPERIENCE: Hang Out at Mission Dolores Park

From Aztec ceremonial dancers to yogis standing on their heads, from Frisbee tossers to questionably talented folk singers (for whom the times they aren't a changin' much), frolicking dogs, and a parade of San Francisco characters—that's the cast at Dolores Park. This 16-acre (6.5 ha) gathering spot is especially popular on sunny weekends and has great views of the city.

Take a cue from the locals, who bring lunches from nearby eateries. Pick up bagels or a breakfast burrito at **Dolores Park Cafe** *(18th & Dolores Sts.).* **Bi-Rite Market** *(3639 18th St., about a block from park)* uses local farm produce and humanely raised meats for its soups and sandwiches. At their creamery across the street, pick up brown sugar ice cream with ginger caramel swirl, or sorbet made from organic fruit. In the park itself, vendors sell cookies, ice pops, and other munchies. (Suggestion: You might inquire what's in the brownies before you eat them . . .)

On the last Saturday of each month *(except Dec.–Feb.),* there's an event with true San Francisco spirit: the **Really Really Free Market.** People bring food, usable items, and their skills to give away, simply for the sake of giving. Dolores Park is one of a kind.

Murals of the Mission District

A long-standing tradition in Latin America, outdoor murals add color to the streets of the Mission District. Some illustrate Latino daily life, family, work, and play. Others give groups without media access a way to express their political views, or to depict the struggles and achievements of their races. Some murals simply celebrate personal fantasies. Hundreds of murals adorn everything from banks to schools.

The 300-foot-long (91.4 m) Carnaval Mural on Harrison Street makes a vibrant sidewalk gallery.

Mural painting has been going on in San Francisco since at least the 1930s, when noted Mexican muralist Diego Rivera created work at the San Francisco Art Institute, the Pacific Exchange, and City College of San Francisco. Another influence was David Alfaro Siqueiros (1896–1974), a Mexican mural painter who depicted political protest and revolution. In the 1960s, he improved the technical methods of outdoor painting. Mural painting in the Mission District took off in the following decade.

Some Mission murals were funded by the city for their cultural and artistic merit; others are spontaneous, funky, and homemade.

Precita Eyes Mural Arts Center *(2981 24th St. at Harrison St., tel 415/285-2287, precita eyes.org)* sells a "Mission Mural Walk Map" and leads walking tours. The Precita Avenue branch *(348 Precita Ave.)* holds classes.

Murals & Where to See Them

Balmy Alley *(off 24th St. bet. Harrison St. & Treat Ave.):* On garage doors, fences, and walls, colorful murals with names such as "Indigenous Eyes" reflect Latin American political concerns. The first murals here were painted by schoolchildren, and in 1984 a group called PLACA (slang for a graffiti artist's "tag") created nearly 30 murals.

Carnaval Mural *(Harrison St. at 19th St., Precita Eyes Muralists):* The 300-foot-long (91.4 m) mural depicts the dancers, costumes, and masks of the Carnaval Festival.

BART Station Mural *(24th St. at Mission St., Michael Rios):* In depicting a BART commuter train running across the bent backs of "the people," this 1975 mural protests the extra sales tax that paid for San Francisco's rapid transit, which in turn threatened the Mission District with high-rise development.

"500 Years of Resistance" *(St. Peter's Church, 24th St. at Florida St., Isaias Mata):* A study of racial and economic struggle, the mural shows Mexico's Padre Miguel Hidalgo and Martin Luther King, Jr.

Clarion Alley Mural Project *(bet. Mission, Valencia, 17th, & 18th Sts.):* This block-long street-art scene reflects social inclusiveness and aesthetic variety. The murals were created by a palette of peoples: Latino, Caucasian, African-American, Native American, Asian, Indian, gay, and disabled. From spray-can murals to pieces in folk-art styles and conceptual projects, the area pops with colorful images, fluorescent graffiti-style lettering, social ideas, and visual variety.

Some murals are political ("Stick It to the Man"); others illustrative, hallucinogenic, or cartoonish. The work began in 1993 with a volunteer artists' collective called CAMP (Clarion Alley Mural Project) and was originally inspired by the murals on Balmy Alley.

"New World Tree" *(Mission Playground pool, 19th St. near Valencia St.; Cervantes, Alicia, Martinez):* A tree with a man, woman, and children suggests an Eden of mixed cultures.

Other murals: Mission Cultural Center *(2868 Mission St.);* Cesar Chavez Elementary School *(22nd St. at Shotwell St.);* Flynn Elementary School *(Harrison St. at Cesar Chavez St.).*

Balmy Alley showcases some of the 200-plus murals that adorn walls and garage doors of the area.

The Castro

The Castro is the rainbow heart of San Francisco's gay and lesbian community. Bounded by Market, Noe, 20th, Diamond, and 17th Streets, it looks much like any other affluent neighborhood—if not in its social life, then in its streets, shops, and houses. On special occasions there's plenty of local color: Just consider the daytime costume party and beerfest that is the Castro Street Fair, held on the first Sunday in October.

The neon of the Castro Theatre, reflected in a car window, serves as a beacon in the gay neighborhood.

The Castro

⬛ Map pp. 196–197

🚌 Bus: 24, 33, 35, 37; Streetcar: F

The neighborhood was definitely in a party mood during the 1970s. "Castro clones" (men with tight jeans and t-shirts, combat boots, and beards or mustaches) cruised the bars and bathhouses. But in the 1980s, the catastrophe of AIDS brought a more sober mood. Social services appeared, promoting safe sex and testing.

Today the Castro draws both straight and LGBT tourists. Stroll along the streets on a Saturday afternoon or see a movie at the Castro Theatre, where the audience often creates a participatory theater of its own.

In this part of town, you'll definitely see things you don't see every day. One comfortable introduction to the colorful

Castro Theatre

Want a perfect place to catch a movie? This vintage cinema palace (*429 Castro St., tel 415/621-6120, castrotheatre.com*), designed by Timothy L. Pflueger in 1922 in Spanish Renaissance Revival style, resembles a Mexican cathedral—if cathedrals had pink-and-blue neon signs. The 1,450-seat auditorium calls to mind a Bedouin tent, with drapery, ropes, and tassels. The vertical neon sign is an addition from the late 1930s.

The theater styles itself as "an acre of seats in a palace of dreams." Films shown here range from indies and campy cult classics to first-run movies and silents. (The digital projection system can mimic the look of an old silent film, speeding up or slowing down the action on screen.)

In 1977, the theater was designated a City of San Francisco registered landmark. It is one of the few remaining movie palaces from the 1920s that is still in operation. A "mighty" Wurlitzer organ is played before shows.

INSIDER TIP:

For native plants and city views, visit Corona Heights Park (*Roosevelt & Museum Ways*); it's next to the Randall Museum, which features natural history.

—KATHY AMENDOLA
Cruisin' the Castro Walking Tours

neighborhood is via **Cruisin' the Castro Walking Tours.**

The neighborhood's main thoroughfare is **Castro Street** (*Market St. to 19th St.*). At the busy intersection with Market Street, **Harvey Milk Plaza** was named for the nation's first openly gay elected official. A former Wall Street financial analyst, Milk became a city supervisor in 1977. He also ran a camera store in the Castro whose sign read: "Yes, We Are Very Open." Milk was responsible for passing a 1978 gay rights ordinance, but was killed that year by former supervisor Dan White. The murder galvanized gay political activity. The 2008 film Milk, starring Sean Penn, was based on his life. During protests and celebrations, traffic at this intersection usually grinds to a halt, with Castroites takin' it to the street. The trees along the street are Canary Island palms.

Along **Market Street** (*Castro St. to Church St.*) shops proffer trendy clothing, home accessories, gay and lesbian books, flowers, and more. Look for shops and bars with revealing, funny names such as Rock Hard and Moby Dick.

Calling itself San Francisco's "queer Smithsonian," the **GLBT History Museum** (*4127 18th St., tel 415/621-1107, glbthistory .org, closed Tues., $$, free 1st Weds.*) explores a century of gay, lesbian, bisexual, and transgender life in the city—the first stand-alone museum of its kind in the United States. The neighborhood and tens of thousands of visitors all come together at June's **San Francisco Lesbian, Gay, Bisexual, Transgender Pride Parade & Celebration** (*tel 415/864-0831, sfpride.org*), an extravaganza that

Cruisin' the Castro Walking Tours

☎ 415/255-1821

💲 $$$$$ (includes access to Castro Theatre)

cruisinthecastro.com

Rainbow flags, whose colors reflect the diversity of the LGBT movement, grace the Castro's streets.

Noe Valley

 Map p. 196
Bus: 24, 48;
Streetcar: J

starts with a parade down Market Street featuring such entrants as several hundred women motorcyclists known as Dykes on Bikes, queer cheerleading squads, zanily costumed revelers, support groups, politicians, and celebrities. The event continues with a celebration around the Civic Center that features music, booths, and food and drink.

Just south on Castro Street is the **village center** around 18th Street. Past 20th Street there's a string of Victorian houses.

If you follow Castro to 24th Street, you reach the main shopping strip in **Noe Valley.** Just south of the Castro, quiet Noe Valley, bounded by 20th, Dolores, 30th, and Douglas Streets, attracts young professionals with families to its Victorian cottages. They replaced the hippies of the 1970s (when the area was nicknamed "Granola Valley") and brought wine shops and latte dispensaries with them. ∎

SF LGBT

San Francisco's gay life dates to the 1908 opening of The Dash, an infamous bar on Pacific Street whose cross-dressing waiters would perform sex acts in the booths. By 1964 *Life* magazine declared the city the "gay capital of America." Yet many still worried that if their sexual orientation came out, they would be shunned or lose their jobs. In 1972 the city's first openly gay bar, Twin Peaks tavern, took down the usual blacked-out windows and installed tall plate glass, hiding no more.

In the 1970s, the city was a center of gay liberation: Activist Harvey Milk was elected supervisor (see p. 203), the city passed the Gay Bill of Rights against housing and employment discrimination, Armistead Maupin wrote of gay life (see p. 36), and a local artist designed the rainbow flag. In 2004, under then mayor Gavin Newsom, the city issued the nation's first same-sex marriage licenses (later annulled). When the U.S. Supreme Court declared same-sex marriages legal nationwide in 2015, San Francisco went wild with celebration. It was a lovely day in the gayborhood.

Nearby landscapes and towns within driving distance from San Francisco that are utterly different

Excursions

An actor playing Buena Vista Winery's founder Agoston Haraszthy greets visitors to the winery.

Excursions

Venture almost any direction from San Francisco and you'll find enriching places filled with cultural wonders and great natural beauty. And you can do more than just look: There are plenty of opportunities for active adventures.

South & East

On the San Francisco Peninsula are the parklike campus of Stanford University and a country estate called Filoli, created by the possessor of a gold rush fortune. In Silicon Valley, where rolling hillsides were once covered in fruit-producing orchards, industrial parks crowd around San Jose, turning out chips and software. For tourists, San Jose's attractions include the Tech Museum of Innovation and the spooky Winchester Mystery House.

Farther south, the Monterey Peninsula is considered by many to be one of the world's most beautiful shores, and it is also home to two intriguing towns. In Monterey's historic quarter you'll find Spanish adobe buildings and Cannery Row, once the haunt of novelist John Steinbeck and now a commercialized tourist magnet. The innovative Monterey Bay Aquarium boasts a million-gallon (3.8 million L) indoor ocean and thousands of sea creatures. Defining the word "quaint" (maybe a bit too insistently), Carmel-by-the-Sea shelters fairy-tale cottages, fine restaurants, galleries, and California's loveliest mission. Nearby Point Lobos unveils a natural realm of rugged shores, basking sea lions, and windblown headlands with Monterey cypress trees.

To the east of San Francisco, in Oakland, you can follow the shore of Lake Merritt to the Oakland Museum of California, which tells the story of the golden state through history, natural science, and art. Facing the busy port, Jack London Square bustles with restaurants, shops, and sites related to its namesake author. Famously liberal Berkeley (birthplace of 1960s student protest) is home to the 36,000-student campus of the University of California, and it also offers an abundance of street life, cafés, restaurants, and campus cultural activities.

North

Across the Golden Gate Bridge in Marin County lies Sausalito, a small harbor town with a sophisticated atmosphere and a Mediterranean look. Beyond trendy Mill Valley stand the thousand-year-old trees of Muir Woods, and beyond them is the tree-covered summit of Mount Tamalpais, reputed to be the birthplace of mountain biking. Along the Pacific shore you'll find beaches, wildlife, lagoons, and 67,000-acre (27,114 ha) Point Reyes National Seashore.

A cypress finds a rocky perch on the 17-Mile Drive (27 km) that winds around Monterey Peninsula.

North & East

This is California wine country: In excess of 400 wineries dot the Sonoma and Napa Valleys, to the east of Marin County, many welcoming visitors with tours and pouring samples to taste. Innovative restaurants and relaxing inns, serving food that complements the local wine, complete the picture. The town of Sonoma has an old Spanish mission and plaza, early hotels, and other buildings. Nearby, Jack London's ranch displays the personal belongings of the author of *The Call of the Wild*. Napa Valley towns include Calistoga, with its hot springs, and St. Helena, the tony hub of wine touring.

Farther Afield

Yosemite National Park in the Sierra Nevada is a kingdom of granite peaks, ancient groves, waterfalls, and wildflower meadows. Also here is the 1927 Ahwahnee Hotel, perhaps the grandest rustic lodge in any national park. Farther north, Lake Tahoe is an alpine lake, so deep that its waters could flood the whole of California to a depth of 14 inches (35.5 cm). Wooded shores, mountain trails, ski areas, historic residences, and gambling casinos on the Nevada shore—there's something here for everyone. Due to their distance from San Francisco, these two excursions are more suitable for a weekend stay than a day trip. ∎

San Francisco Peninsula & Silicon Valley

San Francisco occupies the northern tip of the peninsula that separates the ocean from the bay. People and their enterprises, from education to high tech, pack this strip of land, which is only a few miles wide.

The Memorial Church at Stanford University

Silicon Valley

🅰 Map p. 209 4C

Filoli

🅰 Map p. 209 4B
✉ Cañada Rd., Woodside
☎ 650/364-8300
☎ Open mid-Feb.–Oct.; closed Mon., tours by reservation
💲 $$$$

filoli.org

Stanford University

🅰 Map p. 209 4B
✉ Palm Dr., Palo Alto
☎ 650/723-2560

visit.stanford.edu

Filoli

California gold-mining heir and utilities magnate William Bowers Bourn II built Filoli (short for his motto, "Fight for a just cause, Love your fellow men, Live a good life"), a 43-room Georgian Revival mansion designed by architect Willis Polk, around 1917. With its French windows and carved moldings, it ranks among the great American country houses. Filoli's enticing gardens (designed by Bruce Porter and Isabella Worn) suggest a series of rooms, variously decorated with foliage and flowers.

From San Francisco, head south on I-280 and turn right at the Edgewood Road exit, then right again onto Cañada Road.

Stanford University

This prestigious private university in northern Silicon Valley has been the incubator for top high-tech companies, from Hewlett-Packard to Instagram. In the 1880s, "Big Four" railroad magnate Leland Stanford (who also served as California's governor and U.S. senator) and his wife, Jane Lathrop Stanford, transformed their horse farm into a university dedicated to their son, who had died of typhoid fever. The landscaping was planned by Frederick Law Olmsted, designer of New York's Central Park. The **visitor center** *(Campus Dr. at Galvez St.)* supplies maps and information, and is the starting point for limited free walking tours.

At the heart of the 8,180-acre (3,310 ha) campus is the Richardsonian Romanesque **quad,** an arched colonnade of sandstone classrooms with Spanish red-tile roofs. Dominating the quad is **Memorial Church** (1903), with Byzantine biblical mosaics and stained-glass windows.

To get the big picture of the campus, ride the elevator *($)* up 285-foot (87 m) **Hoover Tower,** designed by Bakewell & Brown;

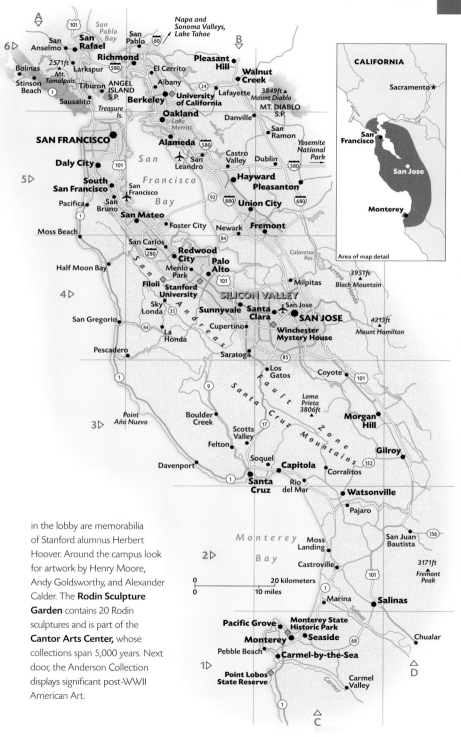

in the lobby are memorabilia of Stanford alumnus Herbert Hoover. Around the campus look for artwork by Henry Moore, Andy Goldsworthy, and Alexander Calder. The **Rodin Sculpture Garden** contains 20 Rodin sculptures and is part of the **Cantor Arts Center,** whose collections span 5,000 years. Next door, the Anderson Collection displays significant post-WWII American Art.

San Jose

⬛ Map p. 209 4C

Visitor Information

✉ 408 Almaden Blvd.

☎ 408/295-9600

🕐 Closed Sat.–Sun.

sanjose.org

Tech Museum of Innovation

✉ 201 S. Market St.

☎ 408/294-8324

💲 $$$

thetech.org

Rosicrucian Egyptian Museum & Planetarium

✉ 1660 Park Ave.

☎ 408/947-3635

🕐 Closed Mon.–Tues.

💲 $$

egyptianmuseum.org

To reach Stanford from San Francisco, head south on US 101 to the Embarcadero exit and turn west. If you're not driving, catch the Caltrain to Palo Alto's California Avenue or Downtown station, from which Stanford's Marguerite shuttle bus runs to campus regularly (6 a.m.–8:25 p.m.).

Silicon Valley

Known "virtually" worldwide, Silicon Valley is the 1960s birthplace of the high-tech and semiconductor industries. Apple and Google are based here. In a quieter past, its main city, **San Jose** (50 miles/80 km SE of San Francisco) began in 1777 as a farming center to supply Spanish soldiers and became California's first capital (1849–1851).

At the **Tech Museum of Innovation** you can play digital sleuth to solve a cyber crime, track your own biometric data while exploring the museum, build a vehicle that harnesses wind to deliver 3-D-printed cupcakes, and enjoy the largest IMAX dome theater in Northern California. The mysterious **Rosicrucian Egyptian Museum & Planetarium** displays mummified priests (and cats!), Egyptian jewelry, and a reproduced rock tomb. The **Winchester Mystery House** (525 S. Winchester Blvd., tel 408/247-2101, winchester mysteryhouse.com, $$$$$) dates to the 1880s, when a spirit medium told wealthy Sarah Winchester she'd live as long as building continued. Over the next 36 years, the Victorian mansion grew to 160 rooms, with doors that open to blank walls, stairs to nowhere, and other oddities.

San Jose attractions also include the **Children's Discovery Museum** (180 Woz Way, tel 408/298-5437, cdm.org, $$$), where kids can tinker with interactive exhibits on the arts and science. The **San Jose Museum of Art** (110 S. Market St., tel 408/271-6840, sjmusart.org, closed Mon., $$) shows contemporary work with a focus on the West Coast. **San Jose History Park** (Kelley Park, 635 Phelan Avenue., tel 408/287-2290, historysanjose.org) fills 14 acres (5.6 ha) with original and reproduced 19th-century houses and businesses, complete with paved streets and running trolleys. **SoFA/South First Area** (So. First St., south of San Carlos St.) is a lively area filled with galleries and food; it hosts a first-Fridays art walk. ∎

Catch SF Football Fever

San Francisco's beloved NFL American football team, the 49ers, plays home games at the 1.85-million-square-foot (171,870 sq m) Levi's Stadium (4900 Marie P. DeBartolo Way, Santa Clara), an hour south of the city. The stadium has 68,500 seats, 9,000 club seats, and 174 suites, and is the world's most technologically advanced (hey, it's Silicon Valley). Cameras feed two enormous video boards (200 by 48 feet/61 by 14.5 m), and a phone app enables real-time game replays and in-seat delivery of food and drinks. For tickets, go online (49ers.com; from $85 for one game to $80,000 for season VIP passes); you'll also find information on stadium tours ($$$$$), tailgating, and parking, plus driving directions. Caltrain runs from San Francisco to Santa Clara station, connecting to a light-rail shuttle on game day (caltrain.com/levisstadium).

Monterey Peninsula

Few places blend nature and history as beautifully as this peninsula 120 miles (193 km) south of San Francisco, with its rocky coastal scenery and long parade of cultures. Here nature comes first: Anyone caught harming a monarch butterfly in Pacific Grove is fined $1,000. Carmel-by-the-Sea prohibits neon signs and billboards. Visitors will find a world-class aquarium, upscale restaurants and cozy inns, and 19 golf courses, including world-famous Pebble Beach.

Fisherman's Wharf, a pier with shops and seafood restaurants, lures boaters to historic Monterey.

Monterey

The capital of California under Spanish, Mexican, and United States flags, Monterey treasures its historic adobes downtown.

Monterey State Historic Park encompasses several of the buildings described below. The **Custom House** (1827), California's oldest public building, displays early cargo. At the Stanton Center, the **Museum of Monterey** looks at maritime history, with model ships and an

1887 Fresnel lighthouse lens of 1,000 prisms, and at local history and art related to the region. Monterey's oldest building is the 1795 **Royal Presidio Chapel** *(Church St. at Figueroa St.),* built of stone and adobe. A touch of New England, **Colton Hall** *(559 Pacific St.)* is where delegates in 1849 framed California's first constitution. Noteworthy houses include the 1835 **Larkin House** *(464 Calle Principal),* an example of the Monterey colonial style that fused

Monterey Peninsula

Visitor Information

-  Map p. 209 1C
- Monterey County Convention & Visitors Center, 765 Wave St., Monterey
- 888/221-1010 or 831/657-6400

seemonterey.com

Monterey State Historic Park

✉ 20 Custom House Plaza

☎ 831/649-7118

💲 $$. Tours Fri.–Sun.

www.parks.ca.gov /mshp

Museum of Monterey

✉ 5 Custom House Plaza

☎ 831/372-2608

🕐 Closed Mon.–Tues.

museumofmonterey .org

Monterey Bay Aquarium

✉ 886 Cannery Row

☎ 831/648-4800 or 866/963-9645 (advance tickets)

💲 $$$$$

montereybay aquarium.org

Spanish adobe construction and New England design; it operates as a house museum. Also look in at the **Robert Louis Stevenson House** *(530 Houston St.),* an 1830s adobe where the Scottish author rented a room in 1879 while courting Fanny Osbourne. A collection of Stevenson memorabilia is on display.

The extraordinary **Monterey Bay Aquarium** reveals the world beneath the sea. Highlights: jellyfish presented as living artworks; a forest of kelp, which can grow 6 inches (15 cm) a day; a million-gallon (3.8 million L) tank whose denizens include sunfish that can weigh 1.5 tons (1.3 tonnes); and giant octopuses, the world's largest species at almost 30 feet long (9.1 m) and 100 pounds (45 kg).

A tidal wave of tourism has now inundated **Cannery Row** *(canneryrow.com),* the site of former sardine canneries along Monterey Bay, leaving a wrack of T-shirt shops, saltwater taffy vendors, and dining spots. From the 1920s to the 1950s (when the sardines gave out), this zone was a place John Steinbeck characterized as "a poem, a stink, a grating noise, a quality of light . . . a dream" (*Cannery Row,* 1945). Steinbeck fans should make a pilgrimage to the **Pacific Biological Laboratory** *(800 Cannery Row),* which was run by Steinbeck's friend and protagonist Ed "Doc" Ricketts.

For a much funkier, less plastic tourist experience than Cannery Row offers, try nearby **Fisherman's Wharf** *(montereywharf .com),* a pier with shops and seafood eateries. ■

The Monterey Bay Aquarium brings sea life up close and personal to landlubbers of all ages.

Carmel-by-the-Sea

An artists colony turned upscale resort, Carmel has a village atmosphere with cottages on tree-lined streets, fancy shopping and dining along Ocean Avenue, inns, art galleries galore, and a curve of white sand on a turquoise ocean.

Mission San Carlos Borroméo de Carmelo has sandstone walls, a Moorish-domed bell tower, and walled gardens. These elements add up to something ineffable, beyond simply a historic mission. Completed in 1797, it captures the romance of mission days in old California. Padre Junípero Serra, founder of the California mission system, chose this as his headquarters and is buried in the sanctuary.

The garden entry to Mission San Carlos Borroméo de Carmelo draws visitors to the historic sandstone shrine.

INSIDER TIP:

For a treat, try the smoked chicken with baby artichokes at Rio Grill *(101 Crossroads Blvd.).* It always astonishes.

—CHARLES KOGOD
National Geographic contributor

Poet Robinson Jeffers designed **Tor House** (26304 Ocean View Ave., tel 831/624-1813, torhouse .org, Fri.–Sat. tours by reservation, $$) to look like a Tudor barn his wife had seen in England. Granite for its walls was hauled up by horses from the cove below; he also built the stone **Hawk Tower.**

From Carmel, the **17-Mile Drive** (27 km) takes you through 8,000-acre (3,240 ha) Del Monte Forest. The road passes multi-million-dollar houses and several legendary golf courses (Pebble Beach, Spyglass Hill, Cypress Point), and traces a windswept and rugged shoreline. The oft-photographed Lone Cypress perches on a rocky point.

An inspiring place three miles (4.8 km) south of Carmel, **Point Lobos State Reserve** *(tel 831/624-4909, pointlobos.org, $$ per car)* protects rocky headlands, tide pools, Monterey-cypress groves, and meadows. Its 750 off-shore acres (303 ha) is one of the state's first underwater preserves. Watch for seals, sea otters, and sea lions (Point Lobos is derived from Punta de los Lobos Marinos). You can walk the winding trails here. ■

Carmel-by-the-Sea
🗺 Map p. 209 1C
Visitor Information
✉ San Carlos St. bet. 5th & 6th Sts.
☎ 831/624-2522
carmelcalifornia.org

Mission San Carlos Borroméo de Carmelo
✉ 3080 Rio Rd.
☎ 831/624-1271
💲 $$
carmelmission.org

17-Mile Drive
✉ Carmel gate: Hwy. 1; Pacific Grove gate: Hwy. 68 W
💲 $$ (per car)

Berkeley

Dubbed the "Athens of the West" in the 1870s, the University of California at Berkeley today defines the city with its academic air and sprawling campus. With the bay in front and craggy hills behind, nature provides a backdrop to a vibrant metropolitan scene.

West Coast creativity enlivens a street scene near the University of California campus.

Berkeley

◪ Map p. 209 6B

Visitor Information

✉ 2030 Addison St., #102

☎ 510/549-7040

🕐 Closed Sun.

🚈 BART: Downtown Berkeley

visitberkeley.com

The city was named in 1866 for Irish prelate George Berkeley (author of the line, "Westward the course of empire takes its way"). The hills showcase regional architecture, including the rustic shingled houses of architects Bernard Maybeck and John Galen Howard in North Berkeley.

On the gastronomic front, the birthplace of California cuisine was Alice Waters's **Chez Panisse** (see Travelwise p. 257) in an area nicknamed Gourmet Ghetto for its restaurants. Telegraph Avenue

(Bancroft Way to Parker St.) offers multicultural people-watching (students, hipsters, retro and aging hippies, counterculture intellectuals), shopping (street vendors, vintage), and world cuisine.

University of California

The central campus consists of some 15 million square feet (1.3 million sq m) of buildings on 180 acres (73 ha). Get your bearings with walking-tour information at the visitor center. The university was the first in the University of California system, moving to Berkeley in 1873, and now has 36,000 students and top graduate programs. During the '60s, the university was the birthplace of the Free Speech Movement and a crucible of Vietnam War protests.

Demonstrations took place on Sproul Plaza, still a soapbox for protesters, preachers, students handing out flyers, and colorful characters such as "Hate Man," an octogenarian former *New York Times* reporter who opted to live on the streets. ("I avoid the term 'homeless.' If I didn't want a BMW, would you say I was 'BMW-less'?") His philosophy urges people to admit they really hate each other, then carry on.

INSIDER TIP:

Lawrence Hall of Science may be geared toward kids, but locals know it's great for all ages. It can convince you that science is fun.

—ERIN STONE
National Geographic contributor

Granite-and-bronze **Sather Gate** serves as the university's ceremonial front door. For a bird's-eye view of the campus, take the elevator *($)* up the 307-foot (93.5 m) **Campanile,** or Sather Tower, designed and completed by John Galen Howard in 1915. The white marble and granite bell tower was inspired by that in Venice's Piazza San Marco.

Museums reflect the university's scholarship. The **Museum of Paleontology** has a few public exhibits, notably a complete skeleton of a *Tyrannosaurus rex.* The **Phoebe A. Hearst Museum of Anthropology** shows artifacts from California, Peru, Egypt, and Mediterranean Europe, as well as items related to Ishi, the last Yahi Indian. Located just outside campus in the downtown arts district, the **Berkeley Art Museum & Pacific Film Archive** draws on its strengths: Qing-dynasty Chinese painting, early American painting, abstract expressionism, and 17,500 films and videos (from Japanese to West Coast avant-garde). Among treasures of the American West at the **Bancroft Library** are the nugget reputed to have started the California gold rush and many of Mark Twain's papers. The **Lawrence Hall of Science** *(Centennial Dr., tel 510/642-5132, $$$)* is filled with holograms and hands-on fun, plus a planetarium.

Other Berkeley Sights

UC Berkeley Botanical Garden

(200 Centennial Dr., tel 510/643-2755, botanicalgarden.berkeley.edu, closed 1st Tues., $$) displays 13,000 kinds of plants found worldwide, most notably cactuses, sunflowers, and orchids. The **First Church of Christ Scientist** *(2619 Dwight Way, tel 510/845-7199, tours 1st Sun. 12:15 p.m.)* was designed by Bernard Maybeck in 1910. Draped with wisteria, the church has been somewhat fancifully described as "a Japanese pagoda in a Gothic forest." ∎

University of California

🄰 Map p. 209 6B

Visitor Information

✉ 101 Sproul Hall, Bancroft Way at Telegraph Ave.

☎ 510/642-5215

🕑 Mon.–Fri.; daily walking tours by online reservation

visitors.berkeley.edu

Museum of Paleontology

✉ Valley Life Sciences Bldg.

☎ 510/642-1821

Phoebe A. Hearst Museum of Anthropology

✉ Kroeber Hall

☎ 510/642-3682

🕑 Closed Mon.–Tues.

hearstmuseum .berkeley.edu

Berkeley Art Museum & Pacific Film Archive

✉ 2155 Center St. (just off campus)

☎ 510/642-0808

🕑 Closed Mon.–Tues.

💲 $$$ museum, $$$ films

bampfa.org

Bancroft Library

✉ Doe Library annex

☎ 510/642-3781

🕑 Closed Sat.–Sun.

Oakland

Named for its oak groves, the city became the western terminus of the transcontinental railroad in 1869. It was linked to San Francisco by the Bay Bridge in the 1930s, then boomed with the Kaiser Shipyards during World War II. But within two decades Oakland was plagued with racial discord (it was the birthplace of the Black Panthers) and serious crime. In 1989, part of I-880 collapsed during the Loma Prieta earthquake.

Jack London Square on the waterfront harks back to the days of the early 20th-century author.

Oakland

⬛ Map p. 209 5B

Visitor Information

✉ 481 Water St.

☎ 510/839-9000

🚆 BART: 12th St./
City Center

visitoakland.org

These days things are looking up in Oakland, with hipsters and artists creating a Brooklyn vibe, a tourism hub at Jack London Square, a fine museum, and a container port that is the fifth busiest in the U.S. With a large black community, Oakland spawned a school of rap music through stars like MC Hammer and Tupac Shakur.

Lovers of Victorian architecture should stroll around **Old Oakland** (bet. Washington St. & Broadway, 8th to 10th Sts.), the original 1870s downtown; its buildings are now occupied by shops and cafés.

Several Victorian houses were moved from the path of I-990 to **Preservation Park** (bet. Castro St. & Martin Luther King Jr. Dr., 12th to 14th Sts.). You can visit the **Pardee Home Museum** (11th St. at Castro St., tel 510/444-2187, $$ tours), an 1868 Italianate house built by an early Oakland mayor.

A classic art deco movie palace (Timothy Pflueger, 1931), the **Paramount Theatre** (2025 Broadway, tel 510/465-6400, tours 1st & 3rd Sat., $$) is faced with a tile mural of marionettes. Inside are bas-relief warriors and maidens and a women's smoking lounge in black lacquer.

In **Lakeside Park** are heart-shaped, 155-acre (63 ha) Lake Merritt (really a tidal lagoon), gardens, and a fun children's fairyland park.

Jack London Square

Along the waterfront *(at the foot of Broadway, jacklondonsquare .com),* this dining, shopping, and entertainment zone commer-cializes the author of *The Call of the Wild,* an Oakland resident for much of his life. As a boy London hawked newspapers at **Heinold's First & Last Chance Saloon** *(48 Webster St., tel 510/839-6761),* built with wood from a whaling ship in 1883; its floors were tilted by the 1906 earthquake. As a Yukon prospec-tor in 1897, the writer lived in a log structure reproduced here as the **Jack London Cabin.**

President Franklin D. Roose-velt's "floating White House," the 165-foot (50 m) **U.S.S. *Potomac*** *(tel 510/627-1215, usspotomac .org, tours Wed., Fri., & Sun., $$; cruises April–Nov.: $$$$$)* is docked close by. Other attractions at the square include ocean activities and a Sunday farmers market.

Oakland Museum of California

This great regional museum fills a three-tiered structure designed in 1969 by Kevin Roche so that the roof of each level becomes a garden and terrace for the one above. The innovative museum looks at California's natural environment, history, and art.

EXPERIENCE: Enjoy Urban Stargazing

"It looks like a doughnut," an observatory volunteer remarks as visitors take turns peering through a 20-inch (51 cm) tele-scope. "But it's the remnant of a dying star that astronomers call the Ring Nebula." A young woman squints into the eyepiece and exclaims: "Wow!"

Thank your lucky stars: Oakland's **Chabot Space and Science Center** *(10000 Skyline Blvd., tel 510/336-7300, chabotspace .org, closed Mon., telescope viewing included with admission Fri.–Sat., $$$)* is one of the nation's few observatories whose power-ful telescopes are open to the public. The hilltop center also has a 36-inch (91 cm) telescope that scientists use to search for everything from asteroids near Earth to signals from extraterrestrial civilizations.

The **Gallery of California Natural Sciences** shows that the state enjoys the greatest bio-logical diversity in the country, but is threatened by pollution, suburbanization, and invasive spe-cies. Exhibits explore a range of diverse habitats: Oakland (urban), Sutter Buttes (central valley), Yosemite (Sierra Nevada range), Coachella Valley (southern deserts), Cordell Bank/Point Reyes (ocean), Mount Shasta (volcanic), and the Tehachapis (southern mountains).

Also on display is the most complete mastodon specimen found in California, discovered when a ranch hand near Mount Shasta dug up what he thought was an arrowhead in a streambed; it turned out to be a mastodon tooth, with the intact skeleton lying nearby.

Oakland Museum of California

✉ 1000 Oak St. at 10th St.

☎ 510/318-8400

🕐 Closed Mon.– Tues.

💲 $$$

🚇 BART: Lake Merritt

museumca.org

Housing more than 2,200 historical artifacts, artwork, ethnographic materials, and photographs, the **Gallery of California History** examines the waves of migration that created the state's cultural mix. Native American collections include Pomo feathered baskets, shell ornaments, and Pacific Northwest carvings. A survey of photography—from daguerreotypes and lantern slides to modern videos—includes rare views of the 1869 transcontinental railroad under construction.

An exhibit at the Oakland Museum of California retraces the journey of settlers to the state during the 1930s Dust Bowl.

Illustrating home life in California, household furnishings range from the kitchen of an 1850s house in the Sierra Nevada to mid-20th-century furniture by designer Charles Eames.

Tool and technology collections showcase Californians at work and include mining equipment from gold rush days; an

entire 1870s assay office; and items from the oil business, Hollywood, the defense industry, and high-tech industry.

The **Gallery of California Art** exhibits paintings, sculpture, prints, illustrations, photographs, and decorative arts by California artists and others who deal with California themes. The collection spans the state's history and is strong in landscape paintings from the 1850s to 1880s (such as Albert Bierstadt's views of Yosemite Valley), art from the gold rush, the arts and crafts style (furniture and decorative arts from the early 20th century), Bay Area figurative painting (Richard Diebenkorn, Elmer Bischoff), and photography (including Dorothea Lange's personal archive of 25,000 negatives and more than 10,000 prints).

Chabot Space and Science Center

The Chabot Space & Science Center (see sidebar p. 217) offers dramatic views of the cosmos via its free viewings *(Fri.–Sat. eve.)* through a 36-inch (91 cm) reflector telescope, one of the world's most advanced planetariums, and a large-screen theater. ■

Marin County

On California's sociological map, Marin is a lotus land colored mellow yellow and sunny green. Residents became famous for grooving on hot tubs, massage, and, of course, themselves. Locals still seek out organic food and any spiritual movement of the moment. But mellow Marin has also become a place of purring BMWs and remarkable wealth. Real estate prices are among the highest in the nation.

In Sausalito, still waters reflect pastel-colored houseboats, alternative residences to those on shore.

Marin County's sunshine and tranquil beauty attract creative corporations and software companies, as well as upscale shops and restaurants for wealthy residents. Yet nearly 40 percent of Marin County has been protected as parks and open space, including Muir Woods and Point Reyes National Seashore.

Cities include Sausalito, trendy Mill Valley, exclusive Ross, and pragmatic San Rafael (home of the **Marin County Civic Center,** designed by Frank Lloyd Wright).

Marin Headlands

Beyond Golden Gate Bridge the Marin Headlands offer nearly 12,000 acres (4,850 ha) of rolling coastal hills with miles of hiking and mountain biking trails, views, and old military installations to explore.

In a cove beneath the Golden Gate Bridge, **Fort Baker** was built to guard the nearby strait. Its Battery Yates (1905–1946) had six rapid-fire guns to trade shots with enemy ships (which never appeared). Some officers' quarters, built between 1901 and 1915 with pressed-tin ceilings and breezy

Marin County
Visitor Information

✉ 1 Mitchell Blvd., Suite B, San Rafael

 415/925-2060

visitmarin.org

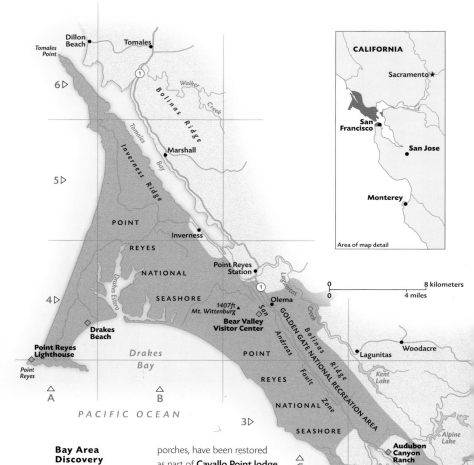

CALIFORNIA

Sacramento ★

San Francisco

San Jose

Monterey

Area of map detail

0   8 kilometers
0   4 miles

Tomales Point

Dillon Beach

Tomales

6 ▷

Walker Creek

Bolinas Ridge

Marshall

5 ▷

Inverness Ridge

Tomales Bay

POINT

Inverness

REYES

NATIONAL

Point Reyes Station

SEASHORE

Lagunitas

4 ▷

Drakes Estero

1407ft Mt. Wittenburg

Olema

Bear Valley Visitor Center

Drakes Beach

Point Reyes Lighthouse

Point Reyes

Drakes Bay

POINT

San Andreas Fault Zone

GOLDEN GATE NATIONAL RECREATION AREA

Bolinas Ridge

Lagunitas

Woodacre

Kent Lake

△ A

△ B

REYES

NATIONAL

△ C

Alpine Lake

PACIFIC OCEAN

3 ▷

SEASHORE

Audubon Canyon Ranch

Bolinas Lagoon

Bolinas

Duxbury Point

Bolinas Bay

Stinson Beach

MOUNT TALMALPAIS STATE PARK

△ D

2 ▷

Bay Area Discovery Museum

🅰 Map p. 221 F2
✉ Fort Baker
☎ 415/339-3900
🕐 Closed Mon.
💲 $$, free 1st Wed.

baykidsmuseum .org

porches, have been restored as part of **Cavallo Point lodge** (see Travelwise p. 257), a luxury retreat complete with a spa and gourmet cooking school. Nearby is a spectacular view of the bridge from below.

Children from infancy to age eight will enjoy the **Bay Area Discovery Museum,** whose hands-on lessons in local history and ecology include a crawl-through sea tunnel.

For spectacular vistas of the bridge and city, follow Conzelman Road along the bluffs westward from the Golden Gate. About

1.8 miles (2.9 km) along, a fire road leads to **Hawk Hill,** where 20,000 birds of prey pass during their fall journey down the coast.

Conzelman Road continues toward Point Bonita, where a short walk takes you to the 1855 **Point Bonita Lighthouse** (closed Tues.–Fri.), which warns fogbound ships away from the rocky shore. (A cannon once boomed every half hour around the clock; now an automated light does the work.)

At Fort Barry the **Marin Headlands Visitor Center** explains the area's natural and human history. Nearby is the nation's only restored **Nike missile launch site** *(closed Sun.–Weds.)*, part of a Cold War defense system from 1954 to 1974. Visitors see a missile raised into firing position. The 5-ton (4.5 tonne) Nike Hercules could fly at more than 3,200 miles an hour (5,150 km/h) and had a range of about 90 miles (145 km).

Sausalito

This town with a Mediterranean feel clings to steep hills above a

yacht harbor. Tourists congregate along Bridgeway, with its shops, restaurants, and bay views. Bars attract a colorful crowd. Locals shop and eat a block from the waterfront on Caledonia Street.

Hundreds of houseboats are moored at Gate 5 and other nearby locations. After World War II, the Bay Area had a surplus of vessels, and adventurous locals turned them into houseboats, creating an artists' colony. These days, young professionals also live in houseboats, as an alternative to sky-high housing prices on shore.

At the **Bay Model Visitor Center** *(2100 Bridgeway Blvd., tel 415/332-3871, closed

---

EXPERIENCE: Angel Island Segway Tours

If you don't care to walk the 7-mile (11 km) perimeter trail around Angel Island, how about riding on a Segway? This amazing two-wheeled electric scooter balances you with a system of gyroscopes, and it moves according to cues from your body language. (Lean forward to go forward, etc.) Guides on the two-hour tours *(tel 415/435-3392, angelisland.com, tours March–Oct. & weekends Nov.–Feb., $$$$$)* tell about island history at popular stops: the U.S. Immigration Station, Battery Ledyard with its view of the Golden Gate Bridge, and East Garrison with its Greek Revival architecture.

Marin Headlands Visitor Center

🗺 Map p. 221 E2

✉ Fort Barry Chapel, Field & Bunker Rds.

☎ 415/331-1540

Nike Missile Launch Site

☎ 415/331-1540

🕐 Closed Sun.–Weds.

Sausalito

🗺 Map p. 221 E2

Visitor Information

✉ Staffed kiosk at ferry landing

☎ 415/331-1093

💲 $$$ (ferry)

⛴ Ferry: 30 min. from Ferry Building at foot of Market St. or Fisherman's Wharf Pier 39

sausalito.org

Angel Island State Park

⛰ Map p. 221 F2

☎ 415/435-5390

⛴ Ferry from San Francisco or Tiburon

💲 $$

parks.ca.gov /angelisland

Muir Woods National Monument

⛰ Map p. 221 E2

☎ 415/388-2596

💲 $$

nps.gov/muwo

Mount Tamalpais State Park

⛰ Map p. 220 D2–D3

Visitor Information

☎ 415/388-2070

💲 $$ (parking)

Mon., also Sun. in winter), a warehouse holds a vast model of the bay that compresses 400 square miles (1,036 km) into a 1.5-acre (0.6 ha) simulation. Researchers used the model to study the effects of floods, drought, and development on the San Francisco Bay.

Sausalito developed as a ferryboat connection to San Francisco, and riding the ferry (see Travelwise pp. 239–240) remains an enjoyable way to visit.

Angel Island State Park

North of Alcatraz, this island rich in beauty and history makes for great hiking, biking, picnicking, and sunbathing. The top of 788-foot (240 m) **Mount Livermore** (a former Nike missile site) has views of the Bay Area.

Named Isla de Los Angeles by mariner Juan Manuel de Ayala in 1775, Angel Island has served as a Spanish cattle ranch, a U.S. military installation, a quarantine station, and the "Ellis Island of the West," an immigration station and detention center for 175,000 Chinese between 1910 and 1940. On a **tram tour** *($$$)* or a walk around the 5-mile (8 km) perimeter road, you'll see historical sites and military garrisons, views, and beaches. Tours *($)* are offered at the immigration station.

Muir Woods National Monument

On the lower slopes of Mount Tamalpais, accessible via the Panoramic Highway, stands the Bay Area's last virgin redwood forest. Some trees here are at least a thousand years old. The redwoods shelter ferns, a creek with crayfish and salmon, and varied trails. **Cathedral Grove** and **Bohemian Grove** have the largest trees: The tallest rises 258 feet (78 m) into the sky; the thickest measures more than 14 feet (4 m) across. The world's tallest living things, redwoods have thrived in northern California for 140 million years and grew when dinosaurs roamed the Earth.

Mount Tamalpais State Park

The most visible point in Marin County is a lofty kingdom of chaparral and oak trees that is laced with more than 200 miles (320 km) of trails. A short path

Redwoods dwarf visitors at Cathedral Grove in Muir Woods.

leads from the East Peak parking lot to a fire lookout on the 2,571-foot (783 m) east summit, where you can scan both the Bay Area and the Pacific Ocean.

Pacific Coast

Along Calif. 1, **Stinson Beach** boasts a 3-mile (4.8 km) stretch of white beach that's safe for swimming; the village makes a good sandwich stop. Just north at **Bolinas Lagoon,** you may see egrets and waterfowl, or spy harbor seals hauled out on Pickleweed Island. Bird-watchers might observe any of 115 species at **Audubon Canyon Ranch**, a 1,000-acre (404 ha) preserve on the lagoon where great blue herons and egrets nest in spring at the tops of redwood trees. At the north end of Bolinas Lagoon look for the road to **Bolinas.** It's a tranquil hideout with an organic-hippie-artistic-countercultural spirit, although it has now become increasingly upscale.

Point Reyes

Where the land juts to meet the ocean at Point Reyes, it seems you've reached the edge of the world. Maybe you have; the peninsula is separated from the mainland by the notorious San Andreas Fault. Situated on the northward-moving Pacific tectonic plate, Point Reyes is heading for Alaska at the rate of 2 inches (5 cm) per year.

Approximately 71,000 acres (28,700 ha) of wild beauty embrace steep cliffs, a thunderous surf and hidden beaches,

Gray Whales in Motion

Each winter, 20,000 gray whales migrate from Alaska along the California coast to their breeding and birthing waters in Baja California. Their 12,000-mile (19,300 km) round-trip trek is the longest annual mammal migration in the animal kingdom. The whales cover 80 miles (129 km) a day. To spot a whale, look for a spout of vaporized water as it surfaces. Gray whales can grow 50 feet (15 m) long and weigh up to 45 tons (41 tonnes).

open meadows of wildflowers, and windswept hillsides. This area is protected as **Point Reyes National Seashore.** Just off Calif. 1 near Olema, the **Bear Valley Visitor Center** gives an overview. Here you can trace the big bad San Andreas Fault.

Fifteen miles (24 km) west, just off Sir Francis Drake Boulevard, **Drakes Beach** offers wind-sheltered sand and a visitor center with exhibits on the ocean environment and 16th-century maritime exploration. You can ponder whether Sir Francis Drake really beached his ship, the *Golden Hind*, in Drakes Bay in 1579, a debate that still occupies historians.

The boulevard goes a few miles farther west to the tip of Point Reyes and the 1870 **Point Reyes Lighthouse,** 296 feet (90 m) above the ocean. The lighthouse is perfect for watching gray whales migrate *(late Dec.–late April).* Exhibits focus on whales and lighthouse gear, including a massive Fresnel lens. Bring a jacket for wind, and be aware that you must walk down (and climb back up) 309 steps to reach the lighthouse. ∎

Stinson Beach

🄰 Map p. 220 D2

☎ 415/868-0734

Audubon Canyon Ranch

🄰 Map p. 220 D3

✉ 4900 Calif. Hwy. 1

☎ 415/868-9244

🕑 Spring to mid-Dec.

🅂 Donation

egret.org

Point Reyes National Seashore

🄰 Map p. 220 B4–B5

Visitor Information

✉ Bear Valley Rd., Point Reyes Station

☎ 415/464-5100

nps.gov/pore

Point Reyes Lighthouse

🄰 Map p. 220 A4

☎ 415/669-1534

🕑 Closed Tues.–Thurs.; summer Tues.–Weds.

Napa Valley

This valley 50 miles (80 km) north of San Francisco produces some of the world's greatest wines, but that's not the only reason readers of *Wine Spectator* have ranked it above Burgundy, Bordeaux, and Tuscany as their "favorite wine region for vacationing in the world." It helps that the valley is bordered by the Coast Range mountains, carpeted with yellow mustard flowers in late winter, and dotted with picturesque wineries that open their tasting rooms to visitors. Charles Krug established the first winery here in 1861; today, more than 400 dot Napa Valley.

Most Napa vineyards and wineries offer wine tastings—above at Domaine Chandon—and tours.

Napa Valley
ⓜ Map p. 229 E2
Visitor Information
✉ 600 Main St., Napa
☎ 707/251-5895
visitnapavalley.com

Charles Krug
ⓜ Map p. 229 B3
✉ 2800 Main St., St. Helena
☎ 707/967-2229
charleskrug.com

The valley boasts epicurean restaurants and such hybrids as the winery/art gallery. Napa Valley is also one of the world's most heavily traveled hot-air balloon corridors. Sunrise ascensions are usually followed by champagne brunch. There are nine golf courses, notably two championship courses at **Silverado Resort and Spa** (*1600 Atlas Peak Rd., Napa, tel 707/257-0200, silveradoresort.com*). Calistoga's

hot springs have attracted visitors since the early 1900s.

Geographically, Napa Valley is a cornucopia of wine grapes that spills southward from 4,343-foot (1,323 m) Mount St. Helena. The rich, porous soil and dry Mediterranean climate provide ideal grape-growing conditions. Many celebrated wineries lie along the valley's main road, Calif. 29, which links the main towns: Napa, Yountville, Oakville, Rutherford,

St. Helena, and Calistoga (see map p. 229). This "rural" highway is often jammed with cars, though, especially in spring, fall, and on weekends. A quieter, less trafficked route is the parallel **Silverado Trail,** to the east. The **Napa Valley Wine Train** (*tel 707/253-2111 or 800/427-4124, winetrain.com, $$$$$*) makes a three-hour round-trip from Napa to St. Helena in 1915–1950 dining, lounge, and Vista Dome cars, with gourmet meals and local wines, and optional winery tours.

INSIDER TIP:

With its breathtaking views, Artesa Vineyards & Winery (*artesawinery.com*) is a gem. The scenery will captivate you.

—ERIN STONE
National Geographic contributor

Napa Valley Wineries

The valley's oldest wine producer is **Charles Krug,** founded in 1861 and now operated by the Peter Mondavi family. **Beringer Vineyards** ranks as the valley's oldest continuously operated winery (1876). Tastings are conducted in a German mansion with a slate roof and stained-glass windows; the wines age in caves tunneled 1,000 feet (305 m) into the hillside.

Fine contemporary art complements the wine at the **Hess Collection Winery. Domaine**

Chandon produces sparkling wine by the classic *methode champenoise*, which involves a second fermentation in the bottle; the method was invented in the 1600s by the blind Benedictine monk Dom Perignon.

Tours at the **Robert Mondavi Winery** range from a 30-minute overview to special sessions on wine tasting and food; the winery presents concerts in summer. New and old meet at **St. Supéry Estate Vineyards & Winery.** Tours and tastings teach visitors about winemaking and such matters as varietal aromas; there's also a Queen Anne–style Victorian house with gardens open for strolling. **Inglenook** focuses around the 1882 stone winery with its grand wooden staircase; the operation, which belongs to moviemaker Francis Ford Coppola, has the air of a European winery.

The 1862 **Schramsberg Vineyards,** the valley's first hillside winery, makes sparkling wines. After Robert Louis Stevenson visited in 1880, he wrote about the winery and founder Jacob Schram in *The Silverado Squatters.*

To visit **Sterling Vineyards,** you ride an aerial tram from the parking lot to the top of a 300-foot (91 m) knoll.

Napa & Yountville

The front door to the valley, Napa grew up on the Napa River as a shipping hub for valley wines. The old part of town is worth a look for its Victorian neighborhoods.

Named for George Yount, who planted the valley's first

Beringer Vineyards
- Map p. 229 B3
- 2000 Main St., St. Helena
- ☎ 707/302-7592
beringer.com

Hess Collection Winery
- Map p. 229 C2
- 4411 Redwood Rd., Napa
- ☎ 707/255-1144
hesscollection.com

Domaine Chandon
- Map p. 229 C2
- 1 California Dr., Yountville
- ☎ 888/242-6366
chandon.com

Robert Mondavi Winery
- Map p. 229 C3
- 7801 St. Helena Hwy., Oakville
- ☎ 888/766-6328
robertmondaviwinery.com

St. Supéry Estate Vineyards & Winery
- Map p. 229 C3
- 8440 St. Helena Hwy., Rutherford
- ☎ 707/963-4507
stsupery.com

Inglenook
- Map p. 229 C3
- 1991 St. Helena Hwy., Rutherford
- ☎ 707/968-1100
inglenook.com

Schramsberg Vineyards

▲ Map p. 229 B4

✉ 1400 Schramsberg Rd., Calistoga

☎ 707/942-4558

schramsberg.com

Sterling Vineyards

▲ Map p. 229 B4

✉ 1111 Dunaweal Ln., Calistoga

☎ 800/726-6136

sterlingvineyards .com

Robert Louis Stevenson Museum

✉ 1490 Library Ln., St. Helena

☎ 707/963-3757

⊕ Closed Sun.– Mon.

stevensonmuseum .org

vineyard in 1833 (and is buried in the pioneer cemetery), the small town of Yountville now caters to an upscale crowd with inns, shops, and restaurants. Exhibits at the **Napa Valley Museum** (*55 Presidents Cir., Yountville, tel 707/944-0500, napavalleymuseum.org, closed Mon.–Tues., $$*) reveal geographical and cultural influences on the valley; artifacts range from Pomo Indian basketry to railroad memorabilia and viticultural tools. Art exhibits feature local and national artists.

St. Helena

Hub of the winegrowing region, St. Helena dates from 1853. Shops and restaurants on historical Main Street occupy buildings of native stone erected before the end of the 19th century. Streetlights were installed

right after being demonstrated at the 1915 Panama-Pacific International Exposition.

Fans of the author shouldn't miss the **Robert Louis Stevenson Museum,** which displays his childhood toy soldiers, together with the author's handwritten manuscript pages, letters, photographs, and first editions. Works by Stevenson (1850–1894) include *Treasure Island, Dr. Jekyll and Mr. Hyde,* and *A Child's Garden of Verses.* In 1880 the writer honeymooned with his bride, Fanny Osbourne, in a cabin on nearby Mount St. Helena (see Robert Louis Stevenson State Park, opposite), which he later described in *The Silverado Squatters.*

You can eat the homework at the **Culinary Institute of America** (*2555 Main St., St. Helena, 707/967-1100, ciachef.edu/ california*), which trains chefs at the former Greystone Cellars, built in 1889 and once operated by the Christian Brothers. Dine at two gourmet restaurants that have institute-trained chefs, or stroll through the herb garden.

A 36-foot (11 m) waterwheel turns at **Bale Grist Mill State Historic Park.** Built by Dr. Edward Turner Bale in 1847, it was used to grind the grain of local farmers. Visitors can see the original grindstones in use, and purchase the flour that they produce.

Calistoga & Beyond

At the north end of the valley, Calistoga is famous for its mineral-rich hot springs and purifying mud baths. Spa treatments are a cottage industry, an

---

EXPERIENCE:
Discover Your Inner Celebrity Chef

The world-famous Culinary Institute of America (*ciachef.edu/enthusiasts*) located in St. Helena offers Saturday classes that cover bite-size subjects from soups to desserts, while culinary "boot camps" are two- to five-day cooking vacations where you can learn everything from making hors d'oeuvres for your next party (hot and cold, with creative garnishing and plating) to in-depth kitchen techniques (knife skills, roasting, sautéing, pan-frying, braising, and more). At baking boot camp, you learn to make specialty and hearth breads. Students even get a chef's jacket, pants, and paper hat.

enterprise that began in 1859 when California's first millionaire, Sam Brannan, built a resort for well-to-do San Franciscans.

INSIDER TIP:

Make sure to visit Oxbow Public Market (610 & 644 1st St., Napa); it's a delicious gourmet food court— one of a kind.

—MERYN CHIMES
National Geographic contributor

Legend says the spa got its name when the colorful Brannan rose to his feet at a banquet after imbibing freely and announced that his resort would be the "Saratoga of California"—at least, that's what he meant to say. His tongue twisted, and he called it the "Calistoga of Sarafornia."

The resort era comes to life at the **Sharpsteen Museum** *(1311 Washington St., Calistoga, 707/942-5911, sharpsteenmuseum .org)* through dioramas created by a Disney artist and a furnished cottage from the old resort.

One of three geysers in the world guaranteed to go off like clockwork (in this case every 20–45 min.), the **Old Faithful Geyser of California** shoots water and steam 40 to 75 feet high (6 to 14 m). About 4,000 gallons (15,140 L) of sulfurous water spew forth at 170°F (77 C°).

The **Petrified Forest** *(4100 Petrified Forest Rd., 707/942-6667, petrifiedforest.org, $$)* resulted from the eruption 3.4 million years ago of a volcano located where Mount St. Helena stands today. Uprooted trees were buried by ash and lava, then permeated by water and silica. Over millennia, this turned the trunks to stone; one measures 105 feet (32 m) in length.

Grapevines, a common sight in the area, greet visitors to Calistoga, well known for its hot springs.

For a vigorous hike or a brush with history, visit **Robert Louis Stevenson State Park** *(tel 707/942-4575)* on Mount St. Helena. A rough trail leads to an abandoned silver mine; the writer honeymooned in a nearby shack. The trail continues to the top (4,343 feet/1,323 m), from which you can see Napa Valley, the Pacific Ocean, the Bay Area, and (if it's clear) the Sierra Nevada. ■

Bale Grist Mill State Historic Park

✉ 3369 St. Helena Hwy., St. Helena
☎ 707/942-4575
$ $$

Old Faithful Geyser of California

▲ Map p. 229 A4
✉ 1299 Tubbs Ln.
☎ 707/942-6463
$ $$$

oldfaithfulgeyser .com

Napa & Sonoma Valley Wines—A Taster's Guide

Wines of the Napa and Sonoma Valleys have achieved a worldwide reputation for excellence. Each part of the valley has its own distinctive wines, produced using a number of different varieties of grape.

Wine tasting involves using your senses.

Top of the line in red grapes is Cabernet Sauvignon. The wine has a full-bodied fruit flavor. Merlot is a smooth, drinkable red wine with a rich fruit taste. The same grapes that the French grow in Burgundy go into California's Pinot Noir. Here, it has a lighter color and body, as well as a fruitier flavor and aroma.

California's premier white wine, Chardonnay has a velvety texture and a flavor that suggests apples or pears. Chardonnay has enough intensity to suit a fine meal; it can also go with a light lunch or picnic.

Wine Tasting Made Easy

There's no reason to be intimidated by a bottle of wine. Just use your senses.

Sight: You can learn a lot about a wine from visual clues. A wine buff holds the glass by the stem, with the base flat on the table, and swirls the wine. Why? When the wine

runs down the sides of the glass, it shows its "legs," a term referring to stripes or columns of liquid. A wine with "good legs" is thicker and has more substance than wine that slides down the glass in sheets (an indication that it is thin). Each wine variety has an ideal color. Chardonnay should be a rich gold; if pale, it probably tastes weak or watery. The staff at a winery tasting room can tell you the ideal color for each variety.

Smell: Another reason for swirling the wine is to mix it with air, which releases chemical compounds you can smell. The nose can detect thousands of different odors in wine. As for wine terms: "Aroma" is the smell of the grape; "bouquet" refers to the fragrances created during winemaking (the yeast used in fermentation, the type of oak used for barrel aging, etc.). The sum of all the aromas in a wine is called its "nose."

Before you drink a bottle of wine, don't forget to sniff the cork: If the wine has turned sour, this is an early warning system.

Taste: Our taste buds detect four flavors: sweet (front of tongue), sour (edges), salty (middle), and bitter (back). To taste sweetness, draw a sip of wine up the middle of your tongue. Wine tastes sweet at a level of 0.7 percent residual sugar; below that, "dry" (which means free of sugar). Roll another sip around the edges of your tongue and notice the acid, which gives a wine tartness; a wine without acid components is called "flabby." If the wine has an agreeable proportion of acidity, sugar, and other elements, it has "balance." To serve a bottle of wine, uncork it a while before serving. This airing gets rid of chemical vapors, adding oxygen to mellow the flavors.

Feel: Warm a sip of wine in your mouth for a moment, then judge its weight, or "body"— how thick or thin it feels. Some wines have a lush feel that tasters try to capture with words like "velvet." The term "big" is used for a wine that fills the senses.

No two people have the same taste buds, so no wine tastes the same to everyone. So remember: If you like it, nothing else matters.

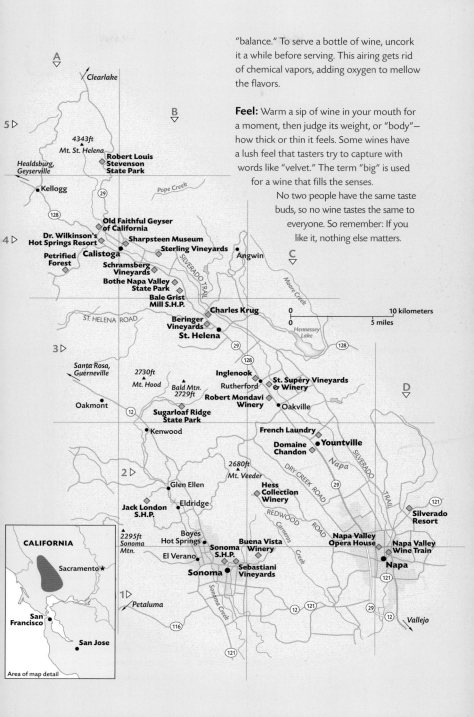

Sonoma Valley

The birthplace of the California wine industry and a producer of world-class vintages, Sonoma Valley (about 10 miles/16 km west of Napa Valley across the Mayacamas Mountains) remains a more easygoing, down-home place than trendy Napa Valley. Farmers grow everything from vine-ripe tomatoes to Christmas trees.

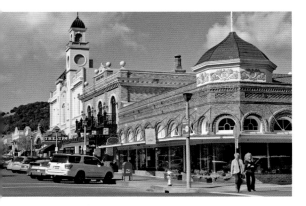

Sonoma Plaza forms part of Sonoma State Historic Park.

Sonoma Valley

◪ Map p. 229 B1–B2

Visitor Information

✉ 453 1st St. E.

☎ 707/996-1090

sonomavalley.com

Sonoma State Historic Park

◪ Map p. 229 B1

☎ 707/938-1519

$ $ (includes all sites)

sonomaparks.org

The town of **Sonoma** dates from 1823, when padres founded a mission here. After Mexico secularized the California missions in 1834, Gen. Mariano Vallejo surveyed the adjacent plaza as part of his charge to establish a pueblo and distribute lands. Sonoma wine growing dates from the 1825 planting of Franciscan mission grapes. Large-scale winemaking began in 1857, when Hungarian nobleman Agoston Haraszthy brought cuttings of Old World grapes to his Sonoma vineyard.

Sonoma State Historic Park

Sonoma Plaza is the largest plaza in California and forms part of Sonoma State Historic

Park. In the plaza's northeast corner, a bronze figure holds a flag to commemorate a ragtag group of Americans who staged the Bear Flag Revolt in June 1846. Thirty horsemen rode into Sonoma, took Mexico's General Vallejo prisoner, and without firing a shot declared California an independent republic. Their muslin flag had a red star and stripe (made from a petticoat), a crudely drawn grizzly bear, and the hand-scrawled words "California Republic." The newly declared republic lasted just 25 days, until U.S. forces stormed the Mexican capital at Monterey and claimed California. In Sonoma, the Stars and Stripes took the place of the Bear Flag. The bear lives on, however, on the state flag of California.

Mission San Francisco Solano (*corner of Spain St. & 1st St. E.*) was the last link in California's chain of 21 Franciscan religious outposts. It lay at the northern end of El Camino Real, the "king's highway" that connected the missions. Uniquely, the Sonoma mission was built under the rule not of Spain but of Mexico, whose government wanted to fend off Russian incursions from Fort Ross, 40 miles (64 km) away. Today, the padres' quarters, adjoining the adobe chapel, is the oldest building in Sonoma (1825). In the 1880s, the mission fell on hard times and was sold; over the years it became a hay barn, winery, and blacksmith shop. Restoration began in 1903.

Across First Street East is the 1841 **Sonoma Barracks,** which housed Mexican and then American soldiers. Inside it now you'll see a history museum, a re-created bunk room, and a film about Mexican General Vallejo. Next door stands the wood-frame **Toscano Hotel,** a former boardinghouse. Nearby, at 133 East Spain Street, the adobe **Blue Wing Inn** was built in 1840. Into its saloon swaggered such Western characters as Kit Carson and bandit Joaquin Murietta.

Half a mile (0.8 km) from the Plaza, via West Spain Street, is General Vallejo's house, **Lachryma Montis** (W. Spain St. at 3rd St. W.), which reveals how the Mexican comandante adapted to American rule. Moving out of his adobe house on the plaza, he built this New England–style house in 1851.

Historic Wineries

Sebastiani Vineyards incorporates some of the mission vineyard. Founded in 1904, the historic winery offers tours and tastings, and displays a huge collection of hand-carved wine casks, some dating from the mid-1800s. In 1857, Count Agoston Haraszthy began premium wine production at what is now **Buena Vista Winery.** Tastings are held in the stone Press House, built in 1862 and thought to be California's oldest winery building.

Valley of the Moon

Twenty minutes north of Sonoma is **Glen Ellen,** site of **Jack London State Historic Park.** The author moved to his ranch here in 1911, having grown "tired of cities and people." He worked to create a model farm raising crops and animals with the latest scientific techniques. Today, you can walk or picnic among the ranch oaks and redwoods. Visit the **House of Happy Walls,** built by London's widow in 1916. It displays the author's mementos, South Pacific artifacts, and publishers' rejection slips. The couple earlier built **Wolf House,** which burned in a mysterious fire before they could move in. Its stone walls still stand. London wrote about Glen Ellen in his 1913 novel, *The Valley of the Moon.* ∎

Sebastiani Vineyards

🅰 Map p. 229 B1

✉ 389 4th St. E., Sonoma

☎ 707/933-3230

sebastiani.com

Buena Vista Winery

🅰 Map p. 229 C1

✉ 18000 Old Winery Rd., Sonoma

☎ 800/926-1266

buenavistawinery .com

Jack London State Historic Park

🅰 Map p. 229 B2

✉ 2400 London Ranch Rd., Glen Ellen

☎ 707/938-5216

💲 $$ (per car)

jacklondonpark.com

Sonoma Character: Author Jack London

The prolific author of more than 50 books between 1900 and 1916, Jack London (1876–1916) penned classics such as *The Call of the Wild* and *The Sea Wolf.* His themes were life and death, and the struggle to survive with dignity. He knew his stuff, having been a prospector, railroad hobo, and war correspondent, as well as sailing his boat, the *Snark,* around the South Pacific in search of the "big moments of living." London spent his later years in Glen Ellen at 1,400-acre (566 ha) Beauty Ranch, where he could "get out of Nature that something which we all need, only the most of us don't know it."

Yosemite National Park

One of Earth's natural cathedrals, Yosemite enshrines a trinity of wonders: Yosemite Valley, groves of sequoias, and the High Sierra. In this beautiful park of nearly 1,200 square miles (3,100 sq km), you can see waterfalls, climb granite peaks, camp under the stars, picnic in wildflower meadows, or just stand awestruck before the scenery.

Granite monolith El Capitan looms above the Merced River in Yosemite National Park.

Yosemite Valley

A mighty granite fortress, Yosemite Valley is edged with cliffs, pinnacles, and rounded domes. Seven miles (11 km) long, it was glacially sculpted; you can tell by its U shape. (River canyons are V shaped.)

Unyielding against the forces that eroded the surrounding terrain, granite **El Capitan** stands as one of the world's largest exposed monoliths. Rising 3,245 feet (990 m) from its base, it is the tallest unbroken cliff on Earth.

Curry Village provides food, accommodations, and camping. Trails from here lead to 317-foot (96 m) **Vernal Fall** and 594-foot (181 m) **Nevada Fall;** both cascades appear to have jumped right off postcards. **Mirror Lake** shows a silvery reflection of surrounding cliffs, a sight popular with photographers. (Shoot pictures on a windless morning or moonlit evening. The lake has water in spring and early summer.)

Above the lake rises legendary **Half Dome.** Originally a complete dome, its cliff face was cracked away by Ice Age glaciers. The summit seems to touch the sky, 4,748 feet (1,447 m) above the valley floor.

Yosemite Village encompasses park headquarters, shops, restaurants, and the **Valley Visitor Center,** with exhibits on natural and human history. Pick up a map while you are here.

A lodge whose architecture is a match for the majestic landscape is the 1927 **Ahwahnee Hotel** (see Travelwise p. 258). For its grand design, architect Gilbert Stanley Underwood called for ten million pounds (4.5 million kg) of native granite, plus "redwood" timbers (actually stained concrete). The interior is decorated with designs from Indian baskets, stylized with art deco. The dining room, with log pillars 40 feet (12 m) high, has floor-to-ceiling windows overlooking Yosemite Valley.

Take the free tram from the visitor center to one of the world's highest waterfalls. **Yosemite Falls** drops 2,425 feet (739 m) in three stages.

Yosemite National Park

 Map p. 233

Visitor Information

✉ Headquarters, Yosemite National Park

☎ 209/372-0200; 801/559-5000, yosemitepark .com (lodging reservations); 877/444-6777, recreation.gov (campground reservations)

💲 $$$$$ (per car)

nps.gov/yose

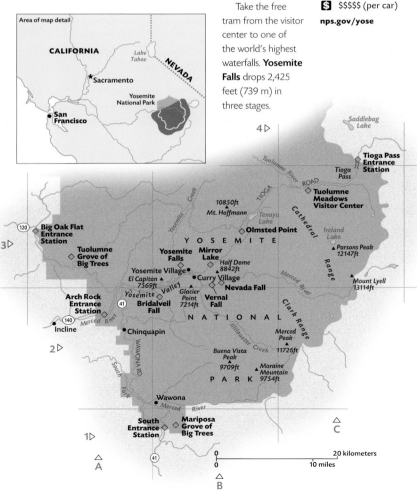

Area of map detail

CALIFORNIA

Lake Tahoe

NEVADA

★ Sacramento

Yosemite National Park

● San Francisco

Mariposa sequoia grove at Yosemite National Park

Mariposa Grove of Big Trees

- Map p. 233 B1
- Closed until Spring 2017
- Shuttle from south entrance (starting Spring 2017)
- $$$$$ (tram tour)

(The Lower Fall alone, at 320 feet/97.5 m, is twice as high as Niagara.) In spring and early summer, the falls roar with snowmelt; by August they're often dry.

Want to stroll through a tree trunk? Visit the **Tuolumne Grove of Big Trees** (at the western end of Tioga Road), a walking route among giant sequoias, ponderosa pines, and incense cedars.

Wawona Road

Take Wawona Road south out of the valley. You'll see **Bridalveil Fall,** dropping 620 feet (189 m) from a "hanging valley," a canyon that was stranded high above the Yosemite Valley floor when glaciers ground away the lower section. Turn up Glacier Point Road to sublime **Glacier Point,** which presents a view unparalleled in the world. Peaks seem to levitate beyond an empty chasm. You can see Half Dome and three waterfalls (Vernal, Nevada, Yosemite). Yosemite Valley lies far below you, at the bottom of a 3,200-foot (975 m) cliff. Imagine the days when the "Firefall" was staged nightly for visitors below in Curry Village. A bonfire was

pushed over the edge, creating a cascade of sparks and fire.

Historic cabins, an 1875 covered bridge, an old jail—all are part of the **Pioneer Yosemite History Center** (in Wawona, to the south of the park on Wawona Road), which shows valley life in the 19th century. In the **Mariposa Grove of Big Trees** some trees are nearly 3,000 years old. These giant sequoias—some weighing more than two million pounds (0.9 million kg)—are the world's largest living things. Yosemite's biggest tree, with a 96-foot (29 m) circumference, is the **Grizzly Giant,** ragged with age after 1,800 years. The 209-foot (64 m) tree stands so high above the forest that it was hit by lightning six times during a storm. You can visit the Mariposa Grove on walking trails.

INSIDER TIP:

The secret of Yosemite is the hidden-in-plain-sight Valley Loop Trail, which links such major landmarks as Yosemite Falls and El Capitan.

—ROBERT EARLE HOWELLS
National Geographic contributor

Tioga Road

Tioga Road leads eastward across the high country. Stop at **Olmsted Point,** where a trail leads to a lookout over Half Dome and Tenaya Lake. There are trailheads leading to the Pacific Crest and John Muir trails. The road crosses 9,945-foot (3,031 m) Tioga Pass before leaving the park. ■

Lake Tahoe

Suspended between the peaks of the Sierra Nevada and the Carson Range at 6,225 feet (1,897 m) above sea level, Lake Tahoe straddles two states, California and Nevada. As the lake deepens from the shore to a depth of 1,645 feet (501 m), its hue changes from aquamarine to rich lapis lazuli.

South Lake

Visitor Information

✉ 3066 Lake Tahoe Blvd., So. Lake Tahoe

☎ 530/541-5255

tahoesouth.com

North Lake

Visitor Information

✉ 100 N. Lake Blvd., Tahoe City

☎ 530/581-6900

gotahoenorth.com

Incline Village Crystal Bay

Visitor Information

✉ 969 Tahoe Blvd., Incline Village

☎ 775/832-1606

gotahoenorth.com

Lake Tahoe has recreation and mountain scenery written large on every page of its calendar. Summer hiking and mountain biking are popular, as are golf and boating on the lake. Winter means skiing. At night, relax in casinos on the Nevada side, which offer gambling and big-name entertainers.

Things to See & Do

South Lake Tahoe is the lake's largest community. The gondola at **Heavenly Mountain Resort** (US 50 W of Stateline, tel 775/586-7000, skiheavenly.com, $$$$$) offers a view of the lake as you ride up Monument Peak.

From here, travel clockwise around the lake to see:

U.S. Forest Service Visitor Center

✉ Visitor Center Rd. off Calif. 89

☎ 530/543-2674

🕐 Closed Nov.–May

Tallac Historic Site

🄰 Map p. 235 B2

☎ 530/541-5227

🕐 Closed mid-Sept. –end of May

💲 $$ (tours)

D. L. Bliss State Park

🄰 Map p. 235 B2

☎ 530/525-7277

🕐 Closed Labor Day–Mem. Day

💲 $$

Ed Z'berg Sugar Pine Point State Park

🄰 Map p. 235 B2

☎ 530/525-7982

💲 $$

Gatekeeper's Museum & Marion Steinbach Indian Basket Museum

✉ 130 W. Lake Blvd., Tahoe City

☎ 530/583-1762

💲 $$

northtahoemuseums .org

The **U.S. Forest Service Visitor Center** lets you look below the surface of Taylor Creek without getting wet. The windows of a "stream profile chamber" reveal salmon, trout, and other creek denizens acting naturally.

The **Tallac Historic Site** preserves rustic mansions built by wealthy San Franciscans. The oldest is the shingled **Pope Estate** (1894), which still has its coffered ceilings and paneling. The log **Baldwin Estate** (1921) evokes the rustic elegance of an early Tahoe summer retreat; there are various exhibits on Washoe Indian culture and local history.

Emerald Bay is the most photographed spot at Lake Tahoe; try shooting from **Inspiration Point** along Calif. 89. Lora Josephine Knight's **Vikingsholm mansion** (*530/525-9530, vikingsholm.com, closed Oct.–May., $$*) stands here, at the head of a bay that resembles a fjord. The 1929 Scandinavian-style castle has 38 rooms and a sod roof where wildflowers bloom. Out in the water, you'll see the lake's only island, Fanette, with an unusual stone teahouse also built by the heiress.

D. L. Bliss State Park has a good beach at Rubicon Bay, an early 1900s lighthouse (the nation's highest at 6,235 feet/1900 m), and the 130-ton (118 tonnes) Balancing Rock. Lumber magnate Bliss once cornered most of Tahoe's lakefront property.

Ed Z'berg Sugar Pine Point State Park shelters around 2,000 acres (809 ha) of its namesake trees, as well as incense cedars and other species. Indian fighter Gen. William Phipps built the 1872 Phipps Cabin, and a San Francisco financier erected the **Hellman-Ehrman Mansion** (*tel 530/525-7982, closed Labor Day–Mem. Day, $$*) in 1902. Join a tour of the interior or picnic on the lawn.

In **Tahoe City** the lake has its sole outlet, the Truckee River. See it from **Fanny Bridge,** so called for the rear view of gawkers leaning over the rail. Tahoe City is a gateway to ski areas at **Alpine Meadows** and **Squaw Valley.** Pioneer relics are displayed at the **Gatekeeper's Museum & Marion Steinbach Indian Basket Museum.** Washoe Indians often came to use the grinding stone in front of the **Watson Cabin** (*560 N. Lake Blvd., 530/583-1762, closed Labor Day–Mem. Day*), the oldest building in town (1909). ∎

Amazing Lake Tahoe

• The nation's largest alpine lake, Tahoe measures 22 miles long by 12 miles wide (35 by 19 km). If you tipped out the lake's contents, the water would flood an area the size of California to a depth of 14 inches (35.5 cm).

• More than 60 streams flow into Lake Tahoe, but only one flows out, the Truckee River. Tahoe loses much of its water to evaporation: If the water that evaporates

every day could be recovered, it could supply the daily requirements of a city the size of Los Angeles.

• Reputedly, the lake's water is 99.99 percent pure, about the same as distilled water. It is so clear that a dinner plate would be visible 75 feet (23 m) below the surface. The lake's legendary clarity is threatened, however, by sediments washed in from developed areas.

Travelwise

A cable car makes its way up
San Francisco's California Street.

TRAVELWISE

PLANNING YOUR TRIP

The city's major walk-in source for information, maps, and brochures is the San Francisco Visitor Information Center *(Lower Level, Hallidie Plaza, 900 Market St., next to cable car turntable at Powell & Market Sts., tel 415/391-2000).* The superb official San Francisco Travel website (see below) offers information on neighborhoods, activities, dining, shopping, nightlife, culture, and events; transportation information and interactive maps; hotel bookings; LGBT travel; and more. The website's "Visitors Planning Guide" can be viewed online, downloaded, or ordered with a separate map as the "Visitor Kit" for mailing. The *San Francisco Chronicle's* "SF Guide" site *(sfgate.com/sfguide)* offers neighborhood profiles and information on dining and things to do.

Useful Websites

San Francisco Travel (official tourism site): sanfrancisco.travel
San Francisco Chronicle **newspaper:** sfgate.com
San Francisco Magazine: modern luxury.com/san-francisco

When to Go/Climate

The weather in San Francisco is temperate year-round, generally ranging from 70°F (21°C) down to 40°F (4.4°C). But the weather isn't predictable. It can sometimes change its mind several times during the course of a day, as fog rolls over the city or burns off under the sunshine. Some summer days top 80°F (26.6°C), yet summer is the foggiest season. Most rain falls from November through March. To prepare for quirky weather, layer your outfits with a sweater

and jacket; leave shorts and summer garb at home.

Most tourists descend on the city in July and August. If they include you, reserve hotel rooms ahead and be prepared to stand in line at tourist spots and cable car stops. Explore the city on weekends (when hotel rates often drop), and visit areas such as Carmel and Napa during the week (when they're less crowded).

Main Events

JANUARY
San Francisco Restaurant Week *(sfrestaurantweek.com)* features more than 100 restaurants offering special menus.

FEBRUARY
Chinese New Year *(tel 415/982-3000, chineseparade.com)* The date of Chinese New Year varies and may fall in late January. Venture into Chinatown to see events such as a parade with firecrackers, a block-long dancing dragon, and the Miss Chinatown USA Pageant.

MARCH
St. Patrick's Day Parade
Parade down Market Street, celebrating the patron saint of Ireland. Live music, dance, beverages.

APRIL
San Francisco International Film Festival *(tel 415/561-5000, sffs.org)* Various venues. Films and videos from many countries.

Cherry Blossom Festival *(Japantown, Civic Center, tel 415/563-2313, sfcherryblossom .org)* Performances, parade, food, crafts, martial arts.

MAY
Carnaval San Francisco *(carnaval sanfrancisco.org)* A two-day Latin American–style festival of dance and music.

Cinco de Mayo *(Dolores Park, sfcincodemayo.com)* A celebration of the Mexican victory at Puebla, complete with a parade, displays of traditional Mexican arts and crafts, food, and music.

Bay to Breakers Race *(tel 415/231-3130, baytobreakers.com)* More than 50,000 entrants race and/or show off wacky costumes during this 12K run, which starts near the Embarcadero and ends at Ocean Beach.

JUNE
San Francisco Jazz Festival *(tel 415/398-5655, sfjazz.org)* Legendary performers and up-and-coming artists perform at SFJAZZ Center and Davies Symphony Hall.

Union Street Festival *(Fillmore, tel 800/310-6563, unionstreet festival.com)* Arts and crafts, food, live music.

Dipsea Race *(tel 415/331-3550, dipsea.org)* A 7.4-mile (12 km) run from Mill Valley to Stinson Beach.

Lesbian, Gay, Bisexual, Transgender Pride Celebration *(tel 415/864-0831, sfpride.org)* Celebration and live music at Civic Center Plaza; parade down Market Street, costumes, dance, art.

Juneteenth Festival *(Fillmore St., Sutter to Turk, tel 510/692-2514, sfjuneteenth.com)* African-American observance of the end of slavery; includes entertainment and parade.

JULY
Cable Car Bell-Ringing Contest Held in Union Square.

San Francisco Marathon *(tel 888/958-6668, thesfmarathon.com)* Entrants run on the 26.1-mile (42 km) route through the city and over the Golden Gate Bridge.

SEPTEMBER
Free Shakespeare in the Park *(tel 415/558-0888, sfshakes .org)* May start in late August.

Performances are held in the Presidio and McLaren Park.

San Francisco Opera opening night (*War Memorial Opera House, tel 415/864-3330, sfopera.com*) Gala with formal ball.

OCTOBER

Castro Street Fair (*tel 800/853-5950, castrostreetfair.org*) Based around Castro and Market Streets, this community event brings together musicians, dancers, artists, and organizations to celebrate the diversity of the Castro, the city's gay neighborhood.

Italian Heritage Parade and Festival (*sfcolumbusday.org*) Held on the Sunday before Columbus Day. Parade and street stalls based around Fisherman's Wharf and North Beach.

Fleet Week (*fleetweeksf.org*) Brings military ships and Blue Angels air shows to the waterfront.

How to Get to San Francisco
From the Airport

San Francisco International Airport (SFO) lies 14 miles (22.5 km) south of the city off US 101 (*Bayshore Fwy.*). For airport ground transportation, including BART (Bay Area Rapid Transit), shuttles, buses, taxis, limousines: tel 800/435-9736 or 650/821-8211, flysfo.com/to-from /overview. BART (*tel 415/989-2278, bart.gov*) operates rail service to San Francisco (*$8.65*) until just before midnight; its station in the International Terminal is accessible from any terminal via the free AirTrain shuttle to the Garage G/ BART station stop. Taxis to San Francisco cost about $45–$65 and can be shared; shuttle vans charge about $17. Uber and Lyft also serve the airport (see "Ride-hailing services" below). SFO has an airport art museum, local restaurants and retailers, and yoga and meditation rooms.

In the East Bay, 17 miles (27 km) from the city, smaller Oakland International Airport (*tel 510/563-3300, flyoakland.com*) has connections to San Francisco by BART (*about $10; take the automated monorail to the BART Coliseum station for connections*), shuttle, and taxi (*about $80*).

By Rail

Amtrak (*tel 800/872-7245, amtrak.com*) runs trains that arrive in Emeryville, near Oakland, and connect by motorcoach to San Francisco.

GETTING AROUND
By Public Transportation

For information, dial toll-free from the Bay Area: 511; toll-free from elsewhere: 888/500-4636; website: 511.org. Useful phone apps for transport: sanfrancisco.travel /best-san-francisco-travel-apps.

Muni: The San Francisco Municipal Railway, aka Muni (*tel 311, sfmta.com*) operates buses, streetcars, light rail, and cable cars. Download maps at sfmta.com/maps. Buses have the widest network and most convenience. Their destinations and numbers appear on the front; bus stops are indicated by signs and street markings. There are six light-rail Muni Metro lines. Two historic streetcars, the E-Embarcadero and F-Market lines, run together from Fisherman's Wharf to the Ferry Building, where the F line turns inland on Market Street to Castro Street, and the E line continues along the Embarcadero to AT&T Park and the Caltrain depot.

Cable cars (indicated by CC in text) follow three routes: The Powell-Hyde and Powell-Mason lines begin at Powell and Market Streets near Union Square; the

former ends at Victorian Park near the Maritime Museum, the latter near Fisherman's Wharf at Bay and Taylor Streets. The California Street line follows California Street from Market Street through Chinatown to Van Ness Avenue. Tips: Board the cable car along the route rather than waiting with a crowd at either terminus. For thrills, the Powell-Hyde line descends the steepest slope (on Hyde Street between Chestnut Street and Bay Street).

Muni fares are $2.25 for buses and streetcars ($1 for seniors or children); free transfers are valid for 90 minutes. Cable cars cost $7 for a one-way ticket. A Muni Passport costs $17 for one day, $26 for three days, and $35 for seven days.

BART: Bay Area Rapid Transit (*tel 415/989-2278, bart.gov*) is a modern rail line with nine San Francisco stations linked to 30 East Bay stations. Maximum fares are $1.85 within the city and $6.45 to the East Bay.

Taxis: Taxi fares run $3.50 for the first fifth of a mile and 55 cents for each additional fifth of a mile. The standard tip is 15 percent. Ask your hotel or restaurant to call you a cab. If calling yourself, try Yellow Cab (*tel 415/333-3333*), Green Cab (*tel 415/626-4733*), Metro Cab (*tel 415/920-0700*), Desoto Cab (*tel 415/970-1300*), or Veteran's Cab (*tel 415/648-4119*).

Ride-hailing services: The increasingly popular Uber (*uber.com*) and Lyft (*lyft.com*) summon private car drivers through an app on your mobile phone. Response time is faster and rates often lower than taxis'.

Ferries: The Blue & Gold Fleet (*Pier 41 & Ferry Building, tel 415/ 773-1188, blueandgoldfleet.com*) runs to Sausalito, Tiburon, Angel Island, Vallejo, Alameda/Oakland, Harbor Bay, South San Francisco, and (on game days) AT&T Park. Golden Gate Ferry *(behind Ferry Building, tel 415/455-2000, golden gateferry.org)* goes to Sausalito, Larkspur and AT&T Park on game days.

Out of Town: Golden Gate Transit *(tel 415/455-2000 or 511, golden gatetransit.org)* runs buses across Golden Gate Bridge to Marin and Sonoma Counties. Caltrain *(4th St. at King St., tel 800/660-4287, caltrain.com)* runs trains between the city and San Jose.

Walking Tours
A remarkable resource, the public library's nonprofit San Francisco City Guides *(tel 415-557-4266, sfcityguides.org)* offers 70 different walking tours per week, covering history, architecture, neighborhoods, art, culture, and local lore; free, but donations welcome.

Driving
Always give the right of way to pedestrians and cable cars. On hills, set your parking brake and curb your wheels: Facing uphill, turn tires toward the street to prevent a runaway vehicle; facing downhill, turn tires toward the curb. Curb colors indicate parking regulations: red (no stopping or parking), green (10-minute limit), yellow (commercial loading zone; check signs for effective hours), white (passenger loading zone), blue (handicapped with permit), tow-away zone (ticket plus towing and storage fees).

Parking garages are situated near San Francisco's major tourist sites. Muni's SF Park program *(sfpark.org or mobile app)* shows available parking garages and metered parking; prices change according to demand.

All major car rental companies operate in San Francisco, with offices in the city and at airports. Obtain phone numbers by dialing 800/555-1212 (toll-free directory).

PRACTICAL ADVICE
Safety
Although San Francisco is a relatively safe city, you should be cautious in—and avoid at night—the Tenderloin. Also be alert in the Lower Haight *(E of Haight-Ashbury),* the Western Addition *(W of Civic Center and S of Japantown),* and the Mission District *(E of Valencia St. and N of 16th St.).*

Apply rules of common sense:
• Do not give your bags to anyone in an airport or train/bus station other than authorized personnel or your taxi driver.
• Be alert to your surroundings, especially in crowds.
• Don't carry large amounts of money. Keep your wallet in your front pocket; hold your purse securely with the clasp facing in.
• Do not use ATMs when there is no one around.
• If you are robbed, don't resist and call 911.
• Don't leave valuables in your car. In case of mishap, contact the Crime Victims Hot Line at 800/842-8467, the police non-emergency line at 415/553-0123, or the District Attorney's Victim Services Division at 415/553-9044 on weekdays.

Earthquakes
If you feel a tremor, step into a doorway or crouch under a table; stay away from windows. If outdoors, move away from buildings, trees, and electrical power lines.

Travelers With Disabilities
For general information, the San Francisco Convention & Visitors Bureau maintains a TDD/TTY line at 415/227-2619.

All Muni buses and streetcars (but not cable cars) are accessible to disabled travelers *(311, TTY 415/701-4730, sfmta.com/getting-around).* Golden Gate Transit offers accessible bus and ferry services to Marin County *(tel 415/455-2000 or 511, TDD 711, goldengatetransit.org/accessibility).*

Parking zones for people with disabilities are marked with signs and blue curbs. By law, public buildings must be at least partially accessible and provide toilets for visitors with disabilities.

Emergencies & Health Care
• For police, medical, or fire emergencies, dial 911.
• Around-the-clock emergency rooms are available at St. Francis Memorial Hospital *(1150 Bush St., tel 415/353-6373, physician referral 800/333-1355),* the Medical Center at the University of California, San Francisco *(505 Parnassus Ave., tel 415/353-1037, physician referral 415/353-1238),* and San Francisco General Hospital *(1001 Potrero Ave., tel 415/206-8111).*
• Other medical care includes walk-in clinics such as Concentra Urgent Care Center *(26 California St., tel 415/781-7077).* The multilingual Traveler Medical Group *(490 Post St., tel 415/981-1102)* makes house calls to hotels.
• The San Francisco Dental Society has a referral service *(tel 415/928-7337).*
• Walgreens has 24-hour pharmacies at 3201 Divisadero St. *(tel 415/931-6417)* and 498 Castro St. *(tel 415/861-3136).* Four-Fifty Sutter Pharmacy *(tel 415/ 392-4137)* delivers prescriptions to hotels.

Hotels & Restaurants

Choose a lavish Nob Hill institution or a fashionable new boutique hotel near Union Square, a reasonably priced motel along Lombard Street or a neighborhood Victorian bed-and-break-fast. Rooms can be reserved through San Francisco Travel, which partners with booking.com: *sanfrancisco.travel/stay.* **Promotions and times of low occupancy can reduce rates, even at luxury hotels; it's always worthwhile to ask for discounts.**

Dining is a major attraction. (San Francisco is regularly named on lists for best United States cities for dining.) More than 4,450 restaurants offer California cuisine (created in the Bay Area), French gastronomy, grills, humble burgers and tacos, and wonderful dishes from Italy, the Pacific Rim, Latin America, and other regions whose people immigrated to the city. For availability and menus for hundreds of restaurants, go to opentable.com. Smoking is banned in all restaurants and bars.

Using This List

Hotels and restaurants are first organized by neighborhood, then alphabetical order according to their price category. Restaurant closing days are included, but try to verify by phone; reservations are recommended. Most hotels, and some restaurants, have parking; check details with individual establishments. Ask hotels and restaurants about the extent of facilities for disabled guests, as these vary. Few hotels have smoking rooms.

At upscale restaurants, lunch will cost at least 25 percent less than dinner, and some offer a prix-fixe menu. All restaurants in San Francisco are nonsmoking.

Credit Cards

AE American Express, D Discover, MC Mastercard, V Visa

■ FINANCIAL DISTRICT

HOTELS

🏨 GALLERIA PARK
$$$$$
191 SUTTER ST., 94104
TEL 415/781-3060
jdvhotels.com
Stylish boutique hotel in a 1911 landmark building. The lobby has art nouveau touches. Rooms are decorated in pale hues. Rooftop park, complete with jogging track.
🛈 177 🅿 Valet 🔁 �''🚭 💺 🚇 🌐 Free 🚫 All major cards

🏨 HYATT REGENCY
$$$$$
5 EMBARCADERO CENTER 94111
TEL 415/788-1234
hyatt.com
This hotel is famous for its 17-story atrium lobby and glass-pod elevators. Floors are arranged in open tiers; many rooms have waterfront views. Decor is rather businesslike. It is situated at the end of the California Street cable car line.
🛈 804 🅿 Valet 🔁 🚭 💺 🌐 Free 🚫 All major cards

🏨 LOEWS REGENCY
$$$$$
222 SANSOME ST. 94104
TEL 415/276-9888
loewshotels.com
Set in a dramatic location with great views of the city, this luxurious hotel consists of

PRICES

HOTELS
An indication of the cost of a double room in the high season is given by **$**. Rates may be lower during slow periods, promotions.

$$$$$	Over $450
$$$$	$350–$450
$$$	$250–$350
$$	$150–$250
$	Under $150

RESTAURANTS
An indication of the cost of a three-course meal without drinks is given by $ signs.

$$$$	Over $50
$$$	$35–$50
$$	$15–$35
$	Under $15

two towers linked by a glass skybridge. It occupies 11 floors of a 48-story tower.
🛈 155 🅿 Valet 🔁 🚭 💺 🌐 Free 🚫 All major cards

SOMETHING SPECIAL

🏨 PALACE HOTEL
🍴 $$$$
2 NEW MONTGOMERY ST. 94105
TEL 415/512-1111
sfpalace.com
This grand old hostelry, dating from 1909, houses the famous **Garden Court** restaurant (with an art-glass ceiling and marble columns); the bar has a must-see Maxfield Parrish mural. There is a skylighted

swimming pool; large rooms have high ceilings.

[i] 556 [P] Valet [⬍] [◐]
[◔] [📺] [📶] [🛜] Charge
[💳] All major cards

🏨 OMNI
$$$–$$$$$
500 CALIFORNIA ST.
94104
TEL 415/677-9494
omnihotels.com
Located on the California cable car line two blocks from Chinatown, this "mini-Ritz" of a hotel, which occupies a 1926 building, offers quiet luxury (plush beds, marble vanities) and modern business amenities.

[i] 362 [P] Valet [⬍] [◐] [◔]
[📺] [🛜] Free in lobby
[💳] All major cards

RESTAURANTS

🍴 MICHAEL MINA
$$$$
252 CALIFORNIA ST.
TEL 415/397-9222
michaelmina.net
With dramatic high ceilings and a menu based on Japanese and European influences, this award-winning restaurant serves seafood (e.g., ahi tuna tartare) and meats (smoked rib-eye with truffle mushroom purée).

[🪑] 110 [P] Valet [🕐] Closed Sat. & Sun. L [💳] All major cards

🍴 QUINCE
$$$$
470 PACIFIC AVE.
TEL 415/775-8500
quincerestaurant.com
Contemporary seasonal cuisine from award-winning chef Michael Tusk, whose tasting menu changes nightly and showcases organic produce and meats, select fish, and caviar.

[🪑] 90 [P] Valet [🕐] Closed L & Sun. [💳] All major cards

🍴 WATERFRONT RESTAURANT
$$$$
PIER 7, THE EMBARCADERO
TEL 415/391-2696
waterfrontsf.com
Contemporary restaurant with Bay Bridge views and a menu emphasizing classic seafood and beef.

[🪑] 160 [P] Valet
[💳] All major cards

🍴 WAYFARE TAVERN
$$$$
558 SACRAMENTO ST.
TEL 415/772-9060
wayfaretavern.com
Traditional American surroundings (gilded eagle logo, lots of wood) for upscale traditional food: creamy deviled eggs, corn soup, chicken fried in buttermilk brine, roasted garlic, crisp herbs, lemon.

[🪑] 58 [P] Valet
[💳] All major cards

🍴 BARBACCO
$$$
220 CALIFORNIA ST.
TEL 415/955-1919
barbaccosf.com
Brick-wall trattoria serving simple Italian dishes at a kitchen bar and communal tables: salt cod fritters; bruschetta; pasta with braised lamb shoulder, Sicilian olives, ricotta.

[🪑] 65 [🕐] Closed Sat. L & Sun.
[💳] All major cards

🍴 BOCADILLOS
$$$
710 MONTGOMERY ST.
TEL 415/982-2622
bocasf.com
Tasty tapas and bocadillos (little sandwiches) inspired by Spain's Basque country. Samples: blistered padron peppers with lemon sea salt; grilled prawns with crispy garlic; grilled hanger steak; spanish anchovies with charred onion-caper salsa and toast;

lamb burger with aioli, tomato, pickle, and chips.

[🪑] 50 [🕐] Closed Sat. L & Sun.
[💳] All major cards

🍴 COTOGNA
$$$
490 PACIFIC AVE.
TEL 415/775-8508
cotognasf.com
A less expensive complement to jointly owned, adjacent **Quince,** offering rustic Italian trattoria cooking and a daily changing menu of spit-roasted or grilled meats and fish, wood-oven pizzas, and pastas.

[🪑] 58 [P] Valet [🕐] Closed Sun.
[💳] All major cards

🍴 KOKKARI ESTIATORIO
$$$
200 JACKSON ST.
TEL 415/981-0983
kokkari.com
With the ambience of a country inn on the Aegean (fireplace, woodwork, flowers), Kokkari showcases seafood and meats. Notable: crispy smelts, grilled chicken with lemon and oregano.

[🪑] 185 [P] Valet [🕐] Closed Sat. & Sun. L [💳] All major cards

🍴 PLOUF
$$$
40 BELDEN PL.
TEL 415/986-6491
ploufsf.com
Specializing in mussels with intriguing sauces, as well as oysters, this French bistro (indoor/outdoor dining) also serves great starters.

[🪑] 65 [🕐] Closed Sat. & Sun. L
[💳] All major cards

🍴 TADICH GRILL
$$$
240 CALIFORNIA ST.
TEL 415/391-1849
tadichgrill.com
Open since 1849, this vintage San Francisco institution is the city's longest continuously operating restaurant. Seafood

includes sole, Hangtown fry, sand dabs, and their famous tartar sauce. No reservations. 120 Closed Sun. MC, V

YANK SING
$$$
101 SPEAR ST.
TEL 415/781-1111
49 STEVENSON ST.
TEL 415/541-4949
yanksing.com
Two words: dim sum. The helpful staff at both locations will explain the delectable items on the trolleys; watch for Peking duck with scallions and plum sauce, Shanghai pork dumplings, and shrimp ha gau.
Spear St. 248, Stevenson St. 92 Closed D
All major cards

■ UNION SQUARE & NOB HILL

HOTELS

CLIFT
$$$$$
495 GEARY ST.
94102
TEL 415/775-4700
clifthotel.com
This classic San Francisco hotel got an artsy makeover from designer Philippe Starck; the lobby features a surreal stool by René Magritte and a coffee table by Salvador Dalí. The 1933 Redwood Room cocktail lounge, whose interior was fashioned from a single tree, has trendy digital paintings. Guest rooms feature pale pastels and Starck-designed beds.
372 Valet Free in Lobby
All major cards

THE FAIRMONT
$$$$$
950 MASON ST.
94108
TEL 415/772-5000
fairmont.com/sanfrancisco
The lobby of this 1907 Nob Hill icon has marble columns and a gilt coffered ceiling. Rooms are decorated in jewel-box colors; the Penthouse Suite fills an entire floor and includes a billiard room done in Persian tiles.
591 Valet
All major cards

RITZ-CARLTON
$$$$$
600 STOCKTON ST.
94108
TEL 415/296-7465
ritzcarlton.com
In a grand 1909 neoclassical building, guest rooms have marble baths and decor inspired by the city's fog (gray, steel blue). The club level has its own concierge and all-day food, with weekend caviar and wine tastings. Spa.
336 Valet Charge
All major cards

SCARLET HUNTINGTON
$$$$$
1075 CALIFORNIA ST.
94108
TEL 415/474-5400
thescarlethotels.com
This venerable hotel has been redone in the bright color accents of the Chinese of Malaysia. The gracious staff remains, as does the Big 4 Restaurant, with its paneled walls and green leather booths, and the Nob Hill Spa with its indoor infinity pool and city-view terrace.
134 Valet Charge
All major cards

TAJ CAMPTON PLACE
$$$$$
340 STOCKTON ST.
94108
TEL 415/781-5555
tajhotels.com
An intimate luxury hotel with stylishly furnished rooms, fine amenities (premium bedding, soaking tubs), and personal service.
110 Valet Free All major cards

THE MARKER
$$$$–$$$$$
501 GEARY ST.
94102
TEL 415/292-0100
themarkersanfrancisco.com
The lobby of this 1910 beaux arts hotel has a grand marble staircase and fireplace. Rooms are done in bright, bold stripes.
208 Valet Free All major cards

HANDLERY UNION SQUARE
$$$$
351 GEARY ST.
94102
TEL 415/781-7800
handlery.com
This is a well-located boutique hotel decorated in neutrals. The Premiere section has large rooms, many overlooking the swimming pool and offering extra amenities.
377 Free All major cards

HILTON UNION SQUARE SAN FRANCISCO
$$$$
333 O'FARRELL ST.
94102
TEL 415/771-1400
hiltonsanfranciscohotel.com
Businesslike rooms are decorated in minimalist contemporary style with dark woods; black tile accents in the baths. "Tower 1" rooms have broad views. Rooftop pool. A convention hotel with personable staff.
1,919 Valet Free in lobby
All major cards

HOTEL REX
$$$$
562 SUTTER ST.
94102
TEL 415/433-4434
jdvhotels.com
Fashioned after bohemian
Paris, this hotel celebrates art,
books. Yellow sunny rooms
have works by local artists.
[i] 94 [P] Valet 🔁 Ⓢ 🔁
🛜 Free 🅰 All major cards

SOMETHING SPECIAL

MARK HOPKINS
INTER-CONTINENTAL
$$$$
999 CALIFORNIA ST.
94108
TEL 415/392-3434
intercontinentalmarkhopkins
.com
A Nob Hill landmark. Large
rooms have views, luxury, and
tech amenities. The famous
Top of the Mark restaurant
and cocktail bar provides a
360° panorama over the city.
[i] 380 [P] Valet 🔁 Ⓢ 🔁 📺
🛜 Charge 🅰 All major cards

SIR FRANCIS DRAKE
HOTEL
$$$$
450 POWELL ST.
94102
TEL 415/392-7755
sirfrancisdrake.com
This landmark 1928 hotel has
a glittery regal lobby (marble,
crystal chandeliers) and rooms
redone in black and tan with
ornate headboards and tech
amenities, some with city views.
[i] 417 [P] Valet 🔁 Ⓢ 🔁 📺
🛜 Charge 🅰 All major cards

STANFORD COURT
$$$$
905 CALIFORNIA ST.
94108
TEL 415/989-3500
stanfordcourt.com
Discreetly tucked away on
Nob Hill, this hostelry has tech

amenities and guest rooms
done in contemporary warm
cream-and-caramel tones,
with luxury bedding; deluxe
rooms have expansive bay
and city views.
[i] 393 [P] Valet 🔁 Ⓢ 🔁 📺
🛜 Free 🅰 All major cards

SOMETHING SPECIAL

WESTIN ST. FRANCIS
$$$$
335 POWELL ST.
94102
TEL 415/397-7000
westinstfrancis.com
The only hotel facing onto
Union Square, this 1904 grande
dame has hosted royalty and
presidents. Renovated rooms
in the original building are
furnished in ecru and brown,
with traditional high ceilings
and crystal chandeliers; many
have views over Union Square.
Modern tower rooms are spacious, with modern paintings
and panoramic windows.
[i] 1,200 [P] Valet 🔁
Ⓢ 🔁 📺 🛜 Charge
🅰 All major cards

DONATELLO
$$$–$$$$
501 POST ST.
94102
TEL 415/441-7100
thedonatellosf.com
Well-located property; all
rooms are studio suites
(king bed, sleeper sofa)
with kitchenettes.
[i] 94 [P] 🔁 Ⓢ 📺
🛜 Free 🅰 All major cards

HOTEL TRITON
$$$–$$$$
342 GRANT AVE.
94108
TEL 415/394-0500
hoteltriton.com
Well-located just outside
the Chinatown gate, this
whimsical hotel—kooky
furniture in the lobby, yoga

mats in your room—is a play-
ground of pop design. Colorful
guest rooms include a celebrity
suite designed by Jerry Garcia;
the Haagen-Dazs Suite is
stocked with complimentary
ice cream. Pets are welcome,
with no extra fee.
[i] 140 [P] Valet 🔁 Ⓢ 🔁 📺
🛜 Free 🅰 All major cards

CARLTON
$$$
1075 SUTTER ST.
94109
TEL 415/673-0242
jdvhotels.com
Bold, simple decor with exotic
international touches. Many
rooms have views; connecting
rooms available for families.
[i] 161 [P] Valet 🔁 Ⓢ
🛜 Free 🅰 All major cards

EXECUTIVE HOTEL
VINTAGE COURT
$$$
650 BUSH ST., 94108
TEL 415/392-4666

🏨 Hotel 🍴 Restaurant [i] No. of Guest Rooms 🔀 No. of Seats [P] Parking 🕐 Closed 🔁 Elevator

executivehotels.net
Themed around the Wine Country, this hotel serves complimentary evening wine beside the fireplace. Rooms in green, cream, and wood.
🛈 106 🅿 Valet 🔁 Ⓢ 🛠 🍸 📶 Free 🅢 All major cards

HOTEL ABRI
$$$
127 ELLIS ST.
94102
TEL 415/392-8800
hotelabrisf.com
Smart urban hotel with a cool vibe, sleek modern decor, stylish fireplace lounge. Amenities include a shopping valet, latest technology.
🛈 91 🅿 Valet 🔁 Ⓢ 🛠 📶 Free 🅢 All major cards

HOTEL CALIFORNIA
$$$
580 GEARY BLVD.
94102
TEL 415/441-2700
hotelcaliforniasf.com
Bright hotel with comfy beds located by the theater district. And yes, you can check out any time you like . . .
🛈 83 🅿 🔁 Ⓢ 🛠 🍸 📶 Free 🅢 All major cards

HOTEL DIVA
$$$
440 GEARY ST.
94102
TEL 415/885-0200
hoteldiva.com
Sleekly designed, fun hotel decorated in charcoal and white, with whimsical touches. Stylish rooms have brushed steel headboards, beds with luxurious white linens, high-tech amenities. Well located across from major theaters.
🛈 116 🅿 Valet 🔁 Ⓢ 🛠 🍸 📶 Free 🅢 All major cards

HOTEL G
$$$

386 GEARY ST.
94102
TEL 415/986-2000
hotelgsanfrancisco.com
When this 1909 hotel was renovated, the original facade, ceiling, and floors were preserved. Simple, smart design in the guest rooms: pale walls, walnut accents. Amenities include Nespresso coffee makers, Mascioni linens.
🛈 532 🅿 Valet 🔁 Ⓢ 🛠 🍸 🅢 All major cards

HOTEL NIKKO
🍽 **$$$**
222 MASON ST.
94102
TEL 415/394-1111
hotelnikkosf.com
This modern hotel with a calm Asian sensibility has a stream of flowing water in the lobby, an atrium swimming pool, and a 10,000-square-foot (930 sq m) health club. Large contemporary rooms. Imperial Club rooms have views and television that plays through the bathroom mirrors. Some packages include lavish breakfast at **Anzu** restaurant.
🛈 114 🅿 Valet 🔁 Ⓢ 🛠 🏊 📶 Free 🅢 All major cards

HOTEL UNION SQUARE
$$$
114 POWELL ST.
94102
TEL 415/397-3000
hotelunionsquare.com
The city's first boutique hotel, built for the 1915 Panama-Pacific International Exposition, has been given a contemporary look and tech amenities. Rooftop penthouses have private view decks.
🛈 131 🅿 🔁 Ⓢ 🛠 📶 Free 🅢 All major cards

HOTEL VERTIGO
$$$
940 SUTTER ST.
94109

TEL 415/885-6800
hotelvertigosf.com
A stylish, eccentric hotel with rooms decorated in white with orange accents. (Why the name? Alfred Hitchcock filmed scenes for the movie here.)
🛈 102 🅿 Valet 🔁 Ⓢ 🍸 📶 Free 🅢 All major cards

INN AT UNION SQUARE
$$$
440 POST ST.
94102
TEL 415/397-3510
unionsquare.com
A stylish small inn. Thoughtful touches include breakfast rooms with fireplaces, complimentary umbrellas, 24-hour concierge service, and down pillows. Classic San Francisco decor in red, cream.
🛈 30 🅿 🔁 📶 Free 🅢 All major cards

KENSINGTON PARK
$$$
450 POST ST.
94102
TEL 415/788-6400
kensingtonparkhotel.com
This 1925 Gothic building has a handsome lobby with Queen Anne furniture and a hand-painted ceiling; rooms feature mahogany pieces and tufted headboards, crisp linens, while Royal Court floors also offer views and special amenities.
🛈 94 🅿 🔁 Ⓢ 📶 Free 🅢 All major cards

NOB HILL INN
$$$
1000 PINE ST.
94109
TEL 415/673-6080
nobhillinn.com
An old-fashioned bed-and-breakfast with fireplaces in some rooms. Although the inn is filled with antiques, it offers bargain rates on smaller rooms; other rooms cost more.
🛈 21 Ⓢ 📶 Free 🅢 All major cards

🏨 ORCHARD GARDEN HOTEL
$$$
466 BUSH ST.
94108
TEL 415/399-9807
theorchardgardenhotel.com
It's easy being green at this stylish hotel. The rooms (natural wood tones, fresh colors) feature eco-friendly keycard energy control systems, and the hotel uses chemical-free cleaning products.
🛏 86 P Valet ⬆ Ⓢ Ⓢ 🎦
🛜 Free ⬥ All major cards

🏨 PETITE AUBERGE
$$$
863 BUSH ST.
94108
TEL 415/928-6000
petiteaubergesf.com
Intimate French country–style inn, with a full breakfast served in the garden room. Many rooms have fireplaces.
🛏 26 P Valet ⬆ Ⓢ
🛜 Free ⬥ All major cards

🏨 PRESCOTT
$$$
545 POST ST.
94102
TEL 415/563-0303
prescotthotel.com
An intimate hotel with impeccable service. Stylish but not stuffy rooms. Club Level guests enjoy complimentary cocktails and hors d'oeuvres.
🛏 164 P Valet ⬆ Ⓢ Ⓢ 🎦
⬥ All major cards

🏨 SERRANO
$$$
405 TAYLOR ST.
94102
TEL 415/885-2500
serranohotel.com
Although decorated with bright colors and a touch of exotica (striped draperies, Moroccan elements), this 1920s hotel retains its original Spanish Colonial style.

🛏 236 P Valet Ⓢ Ⓢ 🎦
🛜 Free ⬥ All major cards

🏨 VILLA FLORENCE
$$$
225 POWELL ST.
94102
TEL 415/397-7700
villaflorence.com
Italian-themed with guest rooms enlivened by warm colors. Situated on the Powell Street cable car line, it adjoins the popular Kuleto's Italian Restaurant.
🛏 189 P Valet ⬆ Ⓢ Ⓢ
🛜 Free ⬥ All major cards

🏨 WARWICK REGIS
$$$
490 GEARY ST.
94102
TEL 415/928-7900
warwickhotels.com /san-franciso
Pleasant boutique hotel with modernized traditional European decor.
🛏 74 P Valet ⬆ Ⓢ Ⓢ
🛜 Charge ⬥ All major cards

🏨 WHITE SWAN INN
$$$
845 BUSH ST.
94108
TEL 415/775-1755
whiteswaninnsf.com
Emulates an English country inn, with floral wallpapers, comfy beds, and fireplaces in the rooms.
🛏 26 P Valet ⬆ Ⓢ 🛜 Free
⬥ All major cards

🏨 ANDREWS
$$
624 POST ST.
94109
TEL 415/563-6877
andrewshotel.com
This 1905 building has a cage elevator. Small rooms with peach walls, lace curtains, and down comforters create a European-inn feeling. Good value; includes continental

breakfast at your door.
🛏 48 ⬆ Ⓢ 🛜 Free
⬥ All major cards

🏨 CHANCELLOR HOTEL
$$
433 POWELL ST.
94102
TEL 415/362-2004
chancellorhotel.com
A good value hotel situated on the Powell cable car line. Small rooms with some nice touches.
🛏 137 P Valet ⬆ Ⓢ Ⓢ
🛜 Free ⬥ All major cards

🏨 CORNELL HOTEL DE FRANCE
$$
715 BUSH ST.
94108
TEL 415/421-3154
cornellhotel.com
A 1910 brick building decorated in French provincial style. Breakfast is included. The weekly package deal is a real bargain, including breakfasts and four dinners.
🛏 48 ⬆ Ⓢ 🛜 Free
⬥ All major cards

🏨 GOLDEN GATE
$$
775 BUSH ST.
94108
TEL 415/392-3702
goldengatehotel.com
A friendly, cozy, turn-of-the-20th-century hotel with Old World charm (claw-foot bathtubs) and modern updates (free Wi-Fi). Fourteen rooms have private bathrooms. Continental breakfast.
🛏 25 ⬆ Ⓢ 🛜 Free
⬥ All major cards

🏨 HOTEL BERESFORD
$$
635 SUTTER ST.
94102
TEL 415/673-9900
beresford.com
Rooms cozily decorated in

🏨 Hotel 🍴 Restaurant 🛏 No. of Guest Rooms 🔷 No. of Seats P Parking 🕑 Closed ⬆ Elevator

Victorian style; continental breakfast, refrigerator. On-site English pub serves meals. Sister property **Beresford Arms** *(701 Post St., tel 415/673-2600)*, with equally charming Victorian flair, has spacious suites with kitchenettes for families and groups, at low rates.

🛈 114 🅿 Valet ⭤ 🛜 Free 🅢 All major cards

🏨 THE GRANT HOTEL
$–$$

753 BUSH ST.
94108
TEL 415/421-7540
granthotel.com

If location (between Union Square and Chinatown) and price both count, here's a no-frills option with clean, simple, small rooms; ask for a quiet one.

🛈 76 ⭤ 🅢 🛜 Free 🅢 All major cards

🏨 ADELAIDE HOSTEL
$

5 ISADORA DUNCAN LN.
(OFF TAYLOR ST.)
94102
TEL 415/359-1915
adelaidehostel.com

In a quiet location on a cul-de-sac, this hostel is popular with Europeans, backpackers, and budget travelers. Private rooms with baths and dorm rooms with shared baths. Free continental breakfast, and kitchen; group events.

🛈 27 ⭤ 🅢 🛜 Free 🅢 All major cards

RESTAURANTS

🍽 ACQUERELLO
$$$$

1722 SACRAMENTO ST.
TEL 415/567-5432
acquerello.com

Two-star Michelin restaurant serves classic and contemporary Italian dishes. Changing prix-fixe and tasting menus. Examples: pork belly with watermelon, radicchio, and apple; risotto with mussels, saffron, fennel, and caviar.

🪑 40 🅿 Valet 🅢 🕐 Closed L & Sun.–Mon. D 🅢 All major cards

🍽 BOURBON STEAK
$$$$

335 POWELL ST.
(IN WESTIN ST. FRANCIS HOTEL)
TEL 415/397-3003
bourbonsteak.com

The American steak house as updated by celebrity chef Michael Mina. Seasonal dishes include (surprise!) steaks, poached in butter before grilling to create a juicy, crusty delight. Favorites: truffled mac 'n' cheese, Maine lobster potpie. Masculine dining room.

🪑 102 🅿 Valet 🅢 🕐 Closed L 🅢 All major cards

🍽 LE COLONIAL
$$$$

20 COSMO PL.
TEL 415/931-3600
lecolonialsf.com

French-Vietnamese food is served in a 1920s atmosphere of overhead fans and palm fronds.

🪑 320 🅿 Valet 🕐 Closed L 🅢 All major cards

🍽 FARALLON
$$$$

450 POST ST.
TEL 415/956-6969
farallonrestaurant.com

Amid Pat Kuleto's undersea fantasy decor (jellyfish-shaped lamps, glowing columns of kelp), the restaurant serves coastal cuisine, meats, and excellent desserts.

🪑 160 🅿 Valet 🅢 🕐 Closed L 🅢 All major cards

🍽 GITANE
$$$$

6 CLAUDE LN.
TEL 415/788-6686
gitanerestaurant.com

With a sexy 1930s cocktails-in-a-cabaret atmosphere, the restaurant serves dishes rooted in southern France, Italy, and Spain, using local ingredients: salmon tartare with avocado mousse; grilled lamb with spiced sausage and beans.

🪑 64 🕐 Closed L & Sun. D 🅢 All major cards

🍽 LIHOLIHO YACHT CLUB
$$$$

871 SUTTER ST.
TEL 415/440-5446
liholihoyachtclub.com

Hawaiian cuisine gets a gourmet treatment here, with entrées such as manila clams with coconut curry, summer squash, snap peas, and garlic naan.

🪑 86 🕐 Closed L & Sun. D 🅢 All major cards

🍽 SWAN OYSTER DEPOT
$$

1517 POLK ST.
TEL 415/673-1101
sfswanoysterdepot.com

Century-old San Francisco institution, serving oysters (popular: mixed dozen) and seafood (combo salad) at a counter. Be prepared to wait.

🪑 18 🕐 Closed D & Sun. 🅢 None

◼ CHINATOWN

HOTEL

🏨 GRANT PLAZA
$$

465 GRANT AVE.
94108
TEL 415/434-3883
grantplaza.com

One of the city's best buys,

---

near the entrance to Chinatown off Union Square. Simply but pleasantly furnished standard rooms.

🏠 71 ⬆ 🅂
🅂 All major cards

RESTAURANTS

🍴 BRANDY HO'S
$$
217 COLUMBUS AVE.
TEL 415/788-7527
brandyhos.com
Hearty Chinese "country food" in Hunan style, emphasizing chili peppers, smoking techniques, shallots, and garlic—as in almond wood-smoked ham with whole garlic cloves.
🪑 140 🅂 All major cards

🍴 GREAT EASTERN
$$
649 JACKSON ST.
TEL 415/986-2500
greateasternsf.com
A busy place known for dim sum and seafood fresh from the tanks along the walls.
🪑 270 🅂 All major cards

🍴 HOUSE OF NANKING
$$
919 KEARNY ST.
TEL 415/421-1429
The House of Nanking's Szechuan cuisine is so good that even the locals put up with the waiting line.
🪑 55 🅂 All major cards

🍴 R&G LOUNGE
$$
631 KEARNY ST.
TEL 415/982-7877
rnglounge.com
Top Cantonese food, particularly R&G Special Beef and salt-and-pepper crab dishes.
🪑 225 🅂 All major cards

■ NORTH BEACH, TELEGRAPH HILL, & RUSSIAN HILL

HOTELS

🏨 HOTEL BOHÈME
$$$
444 COLUMBUS AVE.
94133
TEL 415/433-9111
hotelboheme.com
Ginsberg poetry and 1950s photos imbue the hotel with North Beach spirit. Stylish bold colors, modern comforts.
🏠 15 🅂 📶 Free
🅂 All major cards

🏨 WASHINGTON SQUARE INN
$$$
1660 STOCKTON ST.
94133
TEL 415/981-4220
wsisf.com
A cozy inn with European decor; many rooms face the park. Continental breakfast, afternoon tea.
🏠 15 🅿 🅂 📶 Free
🅂 All major cards

RESTAURANTS

🍴 COI
$$$$
373 BROADWAY
TEL 415/393-9000
coirestaurant.com
A 12-course tasting menu based on available ingredients. Sample: wild king salmon wrapped in charred cabbage with dried scallop-ginger sauce.
🪑 48 🅿 Valet 🕐 Closed L & Sun.–Mon. D
🅂 All major cards

🍴 SCOMA'S
$$$$
PIER 47, NEAR JONES & JEFFERSON STS.
TEL 415/771-4383

scomas.com
This family-owned mainstay of the wharf features bay views, Dungeness crab cakes, cioppino, crab Louis salads, grilled sand dabs. Fresh, sustainable seafood.
🪑 350 🅿 Valet
🅂 All major cards

🍴 TOSCA CAFÉ
$$$$
242 COLUMBUS AVE.
TEL 415/986-9651
toscacafesf.com
Venerable North Beach eatery now overseen by top New York chef. Popular: crispy pig tails, bucatini, roasted chicken, cappuccino with bourbon. Italian murals, red leather.
🪑 49 🕐 Closed L
🅂 All major cards

🍴 CAFÉ JACQUELINE
$$$
1454 GRANT AVE.
TEL 415/981-5565
A small charming place

focused on fabulous soufflés (e.g., salmon and asparagus); also great French onion soup.
➕ 24 🕐 Closed L & Mon.– Tues. 🚭 All major cards

🍴 ROSE PISTOLA
$$$
532 COLUMBUS AVE.
TEL 415/399-0499
rosepistolasf.com
Fine Genoese and Ligurian cooking. Local fish, cioppino, wood-fired pizzas, and chicken grilled under a brick. Serves weekend brunch.
➕ 135 🅿 Valet 🕐 Closed Sat.–Sun. L. 🚭 All major cards

🍴 ORIGINAL JOE'S
$$–$$$
601 UNION ST.
TEL 415/775-4877
originaljoessf.com
Red leather booths, classic 1950s cocktails, and Italian-American food–Original Joe's invented this concept. Serves hearty portions of specialties such as eggplant parmigiana, chicken, veal, seafood, and pasta. Family owned, a beloved San Francisco institution.
➕ 256 🅿 Valet 🚭 All major cards

🍴 CAFFE SPORT
$$
574 GREEN ST.
TEL 415/981-1251
caffesportsf.com
Great rural Sicilian pasta and seafood served in an eclectic atmosphere.
➕ 45 🕐 Closed L & Mon. D 🚭 MC, V

🍴 MAMA'S
$$
1701 STOCKTON ST.
TEL 415/362-6421
mamas-sf.com
Serving breakfasts for more than 50 years: fluffy omelettes, French toast,

benedicts, homemade jam, fresh-baked breads and pastries. Note: long lines.
➕ 39 🕐 Closed Mon. 🚭 None

🍴 TOMMASO'S
$$
1042 KEARNY ST.
TEL 415/398-9696
tommasos.com
Tommaso's has been serving wood-fired, brick-oven pizza since the 1930s. Also calzone, carpaccio, veal.
➕ 60 🕐 Closed L & Mon. 🚭 All major cards

🍴 MARIO'S BOHEMIAN CIGAR STORE
$–$$
566 COLUMBUS AVE.
TEL 415/362-0536
A comfy neighborhood spot famous for focaccia sandwiches and cappuccino.
➕ 65 🚭 MC, V

🍴 MO'S GRILL
$–$$
1322 GRANT AVE.
TEL 415/788-3779
mosgourmethamburgers.com
The burgers are among the city's best. Also breakfast, steaks, chicken.
➕ 40 🚭 MC, V

■ FISHERMAN'S WHARF

HOTELS

🏨 ARGONAUT
$$$$$
495 JEFFERSON ST.
94109
TEL 415/563-0800
argonauthotel.com
Boutique hotel retains the bricks and wooden beams of a 1909 warehouse restored in smart nautical style. Many

rooms and suites have views.
ⓘ 252 🅿 Valet 🔄 🚭 🕐 📺 🛜 Free 🚭 All major cards

🏨 HOTEL ZEPHYR
$$$$
250 BEACH ST.
94133
TEL 415/617-6555
hotelzephyrsf.com
At this colorful hotel aimed at younger, prosperous travelers, rooms feature bar-height work stations, window benches (some with water views), smart-TV streaming, even dartboards. The industrial-chic lobby has shipping containers as walls and gathering spots with contemporary furniture.
ⓘ 361 🅿 🔄 🚭 🕐 📺 🛜 Free in lobby 🚭 All major cards

🏨 SAN REMO
$$$
2237 MASON ST.
94133
TEL 415/776-8688
sanremohotel.com
Built in 1906 for homeless earthquake victims, this hotel has pension-style rooms with shared baths (except the penthouse, which has great views and is booked well in advance). Think European/Victorian and ultraclean.
ⓘ 62 🅿 🚭 🛜 Free 🚭 All major cards

🏨 WHARF INN
$$$
2601 MASON ST.
94133
TEL 415/673-7411
wharfinn.com
This independently owned inn (motel-like but nicely updated) offers free parking. Quieter than the usual Fisherman's Wharf accommodations.
ⓘ 51 🅿 🔄 🚭 🛜 Free 🚭 All major cards

RESTAURANTS

🍴 ALBONA RISTORANTE ISTRIANO
$$$$

545 FRANCISCO ST.

TEL 415/441-1040

albonarestaurant.com

Rare Istrian cuisine—Italian, with accents from Austria to Turkey—features such dishes as pork loin stuffed with sauerkraut, prosciutto, and apples.

🔧 44 🕐 Closed Sun.–Mon. & L 🅂 All major cards

🍴 RESTAURANT GARY DANKO
$$$$

800 NORTH POINT ST.

TEL 415/749-2060

garydanko.com

Chef/owner Gary Danko's contemporary California/French food stars at what is often ranked the city's best restaurant. The fixed-price menu (you can choose within categories) offers such dishes as horseradish-encrusted salmon with dilled cucumbers. The food, flowers, and attentive service create a memorable dining experience.

🔧 75 🅿 Valet 🅂 All major cards

SOMETHING SPECIAL

🍴 STATE BIRD PROVISIONS
$$$

1529 FILLMORE ST.

TEL 415/795-1272

statebirdsf.com

Quirky and imaginative, winner of the James Beard Award for best new restaurant in America, and decorated like an industrial art gallery, the restaurant serves food from carts wheeled through the dining room, a la dim sum. Dishes might include air-dried beef with red chili vinaigrette, smoked trout-avocado chip-and-dip, Kung Pao beef

tongue and sweetbreads with bacon, nuts, and seeds. For dessert: apple pudding cake with cocoa nib cream and fig.

🔧 60 🕐 Closed L 🅂 All major cards

▪ MARINA DISTRICT

HOTELS

SOMETHING SPECIAL

🏨 INN AT THE PRESIDIO
$$$–$$$$

42 MORAGA AVE.

94129—MAIN POST

TEL 415/800-7356

innatthepresidio.com

A haven set amid 1,500 forested acres (607 ha), the first hotel to open in the historic Presidio occupies handsomely restored 1903 bachelor officers' quarters. The redbrick inn celebrates the past with Presidio memorabilia complemented by comfortable, contemporary furniture in linen and natural leather. Suites have gas fireplaces; third-floor rooms have views of the Golden Gate Bridge. Nearby, a Victorian house adds four bedrooms with a common living room, dining room, and porch. Continental breakfast, high-tech amenities.

ⓘ 26 🅿 🔄 🅂 📶 Free 🅂 All major cards

🏨 MARINA INN
$–$$

3110 OCTAVIA

94123

TEL 415/928-1000

marinainn.com

Affordable English country-style hotel, with pine beds, floral wall coverings, and junior suites suitable for families. Includes continental breakfast.

ⓘ 40 🔄 🅂 📶 Free 🅂 All major cards

🍴 GREENS
$$$–$$$$

BLDG. A, FORT MASON CTR.

TEL 415/771-6222

greensrestaurant.com

Famed for its vegetarian organic gourmet food and fine wine list. The airy dining room has bay views. Saturday and Sunday brunch.

🔧 150 🅿 🕐 Closed Mon. L 🅂 All major cards

🍴 A16
$$$

2355 CHESTNUT ST.

TEL 415/771-2216

a16sf.com

Serving wood-fired pizzas and other specialties of Campania, Italy (A16 is the motorway there), this rustically chic restaurant also offers some 500 Italian wines.

🔧 90 🕐 Closed Sat.–Tues. L 🅂 AE, MC, V

🍴 PRESIDIO SOCIAL CLUB
$$$

563 RUGER ST., PRESIDIO

TEL 415/885-1888

presidiosocialclub.com

Just inside the Lombard Gate in a converted 1903 barracks, the Club serves seasonal food: grilled steaks, Gruyère macaroni and cheese, seafood. Also cocktails and Sat.–Sun. brunch.

🔧 117 🅂 All major cards

🍴 ACE WASABI'S ROCK 'N' ROLL SUSHI
$$

3339 STEINER ST.

TEL 415/567-4903

acewasabisf.com

Hip spot serving innovative dishes: Japanese tapas and specialty rolls such as Albacore Tataki (seared albacore, shaved sweet onions, daikon sprouts).

🔧 85 🕐 Closed L 🅂 AE, MC, V

🍴 HOME PLATE

$

2274 LOMBARD ST.

TEL 415/922-4663

Big, delicious breakfasts: scones, potato pancakes with sour cream and apple sauce, homemade chicken sausage, fluffy pancakes, omelettes, crab cake Benedict.

🛏 35 🕐 Closed D 🇸 All major cards

🍴 PLUTO'S

$

3258 SCOTT ST.

TEL 415/775-8867

plutosfreshfood.com

A fun spot for choose-it-yourself wholesome food, featuring a salad bar with myriad add-ons: vegetables, nuts, grilled beef, herb-roasted turkey, portobello mushrooms. Also sandwiches and tasty sides: macaroni and cheese, garlic potato rings.

🛏 40 🇸 AE, MC, V

■ PACIFIC HEIGHTS & JAPANTOWN

HOTELS

🏢 HOTEL DRISCO

$$$$–$$$$$

2901 PACIFIC AVE.

94115

TEL 415/346-2880

hoteldrisco.com

Built in 1903 and offering broad bay views, this upscale hotel offers a pillow menu, Nespresso machines, shopping bags, chauffeur service, and a gourmet continental breakfast.

ℹ 48 🔄 🇸 🇾 🇸 Free 🇸 All major cards

🏢 HOTEL KABUKI

$$$

1625 POST ST.

94115

TEL 415/922-3200

jdvhotels.com

A serene and luxurious hotel, with a Japanese garden and koi pond off the lobby. Deep soaking tubs in most rooms.

ℹ 218 🅿 Valet 🔄 🇸 🇸 🇾 🇸 Free 🇸 All major cards

🏢 HOTEL MAJESTIC

🍴 $$$

1500 SUTTER ST.

94109

TEL 415/441-1100

thehotelmajestic.com

Rooms (and suites with fireplaces) have antiques, four-poster beds, and marble baths with claw-foot tubs. Situated away from the downtown bustle.

ℹ 57 🅿 Valet 🔄 🇸 🇸 Free 🇸 All major cards

🏢 LAUREL INN

$$$

444 PRESIDIO AVE.

94115

TEL 415/567-8467

jdvhotels.com

Contemporary-style inn with rooms like studio apartments, some with views and kitchenettes. At the edge of Pacific Heights.

ℹ 49 🅿 🔄 🇸 🇸 Free 🇸 All major cards

🏢 QUEEN ANNE HOTEL

$$$

1590 SUTTER ST.

94109

TEL 415/441-2828

queenanne.com

This 1890 hostelry has a Victorian parlor. Some guest rooms have fireplaces or bay windows. Includes breakfast.

ℹ 48 🅿 🔄 🇸 🇸 Free 🇸 All major cards

🏢 UNION STREET INN

$$$

2229 UNION ST.

94123

TEL 415/346-0424

unionstreetinn.com

This airy bed-and-breakfast in a 1904 Edwardian building has antique furnishings and a scented garden; cozy carriage house. Full breakfast.

ℹ 6 🇸 Free 🇸 All major cards

RESTAURANTS

🍴 DOSA

$$$$

1700 FILLMORE ST.

TEL 415/441-3672

dosasf.com

An adventure in South Indian cuisine, with bold flavors and organic ingredients. Examples: masala dosa, spicy basil prawns, seared scallops with roasted pepper chutney, cocktails made with Indian spices (cardamom, chili, ginger). Dramatic high-ceilinged dining room with imaginative hanging lights. There's a smaller branch in the Mission District (995 Valencia St., tel 415/642-3672).

🛏 118 🕐 Closed Mon.– Tues. L 🇸 All major cards

🍴 SPQR

$$$$

1911 FILLMORE ST.

TEL 415/771-7779

spqrsf.com

Italian seasonal cuisine from award-winning chef might include nettle and mushroom cannelloni, sausage-stuffed quail. Top Italian wines.

🛏 56 🕐 Closed Mon.–Fri. L 🇸 AE, MC, V

🍴 SPRUCE

$$$$

3640 SACRAMENTO ST.

TEL 415/931-5100

sprucesf.com

Urbane neighborhood

restaurant serving contemporary American food in a former auto garage done up handsomely in chocolate mohair-upholstered walls and big faux ostrich chairs. On the menu: pork loin with sweet corn galette; notable charcuterie plate. Desserts include beignets with *crème anglaise*.

🛏 70 🅿 Valet
🕐 Closed Sat.–Sun. L
🆑 All major cards

🍴 ELITE CAFÉ
$$$
2049 FILLMORE ST.
TEL 415/364-8400
theelitecafe.com
American cooking with a New Orleans accent includes barbecued shrimp with sourdough baguette, meetinghouse biscuits, red beans and rice. Brunch on Saturday, Sunday. Art deco interior.

🛏 85 🅿 Valet 🕐 Closed L
🆑 All major cards

🍴 FLORIO
$$$
1915 FILLMORE ST.
TEL 415/775-4300
floriosf.com
A warm neighborhood bistro where you can linger over Italian seafood, a gourmet burger, steak *frites*, or roasted chicken.

🛏 64 🕐 Closed L
🆑 AE, MC, V

🍴 ELLA'S
$–$$
500 PRESIDIO AVE.
TEL 415/441-5669
ellassanfrancisco.com
Popular breakfast spot. Try the chicken hash, homemade sticky buns, fluffy pancakes, brandied orange French toast. Hearty lunches (chicken potpie, beef stew). Both replaced by brunch on Saturday, Sunday.

🛏 70 🕐 Closed D
🆑 All major cards

🍴 MIFUNE
$
1737 POST ST.
TEL 415/922-0337
Inexpensive and popular, with delicious hot or cold noodles (traditional udon and soba).

🛏 82 🆑 All major cards

■ HAIGHT-ASHBURY & GOLDEN GATE PARK

HOTELS

🏨 THE PARSONAGE
$$$
198 HAIGHT ST.
94102
TEL 415/863-3699
theparsonage.com
Charming hosts and an 1883 landmark Victorian house make this a refuge. Rooms have marble baths, goose-down comforters, some fireplaces, lots of character. Parlors, cozy library; home-made breakfast changes daily. Located east of Haight-Ashbury in Hayes Valley.

🚪 5 🔁 🚫 📶 Free 🆑 MC, V

🏨 STANYAN PARK HOTEL
$$$
750 STANYAN ST.
94117
TEL 415/751-1000
stanyanpark.com
A restored Victorian across from Golden Gate Park. Some suites have kitchens, living rooms, and dining rooms. Continental breakfast.

🚪 36 🔁 🚫 📶 Free
🆑 All major cards

RESTAURANTS

🍴 NOPA
$$$
560 DIVISADERO ST.
TEL 415/864-8643
nopasf.com

This celebrated eatery serves "urban rustic" food: intriguing starters (smoked trout with ricotta, tomato, and rye toast), main dishes from the grill or wood-burning oven (herbed rotisserie chicken, grilled grass-fed beef hamburger), and desserts (cornmeal shortcake with basil ice cream). Also weekend brunch (custard French toast with strawberries). Near Haight-Ashbury in the area "North of the Panhandle."

🛏 130 🕐 Closed L
🆑 All major cards

🍴 CHA CHA CHA
$$
1801 HAIGHT ST.
TEL 415/386-7670
cha3.com
The menu at this tapas bar draws on Mexican, Caribbean, and Cajun cuisines to create intriguing dishes such as jerk chicken, marinated steak, and fried *platanos* with black beans.

🛏 100 🆑 All major cards

⊞ RAGAZZA
$$
311 DIVISADERO ST.
TEL 415/255-1133
ragazzasf.com
Excellent Neapolitan thin-crust pizzas, plus antipasti, salads, baked pasta, and roasts, served in a convivial neighborhood dining room.
🔲 40 🕐 Closed L 🕭 MC, V

■ CIVIC CENTER, SOMA, & THE EMBARCADERO

HOTELS

⊞ FOUR SEASONS
$$$$$
757 MARKET ST.
94103
TEL 415/633-3000
fourseasons.com
Large rooms with marble bathrooms, huge windows; attentive staff. Guests have access to a large fitness facility, pool, and spa.
ⓘ 277 🅿 Valet 🕭 🕭 🕭 🕭 🕭 Charge 🕭 All major cards

⊞ ST. REGIS
$$$$$
125 3RD ST.
94103
TEL 415/284-4000
stregissanfrancisco.com
Luxuries at this stylish 40-story tower hotel include 24-hour butler service (in the suites, butlers will even unpack and press your clothes) and a 9,000-square-foot (835 sq m) spa. Rooms feature leather-stitched walls, large windows.
ⓘ 260 🅿 Valet 🕭 🕭 🕭 🕭 Free 🕭 All major cards

⊞ HARBOR COURT
$$$$
165 STEUART ST.
94105

TEL 415/882-1300
harborcourthotel.com
A 1907 building with small rooms in warm earth tones; many have bay views.
ⓘ 131 🅿 Valet 🕭 🕭 🕭 🕭 🕭 Free 🕭 All major cards

⊞ HOTEL ZETTA
$$$$
55 5TH ST.
94103
TEL 415/543-8555
hotelzetta.com
Hotel Zetta draws a young, style-seeking, and techie crowd with graffiti murals, a playroom with game consoles and giant Jenga, and guest rooms in sleek black-and-white and wood, with sitting/standing desks.
ⓘ 116 🅿 Valet 🕭 🕭 🕭 🕭 🕭 Free in lobby 🕭 All major cards

⊞ W SAN FRANCISCO
$$$–$$$$$
181 3RD ST.
94103
TEL 415/777-5300
wsanfrancisco.com
Hip urban style is everything here, with arty public areas and lavish comforts: feather beds, pillow menu, spa, great service. Trendy crowd.
ⓘ 410 🅿 Valet 🕭 🕭 🕭 🕭 🕭 Free in lobby 🕭 All major cards

⊞ HOTEL GRIFFON
⊞ **$$$–$$$$**
155 STEUART ST.
94105
TEL 415/495-2100
hotelgriffon.com
Rooms, in masculine browns, have plush beds and some have bay views.
ⓘ 62 🅿 🕭 🕭 🕭 All major cards

⊞ HOTEL ZELOS
$$$–$$$$
12 4TH ST.
94103

TEL 415/348-1111
hotelzelos.com
This boutique hotel for the hip and young is located five stories above downtown's busy streets, its rooms decorated in neutrals with persimmon accents. The courtyard has a fire pit and fountains. Rooftop restaurant and terrace.
ⓘ 202 🅿 Valet 🕭 🕭 🕭 🕭 Free 🕭 All major cards

⊞ INN AT THE OPERA
$$$
333 FULTON ST.
94102
TEL 415/863-8400
shellhospitality.com/inn-at-the-opera
Convenient to venues for opera, symphony, and ballet; French ambience and continental breakfast.
ⓘ 48 🅿 Valet 🕭 🕭 🕭 Free 🕭 All major cards

⊞ PHOENIX HOTEL
$$$
601 EDDY ST.
94109
TEL 415/776-1380
jdvhotels.com
This spoofed-up 1950s motel with bungalow decor and a tropical courtyard pool attracts rock musicians and hip celebrities. Located at the edge of the unsavory Tenderloin district.
ⓘ 44 🅿 🕭 🕭 🕭 Free 🕭 All major cards

⊞ THE MOSSER
$$–$$$
54 4TH ST.
94103
TEL 415/986-4400
themosser.com
"Victorian/modern" hotel has very small rooms decorated in brown and red. For budget travelers, there are shared-bath rooms. All have platform beds. On-site recording studio.
ⓘ 166 🅿 Valet 🕭 🕭 🕭 Free 🕭 All major cards

🕭 Nonsmoking   🕭 Air-conditioning   🕭 Indoor Pool   🕭 Outdoor Pool   🕭 Health Club   🕭 Wi-Fi   🕭 Credit Cards

RESTAURANTS

🍴 AME
$$$$$
689 MISSION ST.
(IN ST. REGIS HOTEL)
TEL 415/284-4040
amerestaurant.com
New American cuisine is filtered through Japanese culinary sensibilities. Showcases sashimi and entrees such as sake-marinated black cod with shrimp dumplings or grilled pork chop with chorizo-corn ragout.
🔲 95 🅿 Valet 🕐 Closed L
◾ All major cards

🍴 BENU
$$$$
22 HAWTHORNE ST.
TEL 415/685-4860
benusf.com
The fixed menu at this Michelin three-star restaurant blends East and West in dishes such as thousand-year-old quail egg in a rich soup spiced with ginger; beef rib with tomato and charred scallion; sea urchin in fermented crab sauce. Minimalist decor.
🔲 54 🅿 Valet 🕐 Closed L &
Sun.-Mon. D ◾ All major cards

🍴 BOULEVARD
$$$$
1 MISSION ST.
TEL 415/543-6084
boulevardrestaurant.com
A culinary landmark on the Embarcadero, this belle epoque dining room serves American food given a French twist, as in the wood-oven roasted pork chop paired with smoked polenta.
🔲 180 🅿 Valet 🕐 Closed
Sat.-Sun. L ◾ All major cards

🍴 JARDINIÈRE
$$$$
300 GROVE ST.
TEL 415/861-5555
jardiniere.com
The seasonal French/California menu includes imaginative treatments of meat and fish, pastries.
🔲 140 🅿 Valet ◾
🕐 Closed L ◾ All major cards

🍴 PROSPECT
$$$$
300 SPEAR ST.
TEL 415/247-7770
prospectsf.com
Daily menu of contemporary American cuisine with unusual starters (Kobe beef tartare with cherry tomato jam, avocado, charred onion vinaigrette) and meat and fish dishes (crispy-skin salmon with golden chanterelles). Ambience: sleek loftlike space done in recycled wood.
🔲 120 🅿 Valet
🕐 Closed Sun. & Sat.–Sun. L
◾ All major cards

🍴 SAISON
$$$$
178 TOWNSEND ST.
TEL 415/828-7990
saisonsf.com
With three Michelin stars, the restaurant focuses on the finest daily ingredients prepared from scratch. Examples: caviar cured with smoked salt; cheese custard with onions; abalone grilled over embers. Open floor plan with "chef's table" ambience.
🔲 18 🅿 Valet 🕐 Closed L &
Sun.–Mon. D ◾ AE, MC, V

🍴 WATERBAR
$$$$
399 EMBARCADERO
TEL 415/284-9922
waterbarsf.com
With a view of the water and Bay Bridge through huge windows, the dramatic dining room has aquariums in towering columns and a cascading raw bar lit through glistening ice. Seafood may include seared Hawaiian ahi

with smashed plantains, grilled pineapple, sweet-pea leaves, and cashews. Serves brunch on weekends.
🔲 200 🅿 Valet 🕐 Closed
Sat.-Sun. L ◾ All major cards

🍴 ASIA SF
$$$–$$$$
201 9TH STREET
TEL 415/255-2742
asiasf.com
As you dine, enjoy shows performed by "gender illusionists"—Asian men dressed as women. Not surprisingly, this is a hot spot for bachelor/bachelorette parties. The Cal-Asia menu ranges from soba noodles to miso-glazed salmon and filet mignon.
🔲 140 🕐 Closed L & Mon.–Tues. D ◾ All major cards

🍴 ABSINTHE
$$$
398 HAYES ST.
TEL 415/551-1590
absinthe.com
Creative brasserie with a California slant.
🔲 120 🅿 ◾ All major cards

🍴 BAR AGRICOLE
$$$
355 11TH ST.
TEL 415/355-9400
baragricole.com
Handcrafted cocktails (five kinds of ice are on hand for connoisseurs) and imaginative food (pork sausages with summer squash, grapes). The designy decor runs to cast concrete and reclaimed wood. Weekend brunch.
🔲 160 🕐 Closed L
◾ All major cards

🍴 FRINGALE
$$$
570 4TH ST.
TEL 415/543-0573
fringalesf.com
An unpretentious warm

🏨 Hotel 🍴 Restaurant 🛈 No. of Guest Rooms 🔲 No. of Seats 🅿 Parking 🕐 Closed ⬌ Elevator

restaurant, serving tasty French bistro food featuring Basque-influenced seafood and meats.

🍴 55 🕐 Closed Sat.–Mon. L
🚭 AE, MC, V

MOMO'S
$$$
760 2ND ST.
TEL 415/227-8660
sfmomos.com
Popular spot when the Giants play at nearby AT&T Park; serves American and Italian food: lamb burgers, maple-glazed chops, chicken potpie. Dine indoors or on the deck.

🍴 276 🅿 Valet
🚭 All major cards

SLANTED DOOR
$$$
FERRY BLDG., MARKET ST.
AT THE EMBARCADERO
TEL 415/861-8032
slanteddoor.com
Celebrated modern Vietnam-ese cuisine that uses organic produce and other health-ful ingredients. Examples: cellophane noodles with Dungeness crab; spring rolls with shrimp, pork, mint, and peanut sauce. Bay views.

🍴 150 🅿 🚭 AE, MC, V

ZUNI CAFÉ
$$$
1658 MARKET ST.
TEL 415/552-2522
zunicafe.com
Much praised California cuisine served in pioneering industrial-chic space with copper-top bar. Lunch tips: Caesar salad, ham-burger on focaccia, shoestring potatoes. Typical dinner entrée: roasted rabbit with smashed chickpeas, turnips, wild nettles, yogurt, chili pepper paste.

🍴 100 🅿 Valet 🕐 Closed Mon. 🚭 AE, MC, V

DOTTIE'S TRUE BLUE CAFÉ
$
28 6TH ST.
TEL 415/885-2767
Fabulous breakfasts: egg scrambles, whiskey-fennel sausage, whole wheat ginger pancakes with maple syrup, black bean cakes with eggs, and chili corn bread; great coffee. Slightly dicey area.

🍴 60 🕐 Closed D & Tues.–Wed. 🚭 D, MC, V

THE MISSION & CASTRO DISTRICTS

RESTAURANTS

FOREIGN CINEMA
$$$$
2534 MISSION ST.
TEL 415/648-7600
foreigncinema.com
Foreign movies are shown on a wall outdoors as you dine on splendid California/Mediterranean seafood; meats, oysters. Inside seating also; weekend brunch.

🍴 250 🅿 Valet 🕐 Closed Mon.–Fri. L 🚭 All major cards

FRANCES
$$$$
3870 17TH ST.
TEL 415/621-3870
frances-sf.com
California farm-to-table food is served in a small neighbor-hood bistro. On the changing menu, starters might include roasted fennel chowder with clams, celery, green olives, and garlic croutons, and such entrées as stuffed quail with charred cucumber, grapes, toasted farro, and tzatziki.

🍴 47 🕐 Closed L & all Mon. 🚭 AE, MC, V

MARLOWE
$$$$
500 BRANNAN ST.
TEL 415/777-1413
marlowesf.com
This meat-centric New American bistro serves a popular burger (beef ground with lamb, topped with caramelized onions, cheddar, bacon, horseradish, and aioli).

🍴 54 🚭 All major cards

RANGE
$$$$
842 VALENCIA ST.
TEL 415/282-8283
rangesf.com
A neighborhood purveyor of market-fresh California dishes, such as the coffee-rubbed pork shoulder with creamy hominy and collard greens. Interesting cocktails include the Bottle Rocket (tequila, strawberry, honey ginger, lime).

🍴 70 🕐 Closed L & Mon. D 🚭 All major cards

AL'S PLACE
$$$
1499 VALENCIA ST.
TEL 415/552-4055
alsplacesf.com
Vegetables take center stage, with meat and fish as "sides." Rich flavors include pickled fries with smoked apple barbecue sauce; fregola pasta in pickled pea broth. ("AL" is chef-owner Aaron London.)

🍴 49 🕐 Closed L & Mon.–Tues. D 🚭 All major cards

DELFINA
$$$
3621 18TH ST.
TEL 415/552-4055
delfinasf.com
With a James Beard award winner as the chef, this neigh-borhood trattoria serves rus-tic Italian food: spaghetti with plum tomatoes, garlic, olive oil, and pepperoncini; roasted chicken with olive oil mashed

potatoes, mushrooms. Decor is warehouse chic. Delfina also has a popular pizzeria next door *(tel 415/437-6800, pizzeriadelfina.com)*.

🍴 90 🕐 Closed L
⊗ All major cards

🍴 CHOW
$$
215 CHURCH ST.
TEL 415/552-2469
chowfoodbar.com
A packed spot for healthy organic comfort food, three meals a day.
🍴 100 ⊗ D, MC, V

🍴 MISSION CHINESE FOOD
$$
2234 MISSION ST. (INSIDE LUNG SHAN RESTAURANT)
TEL 415/863-2800
missionchinesefood.com
Minimal atmosphere but fantastic flavors. Popular: lamb noodle soup, and thrice-cooked bacon with rice cakes, bitter melon.
🍴 60 🕐 Closed Tues.–Wed.
⊗ All major cards

🍴 LA TAQUERIA
$
2889 MISSION ST.
TEL 415/285-7117
Scrumptious burritos (many say the best in San Francisco), crispy tacos, fruit drinks.
🍴 80 ⊗ None

■ EXCURSIONS

BERKELEY

🍴 CHEZ PANISSE
$$$$
1517 SHATTUCK AVE.
TEL 510/548-5525
chezpanisse.com
The legendary birthplace of California cuisine presided over by Alice Waters. The

prix-fixe menu features local organic ingredients and French technique. À la carte meals available at the café *(tel 510/548-5049)*.

🍴 Restaurant 50, café 50
🕐 Closed Sun.
⊗ All major cards

🍴 RIVOLI
$$$
1539 SOLANO AVE.
TEL 510/526-2542
rivolirestaurant.com
Top-rated fresh, seasonal cuisine served beside a magical garden: Examples: wild mushroom croquettes, yukon crusted ling cod.
🍴 54 🔧 🕐 Closed L
⊗ All major cards

CALISTOGA

🏨 DR. WILKINSON'S HOT SPRINGS RESORT
$$$
1507 LINCOLN AVE.
TEL 707/942-4102
drwilkinson.com
Fifties-style motel, bungalows, and Victorian house accommodations, with hot springs, volcanic ash mud baths, and spa treatments—the opposite of a typical glitzy Napa spa.
🛏 40 🅿 🔧 🏊 🛜 Free
⊗ AE, MC, V

🍴 SOLBAR
$$$$
1755 SILVERADO TRAIL, IN SOLAGE RESORT
TEL 707/226-0800
solagecalistoga.com/dine
Woodsy-chic dining with poolside patio for all meals and weekend brunch; acclaimed California cooking. Lunch tip: "Lucky Pig," a slow-roasted shoulder of pork with black sesame crepes, pickled pineapple, Mongolian peanuts.
🍴 223 🅿 Valet 🔧
⊗ All major cards

PRICES

HOTELS
An indication of the cost of a double room in the high season is given by **$**. Rates may be lower during slow periods, promotions.

$$$$$	Over $450
$$$$	$350–$450
$$$	$250–$350
$$	$150–$250
$	Under $150

RESTAURANTS
An indication of the cost of a three-course meal without drinks is given by **$** signs.

$$$$	Over $50
$$$	$35–$50
$$	$15–$35
$	Under $15

CARMEL-BY-THE-SEA

🏨 MISSION RANCH
$$$
26270 DOLORES ST.
TEL 831/624-6436
missionranchcarmel.com
Rooms are located in a rustic bunkhouse, 1850s farmhouse, and new compounds with whirlpool tubs and fireplaces, set on 22 acres (9 ha) with spectacular views of Point Lobos and the Pacific Ocean. Extensive tennis facilities. Owned by former Carmel mayor Clint Eastwood.
🛏 31 rooms 🅿 📺 🛜 Free
⊗ All major cards

🍴 CASANOVA
$$$$
5TH AVE. BET. MISSION ST. & SAN CARLOS ST.
TEL 831/625-0501
casanovarestaurant.com
Acclaimed rustic cuisine of France and Italy, served in maze of small rooms and a

---

🏨 Hotel 🍴 Restaurant 🛏 No. of Guest Rooms 🍴 No. of Seats 🅿 Parking 🕐 Closed 🔧 Elevator

patio; hand-dug wine cellar holds 30,000 bottles.

🛏 275 💳 All major cards

🍴 VILLAGE CORNER
$$–$$$
DOLORES AT 6TH ST.
TEL 831/624-3588
villagecornerbistro.com
A bistro with a flower-bedecked, dog-friendly patio, good for a casual breakfast. Later the kitchen hits a different (and more expensive) stride, with such offerings as salmon with peppered pistachio crust, seafood butter, and wasabi cream.

🛏 70 💳 All major cards

🍴 PATISSERIE BOISSIERE
$$
MISSION ST. BET. OCEAN AVE. & 7TH AVE.
TEL 831/624-5008
patisserieboissiere.com
Resembling a French country house with a tiled fireplace, it draws a local lunch crowd for onion soup, chicken potpie, and pastries baked on the premises. Take-out picnics.

🛏 49 🕐 Closed Mon.–Tues. D 💳 AE, MC, V

LAKE TAHOE

🏨 THE LANDING
$$$$$
3300 LAKESHORE BLVD.,
SOUTH LAKE TAHOE
TEL 530/541-5263
thelandingtahoe.com
Lakefront hotel; handsome rooms with stone fireplaces, some with lake views; spa.

🚪 77 🅿 Valet 🚭 ❄ 🏊 🏊 🏋 ❓ Free 💳 All major cards

MONTEREY

🏨 SEVEN GABLES INN
$$$$
555 OCEAN VIEW BLVD.,
PACIFIC GROVE
TEL 831/372-4341
thesevengablesinn.com
An 1886 Victorian mansion and cottages converted to a bed-and-breakfast, with European antiques, gardens, and ocean views.

🚪 25 🅿 ❓ Free 💳 AE, MC, V

🍴 MONTRIO
$$$$
414 CALLE PRINCIPAL
TEL 831/648-8880
montrio.com
An early 1900s firehouse is the setting for California bistro cuisine, with touches of France and Italy: crab cakes with remoulade, braised boneless short rib.

🛏 200 🕐 Closed L 💳 All major cards

🍴 TARPY'S ROADHOUSE
$$$$
2999 MONTEREY-SALINAS HWY.
TEL 831/655-2999
tarpys.com
An atmospheric ivy-clad house serving American country cuisine such as a beef burger with brie, bacon, lobster, and aioli.

🛏 300 💳 All major cards

NAPA

🍴 CELADON
$$$$
500 MAIN ST.
TEL 707/254-9690
celadonnapa.com
"Global comfort food" served in historic mill. Tips: macadamia-crusted goat cheese with poached figs; seared scallops on mashed potatoes; vanilla crème brûlée.

🛏 123 🅿 🕐 Closed Sat.–Sun. L 💳 All major cards

OAKLAND

🍴 WOOD TAVERN
$$$
6317 COLLEGE AVE.
TEL 510/654-6607
woodtavern.net
Popular at this American brasserie are pork chops, gnocchi, and burgers; large wine selection.

🛏 55 🕐 Closed Sun. 💳 AE, MC, V

🍴 PIZZAIOLO
$$–$$$
5008 TELEGRAPH AVE.
TEL 510/652-4888
pizzaiolooakland.com
This eatery in a former hardware store has popular wood-fired pizza.

🛏 185 🅿 🕐 Closed L & Sun. D 💳 AE, MC, V

🍴 PLUM BAR & RESTAURANT
$$
2216 BROADWAY
TEL 510/444-7586
plumoakland.com
Popular pulled pork sliders, nibbles. Droll "happy meal" (half-cheeseburger, smoked fries, beer, shot of bourbon).

🛏 45 🕐 Closed Sat. L & Sun. D 💳 All major cards

PALO ALTO

🍴 EVVIA ESTIATORIO
$$$$
420 EMERSON ST.
TEL 650/326-0983
evvia.net
Superb, simple Greek food made with fresh seasonal ingredients. Popular: grilled lamb chops with lemon, olive oil, oregano.

🛏 100 🅿 Valet 🕐 Closed Sat.–Sun. L 💳 All major cards

SAUSALITO

🏨 CAVALLO POINT LODGE
$$$$$

601 MURRAY CIRCLE,
AT FORT BAKER
TEL 415/339-4700
cavallopoint.com
This early 1900s fort
has been revamped as a
luxury lodge at the foot of
the Golden Gate Bridge,
with rooms in charmingly
restored officers' quarters
and new contemporary
accommodations, many with
bridge, water, or city views.
The spa offers everything from
massages to a tea bar and
visiting shaman (!). Also
gourmet cooking lessons.

🛏 142 🅿 Valet 🚭 📺 📶 Free
🎴 All major cards

🏨 THE INN ABOVE TIDE
$$$$–$$$$$

30 EL PORTAL
TEL 415/332-9535
innabovetide.com
The Bay Area's only hostelry
on the water has rooms
with wide bay views. Many
have decks and fireplaces.
Binoculars, loaner bikes,
luxurious amenities.

🛏 31 rooms & suites
🅿 Valet 🚭 🚭 📶 Free
🎴 All major cards

🍴 SUSHI RAN
$$$$

107 CALEDONIA ST.
TEL 415/332-3620
sushiran.com
Inventive Japanese and
California cuisine: sushi,
maki (popular: crunch roll,
creamy scallop roll), shaking
beef. Large wine and sake
list. Casual environment
with sophisticated service.
Fresh fish daily, local or from
Tokyo's Tsukiji market.

🪑 100 🕐 Closed Sat.–Sun. L 🎴 AE,
MC, V

SONOMA

🍴 EL DORADO
$$$–$$$$

405 1ST ST. W.
TEL 707/996-3030
eldoradosonoma.com
A small hotel overlooking
the Plaza Sonoma where
the Bear Flag revolt (see
p. 230) was staged. Stylish
Californian guest rooms.
The El Dorado Kitchen
serves contemporary
California cuisine from
local farms.

🛏 200 🅿 🚭 🚭 📶 Free
🎴 All major cards

🍴 CAFÉ LA HAYE
$$$

140 E. NAPA ST.
TEL 707/935-5994
cafelahaye.com
Just off the historic plaza,
this café features fresh vegetables, fish, meat. Popular:
roasted chicken with citrus-
fennel salsa.

🪑 35 🕐 Closed L & Sun.–
Mon. D 🎴 D, MC, V

YOSEMITE VALLEY

🏨 AHWAHNEE HOTEL &
🍴 RESTAURANT
$$$$$

1 AHWAHNEE WAY,
YOSEMITE NATIONAL PARK
TEL 801/559-4884
yosemitepark.com
Make reservations several
months ahead for this
1920s mountain lodge,
which boasts Native Amer-
ican decor. Book ahead for
the restaurant too—California cuisine.

🛏 123 🅿 Valet 🚭 🚭
🚭 📶 Free
🎴 All major cards

YOUNTVILLE

🏨 HOTEL YOUNTVILLE
$$$$$

6462 WASHINGTON ST.
TEL 707/967-7900
hotelyountville.com
Fieldstone fireplaces, elegant
linens, and some rooms with
private patios. Rustic setting,
lavish spa.

🛏 80 🅿 🚭 🚭 🚭 📶 Free
🎴 All major cards

SOMETHING SPECIAL

🍴 THE FRENCH LAUNDRY
$$$$

6640 WASHINGTON ST.
TEL 707/944-2380
frenchlaundry.com
Called the "most excit-
ing" restaurant in America.
Reservations available two
months ahead. The prix-fixe
French-California menu may
include moulard duck foie gras
or pearl tapioca with oysters
and caviar.

🪑 74 🅿 🕐 Closed Mon.–
Thurs. L 🎴 All major cards

🍴 MUSTARD'S GRILL
$$$$

7399 ST. HELENA HWY.
TEL 707/944-2424
mustardsgrill.com
A cradle of Napa cuisine,
Mustard's offers dishes
such as baby back ribs,
seafood tostadas, and
delicious hamburgers.

🪑 90 🅿 🎴 All major cards

🏨 Hotel 🍴 Restaurant 🛏 No. of Guest Rooms 🪑 No. of Seats 🅿 Parking 🕐 Closed 🛗 Elevator

Shopping in San Francisco

The character of a San Francisco store is bound up with its neighborhood, each district having its own spin that is reflected in clothes, home furnishings, books, and so on. Shopping is a great excuse to explore these different worlds.

Neighborhoods

Union Square has department stores and exclusive designer boutiques. Don't forget Maiden Lane *(an alley off Kearny),* with its elegant shops. In nearby China-town, shops sell mostly ticky-tack for tourists, as well as electronics, linens, and arts. Jackson Square in the Financial District is home to galleries and antiques shops. North Beach has eclectic, highly individual shops. Hayes Valley *(Hayes St., from Gough to Laguna)* is a happening area with a local feel and has fun and funky clothes, jewelry, crafts, furniture, and boutiques.

Along Upper Fillmore Street *(Broadway to Ellis St.)* lies a strip of upscale shops for gifts, home furnishings, and the like, as well as great thrift shops that sell high-quality cast-off clothes. Union Street in Cow Hollow furnishes young, well-to-do San Franciscans with chic clothes, housewares, antiques, jewelry, designer eye-glasses, and such. Funky, psyche-delic Haight Street overflows with vintage clothes, books, music, and retro hippie parapher-nalia. The Mission District along Valencia and Mission Streets *(from 16th to 24th)* has new and second-hand clothes, furniture, and arts, and items that reflect the neigh-borhood's Hispanic culture, such as Day of the Dead decorations. In SoMa, you'll find discount outlet warehouses.

Malls: Westfield San Francisco Centre *(Market St. at 5th St.)* is anchored by a colossal Nordstrom department store; there are many upscale shops. In the Financial District, the Crocker Galleria *(bet.*

Post, Kearny, Sutter, & Montgomery Sts.) shelters dozens of shops under a vaulted glass roof. The multiple buildings of the Embarcadero Center *(foot of Sacramento St.)* con-tain numerous shops. Ghirardelli Square *(W end of Fisherman's Wharf)* is a complex of shops selling bath products, toys, clothes, and, of course, chocolate.

Most of the businesses listed below are unique to San Francisco and the Bay Area.

Antiques & Collectibles

Bonhams 220 San Bruno Ave. (SoMa), tel 415/861-7500, bonhams.com. Check online or call ahead for information about auctions.

Foster-Gwin, 38 Hotaling Pl. (Jackson Square), tel 415/397-4986. Tasteful gallery with 17th- and 18th-century European furniture, contemporary art, Mediterranean antiques.

Grand Central Station Antiques, 360 Bayshore Blvd. (Bayview-Hunters Point), tel 415/252-8155, gcsantiques.com. Spacious store filled with Euro-pean antiques, primarily.

Mureta's Antiques, 2418 Fill-more St. (Pacific Heights), tel 415/922-5652. Estate jewelry, silver, crystal.

Stuff, 150 Valencia St. (SoMA), tel 415/864-2988. More than 70 dealers fill 18,000 square feet (1,670 sq m) of space with everything from mid-century and Danish modern furniture to vinyl records, artwork, lighting, col-lectibles, vintage dresses, home décor, and old signs. Tip: pricey, so make sure to bargain.

Apparel

Acrimony, 333 Hayes St. (Hayes Valley), tel 861-1025. Minimalist boutique for non-mainstream designers of fashions and acces-sories for men and women.

Ambiance, 1458 Haight St. (Haight-Ashbury), tel 415/552-5095. Kicky party dresses, accessories, and shoes.

Bell Jar, 3187 16th St. (Mission), tel 415/626-1749. Jewelry, accessories, dresses, beauty products, gifts.

Britex Fabrics, 146 Geary St. (Union Sq.), tel 415/392-2910. A vast collection of fine fabrics and accessories (more than 1,000 silks, 5,000 woolens, and 30,000 buttons in stock).

Brooks Brothers, 240 Post St. (Union Sq.), tel 415/402-0476. Conservative suits, button-down shirts, and sportswear for men; women's department.

Buffalo Exchange, 1555 Haight St. (Haight-Ashbury), tel 415/431-7733; 1210 Valencia St. (Mission), tel 415/647-8332. Used clothes with style at low prices or trade.

Burberrys Ltd., 225 Post St. (Union Sq.), tel 415/392-2200. Trench coats, scarves, and more for men and women.

Burlington Coat Factory, 899 Howard St. (SoMa), tel 415/495-7234. Coats and home items at low prices.

Chanel Boutique, 156 Geary St. (Union Sq.), tel 415/981-1550. Find out how the other one percent lives at this ultraluxe purveyor of classic clothes, jewelry, and perfume.

Cielo, 2225 Fillmore St. (Pacific Heights), tel 415/776-0641. Ultra-high-end European and Japanese designer fashions for women.
Dottie Doolittle, 3680 Sacramento St. (Presidio Heights), tel 415/673-1334. Upscale clothes for little girls, boys, and infants.
Elizabeth Charles, 2056 Fillmore St. (Pacific Heights), tel 415/440-2100. Pricey, multi-brand boutique for hard-to-find women's clothing; celebrity clientele.
Freda Salvador, 2416 Fillmore St. (Pacific Heights), tel 415/872-9690. Contemporary, cutting-edge yet walkable shoes made in Spain.
Gimme Shoes, 416 Hayes St. (Hayes Valley), tel 415/864-0691; 2358 Fillmore St. (Upper Fillmore), tel 415/441-3040. Chic European shoes and sports footwear for men and women.
Giorgio Armani, 278 Post St. (Union Sq.), tel 415/434-2500. Sleek couture for men and women. (The less expensive, younger style **Emporio Armani** is at 1 Grant Ave, tel 415/677-9400.)
Goodbyes, 3483 Sacramento St. (Presidio Heights), tel 415/674-0151; men's, 3462 Sacramento St., tel 415/346-6388. On consignment at bargain prices: men's and women's designer apparel, shoes, accessories.
Jessica McClintock, 180 Geary St., 4th Fl. (Union Sq.), tel 415/398-9008. Formal and bridal fashions.
Metier, 546 Laguna St. (Hayes Valley), tel 415/590-2998. Young designer jewelry, high end.
TSE, 60 Maiden Ln. (Union Sq.), tel 415/391-1112. Cashmeres: sweaters, skirts, coats, dresses, jackets; men, women, children.
Urban Outfitters, 80 Powell St. (near Union Sq.), tel 415/989-1515. Chain stocking men's and women's clothing, plus furnishings, jewelry, and unique gifts.

Wasteland, 1660 Haight St. (Haight-Ashbury), tel 415/863-3150. A fashionable place to buy vintage and trendy second-hand clothes at high prices. Also new designs.
Wilkes Bashford, 375 Sutter St. (Union Sq.), tel 415/986-4380. Traditional, trendy, and sophisticated American and European fashions of high quality; men and women.

Arts, Crafts, & Gifts
Catharine Clark Gallery, 248 Utah St. (Potrero Hill), tel 415/399-1439, cclarkgallery.com. Emerging and mid-career contemporary artists in a wide range of media, emphasizing content-driven work, new media, video, and room installations.
Gump's, 135 Post St. (Union Sq.), tel 415/982-1616, gumps.com. Classic San Francisco emporium showcases dinnerware, gifts, home furnishings, crafts, jewelry, jade.
Hang Art, 567 Sutter St. (Union Sq.), tel 415/434-4264, hangart.com, Paintings, sculpture, and works on paper by San Francisco area artists.
Twig Gallery, 2162 Union St. (Cow Hollow), tel 415/928-8944, twiggallerysf.com. Home accessories, jewelry, ceramics, art glass.

Books
Book Passage, Ferry Building, The Embarcadero at Market St. (The Embarcadero), tel 415/835-1020, bookpassage.com. Books on local travel, food, cooking, ecology, and photo and gift books about the Bay Area. Author events.
Bound Together Anarchist Collective Bookstore, 1369 Haight St. (Haight-Ashbury), tel 415/431-8355. Anarchist, leftist, and subversive literature.

City Lights, 261 Columbus Ave. (North Beach), tel 415/362-8193, citylights.com. Landmark literary bookstore founded by poet Lawrence Ferlinghetti.
Green Apple Books, 506 Clement St. (Richmond District), tel 415/387-2272, greenapplebooks.com. Highly regarded for new, used, and rare books.
Smoke Signals, 2223 Polk St. (Russian Hill), tel 415/292-6025. All kinds of magazines and newspapers from all over—the city's best selection.
William Stout Architectural Books, 804 Montgomery St. (Jackson Sq.), tel 415/391-6757, stoutbooks.com. For books on both architecture and design. Highly regarded.

Department Stores
Macy's, Stockton St. at O'Farrell St. (Union Sq.), tel 415/397-3333. Occupies a whole city block: comprehensive selection from clothes to housewares, thronged with shoppers.
Neiman-Marcus, 150 Stockton St. (Union Sq.), tel 415/362-3900. Fine clothing, flash, big-name designers.
Nordstrom, Westfield Centre, 5th St. at Market St. (Union Sq.), tel 415/243-8500. Five floors with great clothing, customer service, and café.
Saks Fifth Avenue, 384 Post St. (Union Sq.), tel 415/986-4300. Quality clothing, couture, for women; men's store, 220 Post St., tel 415/986-4300.

For the Home
Biordi Art Imports, 412 Columbus Ave. (North Beach), tel 415/392-8096. Italian majolica ceramics for table and home.
Nest, 2300 Fillmore St., tel 415/292-6199. Quirky, arty items for the home; offbeat jewelry.

Scheuer Linens, 340 Sutter St. (Union Sq.), tel 415/392-2813. Elegant sheets with high thread counts, table linens; European and U.S. makers.

Sur La Table, Westfield Centre, 5th St. at Market St. (Union Sq.), tel 415/814-4691; Ferry Building, the Embarcadero at Market St. (the Embardacero), tel 415/262-9970. Items for professional and home chefs.

Zinc Details, 1905 Fillmore St. (Pacific Heights), tel 415/776-2100. Local and world designers: housewares, textiles, furniture.

Jewelry

Bulgari, 200 Stockton St. (Union Sq.), tel 415/399-9141. Exclusive designs from a renowned Rome jeweler.

Love & Luxe 1169 Valencia St. (Mission), tel 415/648-7781. Handcrafted jewelry, custom wedding bands, bags, accessories.

Union Street Goldsmith, 2118 Union St. (Cow Hollow), tel 415/776-8048. Locally made gold and platinum jewelry; colored stones.

Leather

Bottega Veneta, 124 Geary St. (Union Sq.), tel 415/981-1700. Italian handbags, luggage, clothes.

West Coast Leather, 290 Sutter St. (Union Sq.), tel 415/362-8300. High-end leather clothing designs for men and women.

Outdoor Markets

Ferry Plaza Farmers Market, Ferry Bldg., Market St. at the Embarcadero (the Embarcadero), tel 415/291-3276, cuesa.org, Tues., Thurs., Sat. Fresh farm products and food items.

Heart of the City Farmers' Market, Market St. between 7th St. and 8th St. (Civic Center), tel 415/558-9455. Wed. & Sun. Fresh local produce, food items.

Records, CDs

101 Music, 513 Green St. (North Beach), tel 415/392-6368. A vast, unorganized stock of used vinyl LPs in the basement makes searching an adventure. Also: secondhand musical instruments and amps, stereo equipment and turntable cartridges, music memorabilia. A second store is around the corner at 1414 Grant, tel 415/392-6369.

Amoeba Music, 1855 Haight St. (Haight-Ashbury), tel 415/831-1200. Vast selection of new and used records and CDs as well as movies.

Explorist International Records, 3174 24th St. (Mission), tel 415/678-5691. Tasteful, organized selection of vinyl records from around the world, ranging from American blues and indie soul to Afro-funk and Cuban jazz, folk, electronic, and more. Also cassette tapes.

Toys & Games

Chinatown Kite Shop, 717 Grant Ave. (Chinatown), tel 415/989-5182. Buy a kite to take to Marina Green or the beach. Hundreds of selections include stunt models; kites decorated as insects, animals, and cartoon characters; airfoils (no frame, easy to pack); dragon kites with long tails.

Marbles: The Brain Store, Westfield Centre, 5th St. at Market St. (Union Square), tel 415/278-0438. Science kits, indoor and outdoor games, puzzles, robots, books, creative activities, arts.

Miscellany

Canton Bazaar, 616 Grant Ave. (Chinatown), tel 415/362-5750. A large and typical Chinatown store chockablock with souvenirs, porcelain, embroidery, arts and crafts.

Clarion Music Center, 816 Sacramento St. (Chinatown), tel 415/391-1317, clarionmusic.com. A huge variety of world instruments, from sitars to didgeridoos, drums, Chinese strings, and gongs.

Ferry Building Marketplace, The Embarcadero at Market St. (The Embarcadero), ferrybuilding marketplace.com. Forage for all kinds of foods, from bread to oysters, from cheese to wine.

FLAX, Bldg. D, Fort Mason (Marina), tel 415/530-3510, flax art.com. San Francisco's best bet for art supplies: stationery, pens, paper, paint, ink, and brushes.

Gity Joon's, 1828 Union St. (Cow Hollow), tel 415/292-7388. Arts and antiques from Asian lands and spiritual traditions, especially religious devotional objects and figures; fountains, jewelry, clothing, books as well.

Golden Gate Fortune Cookie Factory, 56 Ross Alley (Chinatown), tel 415/781-3956. Freshly baked fortune cookies by the bag. For custom orders, bring your own fortunes to be inserted in cookies

Misdirections Magic Shop, 1236 9th Ave. (Sunset), tel 415/566-2180, shop.misdirections.com. For beginning conjurors as well as professional magicians, well stocked with tricks, books, and professional videos.

Pipe Dreams, 1376 Haight St. (Haight-Ashbury), tel 415/431-3553, pipesinthecity.com. If you just *have* to visit a head shop, with its psychedelic posters and display cases of '60s-style paraphernalia, this is the oldest in the Haight.

UnionPostSF, 237 Kearny St. (Financial District), tel 415/593-0330, unionpostsf.com. Will pack and ship your purchases, especially valuable, fragile, awkward items.

Wine Club, 953 Harrison St. (SoMa), tel 415/512-9086. Reduced prices on wines and spirits.

Entertainment & Activities

In the performing arts, San Francisco entertainment venues present everything from world-class opera to cutting-edge theater, from dance to comedy to rock. Nightlife is as varied as the city and its residents. Whether it's an old-time jazz club, a funky blues bar, a dance club for gay leather boys, a hotel ballroom with a big band and a city view, or a concert by rock-and-roll superstars, you'll find it in San Francisco.

Information & Tickets

TIX *(tel 415/433-7827, tixbayarea .org)* sells tickets to theater, dance, and music events at up to 50 percent discounts. A TIX booth for walk-up sales is located at 350 Powell Street *(bet. Geary & Post Sts., Union Sq.)*; a touch-screen kiosk is located at Pier 39 *(Fisherman's Wharf)*. Tickets are also available through City Box Office *(tel 415/392-4400, www.cityboxoffice .com)* at 180 Redwood Street *(near Civic Center performance venues)*.

Theater

Productions run the gamut from big-name musicals and dramas in the downtown theater district and Civic Center to experimental works in neighborhood theaters.

Theater District

American Conservatory Theater/A.C.T., Geary Theatre, 415 Geary St., tel 415/749-2228, act-sf.org. Nationally recognized, Tony Award–winning repertory company; from Shakespeare to Tennessee Williams, plus premieres of new works. The 1909 theater is a national historic landmark. A.C.T.'s second home is an architectural showstopper, the 1917 Strand Theater, revamped with a dramatic two-story lobby by Skidmore, Owings & Merrill; located at 1127 Market St. (Civic Center).
Curran Theatre, 445 Geary St., tel 415/551-2000, shnsf.com. Has been undergoing renovation; search online for updates.
Lorraine Hansberry Theatre, 450 Post St., tel 415/474-8800, lhtsf.org. African-American theater that ranges from classical to experimental.

Other Locations

Beach Blanket Babylon, Club Fugazi, 678 Green St. (North Beach), tel 415/421-4222, beachblanketbabylon.com. Zany, long-running musical spoof of San Francisco and pop culture; outlandish hats and costumes.
Magic Theatre, Fort Mason, Bldg. D, Marina Blvd. at Buchanan St. (Marina District), tel 415/441-8822, magictheatre.org. American playwrights stage new works; performers range from stars to unknowns.
The Marsh, 1062 Valencia St. (Mission District), tel 415/282-3055, themarsh.org. Avant-garde, hip productions and solo works.
Theatre Rhinoceros, at Eureka Theatre, 215 Jackson St. (Financial District), tel 800/838-3006, therhino.org. Nation's oldest gay and lesbian theater company.

Music

Grace Cathedral Concerts, Grace Cathedral, 1100 California St. (Nob Hill), tel 415/749-6350, gracecathedral.org. Fine choral and instrumental music, lovely surroundings and acoustics.
San Francisco Opera, War Memorial Opera House, 301 Van Ness Ave. (Civic Center), tel 415/864-3330, sfopera.com. Spectacular, star-studded productions in renovated opera house. Season runs September through December and June through July.
San Francisco Symphony, Louise M. Davies Symphony Hall, 201 Van Ness Ave. (Civic Center), tel 415/864-6000, sfsymphony.org. Michael Tilson Thomas is the music director. The high standards attract top guest soloists. Runs September through July.
SFJAZZ Center, 201 Franklin St. (Civic Center), tel 866/920-5299, sfjazz.org. Major jazz acts, world music, classical; no seat in the house is more than 50 feet (15 m) from the stage.

Dance

San Francisco Ballet, War Memorial Opera House, 301 Van Ness Ave. (Civic Center), tel 415/865-2000, sfballet.org. The nation's oldest ballet company presents classical and contemporary works. Runs January through May; also Christmas season *The Nutcracker.*

Nightlife

1015 Folsom, 1015 Folsom St. (SoMa), tel 415/991-1015, 1015.com. Huge dance club with theme environments.
Bimbo's 365 Club, 1025 Columbus Ave. (North Beach), tel 415/474-0365, bimbos365club .com. Plush environment for rock and jazz, big names.
Biscuits and Blues, 401 Mason St. (Union Sq.), tel 415/292-2583, biscuitsandblues.com. Intimate, casual blues club.
Boom Boom Room, 1601 Fillmore St. (Japantown), tel 415/673-8000, boomboomroom .com. The late bluesman John Lee Hooker's down-home club presents R&B, roots, funk, and more.

Cobb's Comedy Club, 915 Columbus Ave. (North Beach), tel 415/928-4320, cobbscomedyclub .com. Small, intimate venue. New talent, big names. Hot spot.

Fillmore Auditorium, 1805 Geary Blvd., tel 415/346-6000, thefillmore.com. Rock concerts at the famous psychedelic '60s dance hall.

Great American Music Hall, 859 O'Farrell St. (Tenderloin), tel 415/885-0750, slimspresents .com. Rock, pop, R&B, and folk in an ornate turn-of-the-20th-century hall.

Harry Denton's Starlight Room, Sir Francis Drake Hotel, 450 Powell St., tel 415/395-8595, starlightroomsf.com. Booze and dancing, with a city view. Sunday brunch features drag queen divas.

Ruby Skye, 420 Mason St. (Union Sq.), tel 415/693-0777, rubyskye .com. Art nouveau theater turned into a dance club, with DJs and live music.

The Saloon, 1232 Grant Ave. (North Beach), tel 415/989-7666. A fun blues dive, in the city's oldest bar.

Slim's, 333 11th St. (SoMa), tel 415/255-0333, slimspresents .com. Boz Scaggs's popular club devoted to blues and roots music, rock; some top performers.

The Warfield, 982 Market St. (Civic Center), tel 888/929-7849, thewarfieldtheatre.com. Major rock groups in an intimate concert venue housed in what was once a vaudeville theater.

Outdoor Activities

From biking to fishing, San Francisco offers diverse options for outdoor enthusiasts. Head to the city's waterfront, parks, and trails, or to environs nearby.

Spectator Sports

Golden State Warriors, Oracle Arena, 7000 Coliseum Way, Oakland, tel 888/479-4667, nba.com/warriors. Basketball.

Oakland A's, The Coliseum, 7000 Coliseum Way, Oakland, tel 877/493-2255 (tickets), oakland .athletics.mlb.com. Baseball.

Oakland Raiders, The Coliseum, 7000 Coliseum Way, Oakland, tel 800/724-3377, raiders.com. American football.

San Francisco 49ers, Levi's Stadium, 4900 Marie P. DeBartolo Way, Santa Clara, tel 415/464-9377, 49ers.com. Football.

San Francisco Giants, AT+T Park, tel 415/972-2000, sfgiants.com. Baseball.

Golf

Courses open to the public:

Lincoln Park Golf Course, 34th Ave. at Clement St., tel 415/221-9911, lincolnparkgolfcourse.com.

Presidio Golf Course, 300 Finley Rd., tel 415/561-4661, presidio golf.com. Privately managed course in the Presidio. See p. 140 for more information.

TCP Harding Park, 99 Harding Rd., tel 415/664-4690, tpc.com/ hardingpark. Municipal course.

Walking, Running, & Biking

Two of the nation's prettiest routes for walking and biking are the Golden Gate Promenade, a 4-mile/6.4 km jaunt along the water with views of yachts and windsurfers, between Aquatic Park and Golden Gate Bridge) and the Coastal Trail (a more rough-and-tumble 9-mile/14.4 km route from the bridge to Lands End). Other good places include the Presidio and Golden Gate Park (whose main road closes to auto traffic on Sundays).

Although a network of bike lanes runs throughout the city, bikers must negotiate steep hills and dodge cars. Mountain biking enthusiasts flock to Marin; the

sport reportedly was invented on trail-laced Mount Tamalpais, which offers stupendous views.

Avenue Cyclery, 756 Stanyan St. (Haight-Ashbury), tel 415/387-3155, avenuecyclery.com. Rent bikes next to Golden Gate Park.

Blazing Saddles, seven city locations, tel 415/202-8888, blazing saddles.com. Rents bikes, offers cycling tours.

Windsurfing

Top-rated among windsurfers, the San Francisco Bay is blown by westerly winds from spring through fall. Best sites include Crissy Field, Fort Point at the southern anchorage of Golden Gate Bridge, Larkspur Landing in Marin, and the waters by Candlestick Park, south of the city. Be cautious of the cold water, strong currents, and boat traffic.

Other Sports

A good spot for boating is Golden Gate Park.

Stow Lake Boathouse, tel 415/386-2531, stowlakeboat house.com. Rent a rowboat, electric boat, or pedal boat by the hour. At the center of the lake is Strawberry Hill, an island with a Chinese pavilion and waterfall.

Another popular Golden Gate Park sport is lawn bowling with the **San Francisco Lawn Bowling Club,** near Sharon Meadow and the Carousel, tel 415/487-8787, sflbc.org. This sport is easy to learn. Free lessons are offered on Wednesdays at noon and at other times by appointment.

Consider a sportfishing expedition from Fisherman's Wharf or pier fishing at Aquatic Park, Fort Mason, or Crissy Field.

Locals and visitors enjoy sailing and sea kayaking for the bay and city views and for the fresh air and exercise. Many commercial operators offer trips and rentals.

INDEX

ACKNOWLEDGMENTS

The author dedicates this book to his mother, Margaret Eastman Dunn.

ILLUSTRATIONS CREDITS

All photographs by Gilles Mingasson unless otherwise noted:

Cover, SOPA/eStock Photo; spine, Gavin Hellier/Robert Harding/Corbis; 2-3, Stefano Politi Markovina/JAI/Corbis; 4, Jean-Pierre Lescourret/Getty Images; 8, Frank van den Bergh/Getty Images; 14-5, Photo by Phillip H. Coblentz/SFCVB; 21, Can Balcioglu/Shutterstock; 22, Lonely Planet/Getty Images; 29, Library of Congress Prints & Photographs Division, LC-USZ62-8197; 30-31, telesniuk/ Shutterstock; 32, Library of Congress Prints & Photographs Division, LC-USZ62-96789; 37, Marcio Jose Sanchez/AP/Corbis; 38, GAB Archive/Getty Images; 44, Henrik Kam; 53, Jason Dewey Photography; 72, Andy Z./Shutterstock; 78, Kelly-Mooney Photography/Corbis; 87, Allen Ginsberg/Corbis; 102, ChameleonsEye/Shutterstock; 108, Randy Duchaine/Alamy Stock Photo; 114, Popperfoto/Getty Images; 118, Leonid Serebrennikov/Alamy Stock Photo; 122, Nancy Hoyt Belcher/Alamy; 125, Library of Congress Prints & Photographs Division, LC-DIG-ppmsca-19051; 129, PatitucciPhoto/Aurora Photos; 137, Gary Crabbe/Enlightened Images/Alamy Stock Photo; 138, cdrin/Shutterstock.com; 139, Cameron Davidson/Corbis; 156, Jean-Pierre Lescourret/Getty Images; 162, Ted Streshinsky/Corbis; 177, Walter Bibikow/Getty Images; 189, Scott S. Warren/National Geographic Creative/Corbis; 190, Collection SFMOMA/Bequest of Elise S. Haas; 193, The Exploratorium, www.exploratorium.edu; 207, Sacheen Metrani/Shutterstock; 232, somchaij/Shutterstock; 234, Steven Castro/Shutterstock.

National Geographic

TRAVELER

San Francisco

Since 1888, the National Geographic Society has funded more than 12,000 research, exploration, and preservation projects around the world. National Geographic Partners distributes a portion of the funds it receives from your purchase to National Geographic Society to support programs including the conservation of animals and their habitats.

National Geographic Partners, LLC
1145 17th Street NW
Washington, DC 20036-4688 USA

Become a member of National Geographic and activate your benefits today at natgeo.com/jointoday.

For information about special discounts for bulk purchases, please contact National Geographic Books Special Sales: ngspecsales@ngs.org

For rights or permissions inquiries, please contact National Geographic Books Subsidiary Rights: ngbookrights@ngs.org

ISBN: 978-1-4262-1700-5

Printed in Hong Kong

16/THK/1

THE COMPLETE TRAVEL EXPERIENCE

With more than 75 destinations around the globe; available wherever books are sold and at www.shopng.com/travelerguides

TRIPS
natgeoexpeditions.com

MAGAZINE

for iPhone®,
iPod touch®,
and iPad®

APPS